Unwin Education Books: 20

MORAL PHILOSOPHY FOR EDUCATION

Unwin Education Books

Series Editor: Ivor Morrish, BD, BA, Dip.Ed. (London), BA (Bristol)

1. Education Since 1800 IVOR MORRISH
2. Moral Development WILLIAM KAY
3. Physical Education for Teaching BARBARA CHURCHER
4. The Background of Immigrant Children IVOR MORRISH
5. Organising and Integrating the Infant Day JOY TAYLOR
6. Philosophy of Education: An Introduction HARRY SCHOFIELD
7. Assessment and Testing: An Introduction HARRY SCHOFIELD
8. Education: Its Nature and Purpose M. V. C. JEFFREYS
9. Learning in the Primary School KENNETH HASLAM
10. Sociology of Education: An Introduction IVOR MORRISH
11. Fifty Years of Freedom RAY HEMMINGS
12. Developing a Curriculum AUDREY and HOWARD NICHOLLS
13. Teacher Education and Cultural Change H. DUDLEY PLUNKETT and JAMES LYNCH
14. Reading and Writing in the First School JOY TAYLOR
15. Approaches to Drama DAVID A. MALE
16. Aspects of Learning BRIAN O'CONNELL
17. Focus on Meaning JOAN TOUGH
18. Moral Education WILLIAM KAY
19. Concepts in Primary Education JOHN E. SADLER
20. Moral Philosophy for Education ROBIN BARROW

Unwin Education Books: 20
Series Editor: Ivor Morrish, BD, BA, Dip.Ed. (London), BA (Bristol)

Moral Philosophy
for Education

ROBIN BARROW
M.A (Oxon.) Ph.D (London)
Lecturer in Philosophy & Education, University of Leicester

London
GEORGE ALLEN & UNWIN LTD
RUSKIN HOUSE MUSEUM STREET

6934

ISBN 0 04 370059 4 hardback
0 04 370060 8 paperback

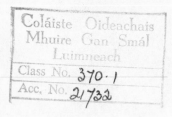
Printed in Great Britain
in 10 point Times Roman type
by Cox & Wyman Ltd,
London, Fakenham and Reading

For Lynn –
Who doesn't want it

Contents

Introduction   *page* 9

PART ONE

1   Philosophy and Education   15
2   Moral Philosophy   41

PART TWO

3   Reasonable and Unreasonable Arguments   59
4   Freedom   71
5   Equality   83
6   Utilitarianism   91

PART THREE

7   Kant and Respect for Persons   119
8   Autonomy   131
9   Rights   141
10 Creativity   146
11 What Is Worthwhile?   156
12 The Free School   175
13 Educational Distribution   184
14 Indoctrination and Moral Values   199

Index   213

Introduction

I call this an introduction rather than a preface, because prefaces tend to be bypassed and these few pages, though hardly stimulating, are important. This book differs in a number of ways from other books on the same theme and I wish to make its plan clear at the outset. It has four features to which attention should be drawn:

1.   It is written primarily for students at colleges of education or university education departments. I might have called it an introduction to the 'philosophy of education' inasmuch as it is an introduction to the technique of philosophy and it uses educational examples. Since the phrase 'philosophy of education' is a chameleon that means all things to all men (or nothing to some), it would not have been an inappropriate title. But it does differ from all other introductions to the philosophy of education in that it concentrates on moral philosophy and moral issues in education.

2.   Despite its use of examples from education, it should serve as an introduction to moral philosophy for anybody interested in the subject. Moral philosophy involves the same procedures and faces the same problems whatever sphere it takes its examples from. Problems about freedom, equality, and so on, are not confined to the educational sphere. Besides, some issues, such as the question of indoctrination, are as relevant to a parent as to a teacher.

3.   It is concerned to combat two heresies. One is the conventional enemy of moral philosophers: the view that a finite list of moral commandments can be put forward and the claim made that they are *known* to be true. The other is the obverse of this view; it is a heresy that seems to be gaining ground at this moment, and one which is perhaps not sufficiently guarded against: the view that it is *known* that moral values are just the fiats of a given society.

4.   Finally, it differs from most other introductions to moral philosophy in that it attempts, with due caution, I hope, to offer a positive moral viewpoint (namely, a modified utilitarianism). I do not bypass philosophical analysis of moral concepts, but I try to avoid what the layman often sees as the analytical sterility of philosophy. I do this partly because this is a book for those who are not professional philosophers but laymen, and partly because it is the application of philosophy to practical issues that is of concern to them. They have to come to some sort of conclusion.

These four considerations have dictated the plan of the book. In Part One I devote more space than is usual to trying to explain what is going on: what the real problems are and why philosophy proceeds in the manner that it does. Chapter 1, which is the one chapter that is perhaps irrelevant to the general reader, is mainly concerned with clarifying what the philosophy of education is concerned to do and explaining why moral philosophy is central to it. I turn a relatively sympathetic eye towards those who find much philosophy of education rather frustrating and even pointless. In Chapter 2 I focus on the main problem in the moral sphere: the difficulty of seeing what would count as moral knowledge. This is an important, though in some ways negative and depressing chapter; its purpose is to clear the ground of unwarranted assumptions.

In Part Two, proceeding by way of examination of the concepts of freedom, equality and happiness, I propose a modified utilitarianism as a reasonable ethical theory. This is the positive part of the book. In Part Three I begin with a brief consideration of Kant's ethical theory in view of its influence on contemporary philosophers of education and its prima facie challenge to utilitarianism. This leads into a discussion of two concepts – both associated with Kant and both of current interest: respect for persons and autonomy. After a brief chapter on the notion of 'rights', I attempt to discuss a number of specific problems in the educational sphere that involve, to a greater or lesser extent, moral judgements: how does one decide the sort of things that should be going on in schools? What is the justification for an emphasis on creative activities? How do we decide the limits of freedom for children? What does equal educational provision involve? How can we avoid moral indoctrination?

It should be stressed that this is a book to be *used*. It is intended that each chapter should begin, and provide substance for, further debate. The purpose of Part Three is not to lay down categorical answers, so much as to indicate what in practice is involved in accepting the proposed ethical viewpoint of Part Two, and how various answers to specific problems presuppose very different ethical assumptions. Part Two itself could in no sense be regarded as definitive or conclusive. But it represents the basis of an argument that I personally regard as convincing.

Although many readers will doubtless find fault with Part Two, it is hoped that this method and, in particular, this division into three parts, will nonetheless help them to appreciate the problems inherent in the moral sphere and to clarify their own position.

It is no part of my concern to offer a review of what other philosophers have to say on the various topics covered in the body of the text. But to compensate for this omission I have added some suggestions for further reading at the end of each chapter. These suggestions are necessarily selective and personal, since no two philosophers are necessarily going to agree on the value of various other books and articles in the field. My selection has been made with the following criteria in mind: (1) The extent to which an article or book is likely to be readily accessible. (2) The extent to which it is likely to be suited to the student. (3) The extent to which it has something of interest to say. (4) The extent to which it has as a matter of fact been widely disseminated.

Part One

Chapter 1
Philosophy and Education

The word 'philosopher' is Greek in origin and means 'a lover of wisdom'. The famous Greek philosophers, such as Plato and Aristotle, did not trouble themselves overmuch about fine and hair-splitting distinctions concerning the limits of the philosopher's role (although Plato went to some lengths to distinguish himself, the real philosopher, from various charlatans; the charlatans, in his view, were those whose concern was simply to *win* an argument by any means to hand). As far as they were concerned, a philosopher was just somebody who was interested in acquiring knowledge and pursuing truth in any sphere. Aristotle, for instance, in our terminology, was a political theorist, an antiquarian, a moral philosopher and a biologist. In his own terminology he was a philosopher, whether he was indulging his antiquarian interests or involved in biological research. For Plato and Aristotle there was no fumbling doubt about what they were professionally entitled to do, or the proper limits of philosophical inquiry. They were looking for answers to every conceivable question that could be raised, they were seeking to explain and understand the world in all its aspects, and ultimately they aimed to lay down the plan for the Good Life for mankind.

Times have changed. In broad terms, philosophers today are left with the task of pursuing the truth only in those areas of human experience that are not being investigated by the various empirical sciences. They tend to be concerned with such questions as whether God exists, how to reconcile the apparent conflict between the desire for freedom and the desire for order, or whether it makes sense to lay down conditions that would have to be met for something to count as a work of art. Such questions cannot be answered simply by conducting experiments, by laboratory tests or by observation. When people meant by the claim that God exists that some supremely powerful being, in more or less human shape, was to be found in some particular place, as some Greeks believed that an anthropomorphic Zeus lived on Mount Olympus, the truth or falsehood of this claim was obviously to be established by empirical research. In theory one only had to climb Olympus and keep watch for a period of time in order to prove that the assertion that Zeus existed was without foundation. However few people today have such a simple and positive notion of God. Their conception of God is so abstract that by definition no amount of empirical research is going to count as evidence against their belief that God exists.

Since they do not mean that there is an old man with a beard sitting in the clouds, when they claim that God exists, the fact that rockets and space-ships may comb every inch of the sky and not run into him is not going to show that God does not exist.

It is at this point that the philosopher steps in. He does so, not because he necessarily either does believe, or does not believe, in the existence of God, but because he is interested in trying to establish whether or not it is true that God exists. However, precisely because claims that God does exist generally seem to involve a notion of God that cannot be touched by empirical findings, the philosopher's first question is likely to be 'Well, what *do you mean* by God?' He will proceed by asking such further questions as what sort of evidence would count one way or the other in this matter and to what extent it makes sense to talk of something that cannot be detected by any of the five senses as 'existing'. Faced with an issue that is beyond the scope of empirical research, he turns to the only other method we have of searching for truth and that is reasoning. In particular he reasons about meaning, for in some areas, such as this, it seems that whether something is true or not will depend very largely, if not entirely, on what precisely is meant. To come down to earth, whether I am a good husband or not will depend partly on the way in which I behave to my wife, but partly, and no less importantly, on what we mean by a 'good husband'.

Philosophers, then, may be defined today as those who are concerned about the truth in those areas of human experience where reason is apparently the only weapon to hand. But besides operating on a smaller stage than philosophers of the past, they also tend in practice to limit their activities still further by dividing philosophy itself into various branches such as the philosophy of religion, the philosophy of art, political philosophy and moral philosophy. These particular divisions have been with us for some time and have acquired a certain respectability through age. More recently a whole spate of new philosophies of this and that have been introduced, including the philosophy of mathematics, the philosophy of action, the philosophy of science and, of course, the philosophy of education.

How real, meaningful or helpful these distinctions are is a matter of opinion. (No sign yet of the philosophy of geography or the philosophy of pop music, for example. Why not?) Some, such as the philosophy of religion, may seem intelligible as distinctive pursuits. One can see that inquiring into the problem of religious truth could be a full-time occupation and that it could properly be conducted without reference to morality, politics, art or mathematics. Others, such as the peculiar beast the philosophy of education, seem to me to have no distinct identity. Given that the sphere of education invites questions about religious education and aesthetic education, for instance, how could one philosophise comprehensively in this sphere without becoming involved in the philosophy of religion and the philosophy of art? One cannot very well start talking about what form religious education ought to take if one has not first looked into the question of what religious belief involves. In particular I do not see how philosophy of education can be divorced from moral philosophy. If one tries to straitjacket the philosophy of education in distinctive clothing, the result, I believe, is a pursuit of very limited value. I shall expand this point and explain why moral philosophy seems to me to be the most important part of the philosophy of education in the next section of this chapter. For the moment I will content myself with saying that I should prefer the phrase 'philosophy applied to education' to 'the philosophy of education'.

Moral philosophy represents a branch of philosophy which may, without undue contortion, be regarded as distinctive. It is concerned with questions about the right and wrong behaviour, good and bad conduct or actions. Anybody who has any understanding of the word 'moral' will appreciate that these terms, particularly 'good' and 'bad', can be used in both a moral and a non-moral sense. For instance, one can talk about a good car, meaning simply a car that functions reliably, and this use of 'good' is obviously quite distinct from its use in a statement such as 'he is a good man'. Equally obviously, moral philosophy is concerned with the moral use of these terms. It is concerned to find out what, if anything, we can establish as true in the moral sphere; or, to be precise, what, if anything, we can establish as true in what various people may regard as the moral sphere.

Moral philosophy is therefore of relevance to anyone who ever asks himself a question such as 'What ought I to do?' or 'Would this be right?'; it is of relevance, too, to anyone who ever makes moral judgements about others, who ever praises or condemns other people's actions. In other words, it is of relevance to virtually everybody.

But it is of particular relevance to teachers. This is not because teachers are necessarily particularly prone to make moral judgements about, or for the presumed benefit of, their pupils. It is not even primarily because the business of education as a whole, in which they are presumed to be interested, is beset by moral questions, although this is certainly so. The two main reasons for regarding moral philosophy as an important pursuit for the teacher are that his own position is fenced in by moral questions and that he is responsible for the moral education of his pupils. On the assumption that he is to some extent a reflective person and that he does not take the easy view that he may as well do whatever he feels like doing, he cannot very well avoid considering questions such as what form of punishment, if any, he may justifiably employ and under what circumstances, whether he is justified in attempting to foster his own values in the children he teaches, to what extent his pupils ought to be free to make their own decisions and where the limits of his obligation to serve his headmaster lie.

The second reason is perhaps the most compelling of all: in most schools at present 'moral education' is not a timetabled subject. There are no 'moral lessons'. Instead all teachers are at all times left to watch over the moral development of their pupils as they see fit. Like it or leave it, they are involved in the upbringing of individuals who will ultimately adopt a variety of moral attitudes and who will themselves have to face up to moral questions and make moral decisions. If the business of moral education is not to be a random charade with the blind leading the blind, the very least we must hope for is that teachers will understand the problems involved in attempting to establish a moral judgement as in some sense correct, and that they will pass on this understanding.

I deliberately stress the idea of understanding the problems involved rather than the suggestion that teachers should know the answers to moral questions, because at this stage it must remain an open question as to whether it makes sense to talk of 'knowing the answers' in this sphere. Many philosophers would say that it does not. And one thing on which all philosophers today would agree is that the moral philosopher's job is not simply to lay down a comprehensive code of conduct telling people how they ought to behave. That is another activity that belongs to a past age of philosophy. Two thousand and more years of moral philosophy seem to have made at least one thing clear, and that is that nobody is very sure how one could substantiate beyond any reasonable doubt that this and only this is the correct answer to the question, 'What ought a man to do in these circumstances?'

The result of this uncertainty is that moral philosophy today, at any rate in the West, tends to proceed in a manner parallel to that employed in the philosophy of religion. It concentrates on analysing the meaning of various moral concepts and examines what lies behind our use of moral terminology. It asks, for instance, in what way moral statements differ from other kinds of statements. It asks what is meant by 'equality'; what we are asking for when we demand equality for all men. Is it a natural right? What is a natural right? We know that the American Declaration of Independence provides examples of natural rights that all men have and that cannot be taken away (freedom, life and the pursuit of happiness), but what is it talking about? Providing examples of what people regard as natural rights does not tell us what it means to say that they are natural rights. 'Natural' could mean a number of things: normal, based on man's nature, found in a state of nature. But what would it mean to say that man has a right to freedom based on his nature? Why couldn't this right be taken away? Fairly obviously it can be, so perhaps we must interpret the claim that it cannot be as meaning that it ought not to be. But what does that mean and why ought it not to be?

These questions are obviously extremely important. One cannot advance far if it is not clear what one is talking about. And no self-respecting moral philosopher would be prepared to bypass them. Nonetheless, it is perhaps understandable that many non-philosophers or students who approach moral philosophy for the first time should feel that by concentrating on the meaning of moral words philosophers are too anxious to avoid saying anything positive, or coming to any conclusions as to what in fact ought to be done. There are very good reasons why philosophers should hesitate to lay down the moral law, and why they abhor the man who rashly makes categorical assertions in an area so uncertain. However, provided that a philosopher makes it quite clear to his audience what is going on, provided he points out and explains the extreme difficulty of being sure of the truth, provided that it is evident that his conclusions cannot be taken for granted as the authoritative pronouncement of some expert, but that they must stand or fall as far as the reader is concerned by his own assessment of the argument, I see no harm in trying to outline a positive view. And that is what I shall try to do in the second part of this book. But in order that the provisos listed above shall be met it is first necessary to clarify the central problem of moral philosophy, which is the question of the extent to which it makes sense to talk of moral knowledge or moral truth. This problem will be considered in Chapter 2. In the remainder of this chapter I shall consider the rationale behind stressing the importance of moral philosophy as a key aspect of the philosophy of education.

The Theory of education

Student teachers are generally required to study the theory of education in some shape or form. Precisely what shape or form differs to some extent from place to place and time to time. It is not my purpose here to get too deeply involved in the argument about how educational theory may best be introduced in colleges and education departments, but rather to say something briefly about the nature of educational theory and its importance in *some* shape or form. However, the way in which it is seen to be important will obviously dictate to some extent the way it should be introduced, just as, for example, one's view of what is important about 'movement' as an educational activity will to some extent dictate one's view of what concentrating on 'movement' with children should involve.

It is not really in dispute today that there is no such thing as a discipline of education itself, as there is a discipline of mathematics or psychology. That is to say, you cannot study educationally as you can study historically; you cannot do education as you can do mathematics. To describe someone as an educationalist, therefore, does not pick him out as somebody with expertise in some particular method of inquiry related to particular kinds of problem, as to describe somebody as a scientist does. Rather, describing somebody as an educationalist picks out only the sphere in which he is interested. But that sphere or field of interest involves many problems and invites many questions which may either be of quite distinct kinds or else depend for their resolution on the application of more than one discipline. In particular, questions of a philosophical, psychological, sociological and historical nature are for ever cropping up in an educational context: why, as a matter of fact, does religious education feature on all school curricula? What factors in our society are contributing to the relatively low correlation between equal educational opportunity and equal educational achievement? How do various children respond to various kinds of punishment? Is it immoral to punish children? Hence the study of education is taken to involve primarily the application of these four disciplines to the educational sphere. 'Educational theory' serves as an umbrella term encompassing philosophical, psychological, sociological and historical inquiry in the field of education. To engage in educational theory is to concentrate on various educational issues and, by a process of distinguishing the different kinds of factor involved in the issue and throwing light on them, to attempt to clarify it and, where possible and necessary, to resolve it. Thus one's immediate concern might be with considering a suitable curriculum for the primary school. If one's intention is to produce a curriculum that is based on reason rather than arbitrary fiat, then, ideally, one will need to make use of the four disciplines, for they ask the questions and seek to provide the answers that, taken together, constitute the relevant sort of reasons for adopting a particular curriculum. As Hirst says, 'To decide matters of curriculum content without due regard to social and psychological, as well as philosophical considerations, is quite indefensible'.[1] And we may add that, although in this particular example history may not seem to be so directly relevant to the issue, it may nonetheless have its use: for example it might cause us to question the importance of some aspect of a curriculum that we had taken for granted, by drawing our attention to the fact that that particular aspect only found its way into the curriculum in the first place by accident.

But now, if this is what educational theory involves, what of those who argue that theory is irrelevant and a waste of the practising teacher's time? It is necessary to distinguish at this point between the claim that theory is by its nature irrelevant to the concerns of the practising teacher and should be expunged from colleges and departments of education (strong thesis), and the entirely different claim that theory should be related very closely to practice (weak thesis).

The strong thesis is surely absurd. It seems to be based on the premiss that thought and action can be totally divorced. Well, perhaps they can be in the case of mindless morons or human automata. Perhaps it is conceivable that an individual should act in certain ways without any kind of reason for so doing. But in fact that is not how we behave, nor is there any obvious reason to wish that it were. No doubt for many of us, much of the time, the reasons that lie behind our actions are muddled, insufficiently worked out or only vaguely formulated in our minds. Nonetheless we choose to act in some ways rather than others and our choices are based on reason – for to make a choice is precisely to opt for one thing rather than another for some kind of reason; that is why in cases where we act in one way rather than another without any obvious reason, if we refer to choice at all, we refer to something like blind or arbitrary choice.

Practice that is not entirely arbitrary, then, presupposes thought. And practice that is well founded equally clearly presupposes informed thought. How then can educational theory be irrelevant to educational practice, since the study of educational theory is the attempt to engage in informed thinking about educational matters? Educational theory, being the application of disciplines that deal in various kinds of reason that are found to be relevant to educational problems, is the sine qua non of informed educational practice. The teacher who practises in ignorance of psychological and sociological data and who lacks any historical perspective or philosophic competence does not thereby indicate that theory and practice can be divorced (still less that they should be); for insofar as he thinks at all he is engaging in theory. It is simply that his educational theorising, being grounded in ignorance and incompetence, will be poor and ill informed.

It follows that in principle educational theory must be relevant to educational practice. I say 'in principle' because, of course, it is always possible for an individual to ignore the logical claims of an argument. It is possible for an individual to become aware of various considerations that constitute good reasons for his changing his practice, but nonetheless refuse to change his practice. But that presumably is the fault of the individual rather than the fault of theory. Assuming that we are concerned with individuals who are not so constituted then there are three important ways in which educational theory is relevant to educational practice.

First, as implied above, theory may lead directly to a change in practice. New psychological or sociological data may very obviously have a bearing on the most appropriate way to deal with particular children in particular situations and may demand a change in the teacher's practice. More generally, simply thinking about what one is doing and why one is doing it may lead to a change in practice, for it may be that on reflection one comes to feel that what one is doing has no obvious rationale and is justified by no specific considerations.

Secondly, theory may improve practice. Again, as a result of engaging in theory we may arrive at a sharper perspective on precisely what we are doing and why we are doing it. By providing us with new information or new ways of looking at our practice, theory may lead directly to our practice being better or more effective, because we are better aware of what is really going on and what we are really trying to do. If it were really true that no amount of study of the various disciplines of education could materially alter or improve the practice in our classrooms, that would be a savage and extraordinary indictment of our teachers, for it would appear to mean that what they actually did was in no way connected with their beliefs, information, conceptual schemes, or, more simply, thoughts. Let us be quite clear about this: the claim that theory is unrelated to practice and therefore logically *cannot* affect it is manifest nonsense. The claim that in fact it *will not* affect practice is in effect the assertion that teachers are somehow incapable of acting as they see reason to act or that they are incapable of developing or changing their beliefs, which is also manifest nonsense. That claim that theory *should not* be the concern of the practising teacher is the demand that practice should proceed without inquiry into the reasons for that particular practice: a most peculiar demand.

So far the tie-up between theory and practice has been seen in terms of a link between the practice and theory of the individual. But there is a third way in which theory may be of relevance to the practising teacher, even without consideration of his practice. For surely, a teacher, being involved in some part of education, both should be and is interested in the wider sphere of education as a whole. The primary school teacher, for instance, commits himself to various objectives and practices; but presumably he does this in the light of some wider educational perspective. He does not teach in the secondary school, but it is of some concern to him what goes on there: he does not want the secondary school to undo all that he has tried to do, for instance, and conversely he wants what he does try to do to make sense in relation to the next stage of the child's education. Furthermore a teacher is not only concerned with his practice: he is concerned that other teachers too should pursue some practices rather than others. It would be most extraordinary for a teacher to be committed to the 'integrated day' but not to mind at all if no other schools based their curriculum planning on the ideal of the integrated day. This is merely to say that even if a particular teacher had perfected both his practice and his argument in favour of that practice, there would still be countless educational issues of some interest to him and involving considerable controversy, the reasoned consideration of which would demand the application of the constituent disciplines of educational theory. A teacher, in other words, seldom sees himself simply as an isolated classroom practitioner; he also sees himself, and it is surely right that he should, as an educationalist or someone whose concern is with the wider sphere of education as a whole.

If the arguments above are sound then the strong thesis is to be rejected on the grounds that theory cannot be divorced from practice, that theory may explicate and hence improve practice, that theory may change practice, and that theory may benefit the individual qua educationalist as well as qua teacher or classroom practitioner.

The weak thesis is an altogether different matter. This is a claim not about whether theory should be studied but about how it should be studied. Specifically I am concerned with the suggestion that the study of the theory of education for students should be 'grounded in the study of schools and classrooms' or related to actual problems, rather than that it should consist of initiation into the constituent disciplines. Thus some would argue that *in fact* much theory of education is irrelevant to practice, because it pursues purely philosophical or psychological paths too far away from the experience of teachers in the classroom, but that it need not be.

Let us start on common ground: all are presumably agreed that the point of theory is to inform practice. Indeed the defence of theory given above consisted in indicating that it can affect practice and that practice cannot be *reasonably* modified except in the light of theory. So we can all agree that that type of educationalist whose theorising apparently bears no relation to what children are like or to the sort of problems that actually beset teachers is to be condemned. Thus when Hirst writes that 'theory must be understood as stemming from practical problems and it must continually be brought to bear on particular complex issues',[2] in essence we agree. Of course theory does stem from practical problems and of course this must be understood if the point of theory is to be grasped. It is because there are practical problems that we engage in theory, and therefore it is also desirable that theory should be applied to practical problems. But *what* 'particular complex issues' should theory examine? And why should it do so 'continually'?

From the undisputed suggestion that theory should be brought to bear upon practical problems that actually do exist, one obviously cannot conclude, as some would have us do, that the study of theory should be rooted in the particular problems that face the students in question. This is not to say that the particular problems of students should be ignored, but there are surely three very good reasons why the study of theory should not necessarily be confined to what arises from the experience of students: (1) Their experience is naturally likely to be relatively narrow. (2) They may be face to face with complex issues that they do not see as complex issues. (3) There may be important complex issues that will require consideration when they arise, but which have not yet arisen. Thus we should interpret the demand that theory be brought to bear on 'particular complex issues' only as the demand that it should be brought to bear on issues that teachers in general may come up against.

What about the claim that theory should 'continually' be related to practice? What does this mean? How often is continually? Let us assume that the implication of the term is something like this: the study of theory should proceed by reference to practical issues; any given lecture or seminar should focus on some specific educational situation. Thus we should not discuss the problem of freedom as a straight philosophical issue, but rather we should discuss a specific educational problem such as 'Ought children to be free to opt out of learning to read if they feel like it?' What is there to be said about such a suggestion?

One thing is absolutely clear: if people are going to have a meaningful discussion about a question such as 'Ought children to be free to do such and such?', then they will need to be familiar with, and to have some ability at handling, the complex questions of what constitutes freedom, how, if at all, value judgements can be substantiated, and, in particular, the meaning and status of claims relating to the value of freedom. In addition they will probably need some acquaintance with psychological and possibly even sociological data; precisely what data will obviously depend on the question. This is merely to say that such a question demands some philosophic competence and familiarity with various other disciplines for its satisfactory resolution. Now, of course, you do not have to have immersed yourself in philosophy, psychology or whatever before you tackle some specific question. You can use a specific question as a way into the relevant disciplines. But at some stage, if the question is really to be examined rather than superficially dismissed, you have to go beyond the purely educational. Sticking with our example, it is inevitable that at some stage the issue of freedom per se will have to be pursued. It cannot finally be adequate to answer a specific question about children's freedom without any understanding of, or reference to, the wider issue of the claims of freedom in general.

That being so, it is very difficult to see what those who are obsessed with starting from the classroom situation are so agitated about. I cannot see that it is a matter of great moment whether the problem of freedom is considered prior to specific questions about children's freedom, or whether it is considered when it arises out of some such specific question. But marginally I incline to the view that the logical order of events is the one to go for, which is to say: introduction to the nature of the various disciplines; initiation into the methods, problems and findings of the disciplines; application of the disciplines to specific educational issues. In support of this approach it may be argued that issues change in a way that disciplines do not, that a proper understanding of the nature of the disciplines facilitates the unravelling of complex practical problems and that too exclusive a preoccupation with the classroom situation may tend to discourage one from examining possibilities beyond the range of the present classroom.

The only objections that I can conceive of to this procedure are that students may feel that it is not answering their immediate questions or problems very quickly or that it is not educational. Neither objection moves me very much: the claim that one is leaving the sphere of education when, for instance, one philosophises about freedom is hardly a compelling objection. Inasmuch as the activity is a necessary prerequisite of examining certain educational problems, its educational relevance is thereby indicated. The weakness in the other objection is the assumption that problems or questions can be quickly solved: the speed with which one can solve a specific problem must depend on one's competence within whatever disciplines are necessary to the resolution of the problem in question. There is no quick answer to a question such as 'Ought children to be free to opt out of learning to read, if they want to?'

In short, my claim is that educational theory, which consists of the application of the four disciplines, philosophy, psychology, sociology and history, to the sphere of education, is necessary to informed and well-founded educational practice. How the theory component may best be handled in colleges and education departments is no doubt debatable up to a point. But one thing is clear and that is that somehow or other it is necessary to become acquainted with and able to move about in each of the four disciplines as disciplines, independently of their application to the educational sphere. Grounding theory in practice is a perfectly reasonable procedure so long as it is not taken to suggest that one can meaningfully discuss all educational issues without moving beyond the immediately educational.

I therefore find the following passage from Stenhouse a little difficult to follow. He argues that, for example,

> 'Curriculum as a field should be grounded in the study of schools and classrooms and cannot be approached by a high-level general application of "the constituent disciplines". If philosophy, psychology, sociology and history are relevant to curriculum studies – as I have no doubt they are – it is through application to the specific problems distinguished by empirical study'.[3]

A brief consideration of this quotation will serve to illustrate most of the points made above. First it is not entirely clear whether Stenhouse is claiming that this is the way educational research in the sphere of curriculum should proceed or whether he is claiming that this is the way that students should approach the sphere. Let us compromise and assume that he is saying that this is how the study of curriculum should be approached in colleges and education departments. But, secondly, what precisely is involved in this approach? What are the empirical studies that will reveal specific problems? Does Stenhouse just mean that the study should start from problems located by people's experiences? What people, and how can anyone locate a problem without some understanding of the various disciplines in question? Of course anyone may find himself in a situation which he feels is problematic or not working, without being adept in any of the disciplines of education. But even to feel that something is not working presupposes some kind of objective or criterion for success, and the claim that something is not working involves the prior claim that a certain objective ought to be met. That prior claim itself, if it is to be soundly based and not merely arbitrary, will depend on a degree of educational theorising particularly, in this case, in the discipline of philosophy. Furthermore it is one thing to locate a problem – to sense that something is wrong, quite another to locate the real nature of the problem: to do that will require an even greater sophistication in educational theory. This is to say, in effect, that to classify something as a problem presupposes some competence in educational theory.

If one had literally no grounding in and no grasp of philosophy, psychology, sociology or history in relation to education on what grounds could one reasonably locate a problem? Even prima facie obvious problems, such as that children are not learning anything, is only a problem given certain educational objectives and certain educational data.

Thirdly it is even more evident that in order to solve an educational problem you need to be competent in the relevant disciplines, for they provide the techniques for dealing with various aspects of such problems and the data that is necessary to resolving them. That is to say that faced with a specific question, such as 'What are we to do about this group of 7-year-olds who are disinclined to learn to read?', to do justice to it one has to ask such questions as 'Does it matter?', 'Why are they disinclined?' and 'Could one find a way of removing their disinclination?' To do justice to these questions in turn demands some competence in the disciplines of education. Of course, as already admitted, one way of acquiring such competence is by means of considering such examples. But that cannot alter the fact that ideally resolution of such problems demands competence in the various disciplines and that therefore in some way, at some stage before one can be in a position to approach the problem in an informed manner, one needs to be initiated into the disciplines themselves.

Finally, and most importantly, Stenhouse's approach would appear to be extraordinarily dangerous, for it makes us prisoners of actuality, servants of the here and now. By waiting on the present or what is the case, we commit ourselves to a slow and piecemeal modification, at best, of the sort of curriculum we start with. But suppose we want to get beyond this, suppose we feel that we are not prepared to concentrate on problems that arise out of the status quo and which must by definition be assessed from the standpoint of the status quo? Suppose we want to question the validity of the whole damned exercise as at present constituted? How can you do that meaningfully without a degree of sophistication in the constituent disciplines, and except by starting with them rather than with the classroom as we know it and attempting to construct with sound reasoning something de novo?

What Stenhouse seems to set his face against is the flight of theoretical fancy indulged in by a radical thinker such as Plato or Rousseau. Now certainly one may find fault with such theorists on the grounds that in places they seem to ignore the reality of what children and the world are like. But insofar as they dream in defiance of what children are like, we may simply say that they are to that extent in error – and, of course, to say that they are in error involves being oneself competent in the sphere of child psychology. Insofar as they dream in defiance of what the world is actually like they are surely to be applauded: their object is to change the world, not reflect it. Surely, provided that one has the competence to move about in the various disciplines and is familiar with whatever data they provide, nothing could be more invigorating or desirable than that one should contemplate possibilities and ideas beyond the range of the here and now.

But I return to my central point which is that informed comment and judgement on educational issues logically demand competence in the constituent disciplines. How such competence may best be acquired is a methodological question on which there is room for argument. But there is not room for argument as to whether it is necessary, and I shall therefore make no further apology for the odd passages in the remainder of this book that pursue a philosophical point beyond the classroom, nor for the fact that in Part Two I deliberately put the emphasis on pursuing an argument in moral philosophy as a prelude to Part Three in which the educational context is brought to the fore.

The Philosophy of Education

Far more widespread than the view that the theory of education is irrelevant to practising teachers, is the limited claim that philosophy has nothing to offer in the sphere of education. To put the point more specifically, it is often argued that what goes on in the name of philosophy of education is not something distinctive; it is something that goes on all the time in intelligent discussion about education; in fact it is nothing more than an attempt at intelligent discussion, and there is something peculiar about treating it as a distinct discipline. Do we not hope and presume that the other disciplines will be conducted intelligently? Why then should there be any need to do the philosophy of education?

Sociology, psychology and history, it may be pointed out, aim to give us verifiable facts about children and schools. They tell us, more or less firmly, that such and such was or is the case, and the evidence for their claims is accessible. There are disagreements between experts in one or other fields from time to time, and no doubt students are sometimes presented with information or factual claims that turn out to have been false. But at least one knows what is going on and, allowing for error, the facts presented have an obvious and immediate relevance to anyone interested in education. Evidence about the tendency of a peer group to influence the child or evidence that children are psychologically incapable of grasping certain concepts at certain stages of development is useful evidence.

By contrast, philosophy does not proceed by giving us a body of tested information. It tells us nothing positive about children; it gives us no useful facts. To the critical observer, it seems merely to carp and quibble about how people use words. Such an observer might argue that one only has to look at a copy of the *Proceedings of the Philosophy of Education Society of Great Britain* to see that philosophers of education spend their time re-defining terms such as 'teaching', 'development' and 'education' itself, to suit their own purposes. They ponder for hours over such questions as whether 'teaching' necessarily implies that someone should learn some-thing. (If the pupil has learnt nothing, should one say that the teacher was 'teaching' him or 'trying to teach' him?) Surely these philosophers must recognise that there is no 'right' answer to such a question and that asking it is not getting us very far. Words are made by men; 'teaching' means what we want it to mean. Whether or not people generally mean to imply that somebody must learn something if 'teaching' is going on is remarkably unimportant compared with the obvious point that we as teachers *intend* that people shall learn something.

The claim that the philosophy of education is primarily concerned with analysis of the meaning of educational terms is substantially correct, and given the general philosophical climate sketched in the previous section, this is hardly surprising. Furthermore, the feeling that this linguistic analysis is a relatively pointless pursuit for the student teacher to spend time on seems to me to be at least understandable, if we are considering the idea of a specific course laid on to concentrate solely on such analysis. In other words, although I would not agree that the sort of thing that philoso-phers of education tend to do is necessarily trivial or unimportant, I would be dubious about the need for a distinctive course called the philosophy of education and for individuals classified as philosophers in colleges of education, if the philosophy of education is to be understood simply as analysis of educational terminology. In order to make this point clear, it is necessary first to consider a typical defence that might be raised against the criticism of the philosophy of education just outlined.

Any competent philosopher would concede at once that language is man-made and hence fluid, but, he would argue, that is precisely why it needs careful scrutiny. Arguments are constructed out of words, and nine times out of ten important arguments contain some highly ambiguous word at a crucial juncture in the reasoning. We might be told, for instance, that education should take account of children's interests, and elaborate programmes of education might be devised on this basis. One's natural unreflecting assumption is that, of course, one should not ignore children's interests. But if one does reflect for a moment one sees that the notion of interest is ambiguous. Is what is in my interest simply what I want, is it what is good for me in somebody else's judgement, or is it what is good for me in my judgement (which might not be the same as what I want). Clearly one needs to sort out what one does mean by 'children's interests' here, for what one means will affect the programme of education that is appropriate, and may even cause one to change one's mind about whether education should take account of interests. Again, one is often told that teachers must avoid indoctrinating, but although most of us have a vague idea of what we mean by indoctrination we should probably need to sharpen up that idea if we were going to be sure of avoiding it. Am I indoctrinating, for instance, when I play Beethoven records to my young son in the hope that he will come to share my tastes? Am I indoctrinating him when by various means I instil some code of manners in his mind? Do the children's books that I provide him with represent a programme of indoctrination? In short, there are certainly some words that often crop up in educational debate that need careful watching; they need analysis so that their ambiguities are laid bare and so that at any given point we know precisely what we are talking about, if we are going to have any real communication and debate.

Philosophers will go on to relate this general point to the claim that the other disciplines give us useful facts to work with. Yes, they certainly do, but these facts are useful only if we understand them and, a second point, if we do not make the mistake of attributing to them more significance than they deserve. The psychologist may tell us, for example, that there is a high correlation between successful performance in a certain test and creativity. Children who do this test well, later show signs of being creative. A fact (let us assume). A fact? A useful fact? It is of no use whatsoever until we know what is meant here by 'creative' and whether we wish to promote, ignore or curb 'creativity', in the sense intended.

'Creative' is an example of what is called a 'normative' word. Normative words are words that both purport to describe something and at the same time imply that whatever is being described is valuable in some way. For example, the adjective 'round' is simply descriptive: one describes something as round without necessarily implying any approval or disapproval.

But the adjective 'brave' is normative: if one describes somebody as brave. one does not only attribute certain types of behaviour to him, one also implies that this behaviour is admirable. Normative words, of which there are many, are the curse of educational debate. Because 'creative' is normative, because one's natural tendency is to assume that it is a good thing to be creative, one can all too easily listen to the psychologist, learn that ability at a certain test indicates a tendency towards creativity, and go away assuming that it must be a good thing to teach children in such a way that they do well at the test in question. But does the psychologist mean what you mean by 'creative', and, despite the normative aspect of 'creative', is what either of you mean by 'creative' a desirable quality to cultivate in the child?

These are important questions. The statement that something is the case, even when one fully understands it, is of strictly limited significance. It does not in itself tell us what to do about it. In practice, of course, we often leap immediately to certain conclusions about what to do, as soon as we are given some factual information. If I am told that Johnny is beating Lucy over the head with a shoe in the next room, I don't hang about contemplating the limited significance of this fact; I go next door and stop it. Nonetheless, the decision or desire to remedy or encourage some state of affairs is obviously quite distinct from the realisation that this is the situation, or that these are the facts of the matter. The historian, the sociologist and the psychologist give us the facts, so far as they are able, but we have to beware of assuming that they can do more. We have to beware of arguments, lectures or whatever that proceed by telling us that this, that or the other is the case, and then imperceptibly drift into a spate of conclusions about what ought to be the case. The business of describing something is logically distinct from the business of prescribing something or evaluating. However odd we might personally find certain views as to what ought to be done in the light of certain facts, there is nothing illogical in itself about saying anything from 'ignore it' to 'change it' in the face of any statement of fact. We may object to the man who says 'Let it burn', when told that his neighbour's house is on fire, but he is not being illogical. One cannot conclude anything about what ought to be done, simply from a statement about what is the case. (Although, of course, the facts of the case will be *relevant* to any decision as to what ought to be done.) And a very usual way in which educationalists tend to make this illegitimate move, quite unconsciously, is by using in their argument normative words which have not been properly clarified.

Philosophers, then, will defend the business of linguistic analysis by pointing out the importance of knowing precisely what somebody means by certain crucial terms before one can reasonably accept or reject his argument. And, although one might respond by saying that some terms are considerably more worth analysing than others, and that philosophers spend too much time worrying about insignificant terms, one must surely accept that this job does need doing. We do need to think carefully and clearly about the possible meanings of words like 'creative', 'interests', 'needs' and 'intelligence'.

And so we arrive at the view that the philosopher should play the part of an umpire or policeman in educational debate. According to this widely held view, his function is to see that others play by the rules of rational discussion. These rules are many: for example, steps in an argument should be logically connected, emotional prejudice should not count as evidence, all relevant evidence should be considered. But the two most subtle breaches of the rules that the philosopher-umpire delights in exposing remain the two that we have considered: the gaining of a point by the use of ambiguous terminology, and the transition from factual description to prescriptive evaluation, generally unsuspectingly achieved by the use of normative terms.

Given this view of the philosopher's role, I do not find it at all surprising that many people feel that philosophers are rather arrogant, and yet essentially doing nothing distinctive that entitles them to a distinctive professional label. What are they doing but claiming to be better than everybody else at detecting suspect or faulty argument? Is this not tantamount to saying that they are better at arguing and, hence, better at arriving at conclusions than other people, or that they are more rational? It is understandable that many people should resent this implication.

Now, of course, the philosopher will hastily point out that it is not so much that he, the person, is better than everyone else at cool and logical reasoning, as that the business of philosophising or the discipline of philosophy *involves* this attempt at detached rationality. Philosophy *is* the exercise of reason, and some philosophers actually define it quite simply as 'the exercise of logical thought', 'an activity of criticism or clarification', 'a technique for thinking' or 'thinking about meaning'. And so, it may be claimed, there is no suggestion that philosophers are more rational than other people, only that people should be philosophical or, in other words, that they should think clearly about the meaning of terms they employ and the coherence of their arguments.

This is all very well and it might give professional philosophers a job to do, perhaps in schools. There they might profitably encourage children to think more deeply about what they mean by describing certain films as 'great' or certain records as 'fabulous'.

But would this view of the philosopher's role justify a philosopher's position in a college of education or an education department? There he is not dealing with children but with adults who are already well aware of the need for clear thinking and rational argument. Now he may well reply, although he will be reluctant to do so too publicly, that although students may be aware of the need, that does not mean that they are very good at it, and, besides, the field of education throws up new terminology that students have probably not considered closely before. In other words, provided that he is prepared to stop stressing that anyone can do philosophy and that he is in no sense an expert or better at it than anyone else, he can begin to make out a reasonable claim to his salary, by arguing that he is teaching students to think more clearly than they would otherwise do about complex and ambiguous educational terms. But will this do?

The discussion that the philosopher-umpire wants to police stems from his colleagues and from other educationalists. We assumed, for example, that the psychologist might talk of 'creativity', without adequate clarification, and then proceed to make evaluative claims. Now certainly he might do this. But how, one might be forgiven for wondering, is a separate philosophical discussion on the concept of 'creativity', which lays bare the ambiguity of the term, going to help us understand what the psychologist means by it? Surely the philosopher has done all that he can do of practical value when he has pointed out that some terms such as 'creative' are (a) obscure and (b) normative. And this point, I think we may safely say, we have now all hoisted in; perhaps we are getting a little tired of hearing it. What is needed now is clarification from the psychologist as to what *he* means by the term in *his* context, and not suggestions from the philosopher as to what somebody *might* mean in various contexts. One begins to fear that the philosopher has dug his own grave by insisting that philosophy is just thinking about meaning. For his colleagues, such as the psychologist, are surely as well aware as he of the need for coherence, clarity and fair play. As those who define philosophy simply as critical thought about meaning freely admit, we are all philosophising whenever we attempt to examine a word, a phrase or an argument closely; we are thinking about meaning.

Once this is admitted, it does not seem unreasonable for the student to ask why, in that case, he should go to the professional philosopher. Why should he supplement his debates with sociologists, psychologists and historians by debates with philosophers? Surely all that is needed is a degree of philosophical rigour on the part of these other specialists: *they* must clarify their use of obscure terms; *they* must avoid the transition from the statement that something is the case to the assumption that it ought to be the case, or that it is a proper state of affairs just because it is the case. How can the philosopher-umpire justify his intrusion, without reverting to that claim to superiority in clear thinking that he was at pains to deny? If he is not prepared to say that he is better at rational argument, how can he justify policing other people's arguments? Surely he cannot. But equally we cannot let him get away with the claim that he is more rational than anybody else, even if he were more disposed than he is to make this claim. Therefore, it is concluded, the philosopher is not needed.

Before commenting on this conclusion I shall summarise the argument of this section. Two distinct charges may be levelled against the 'philosophy of education', understood as critical examination of educational terminology. One is that the sort of thing that it does is not worth doing. The other is that it is worth doing, but that it does not require a distinctive course to do it. This latter argument may imply the limited thesis that professional philosophers have no special powers that enable them to do the job particularly well, or it may imply the stronger thesis that not only are they not specially qualified, but that in any case the only point in analysing a concept such as 'creativity' is in relation to some context – in other words, with reference to the specific use of the term by specific people, such as the resident psychologist, in which case we need *his* analysis and not somebody else's.

The first argument does not strike me as convincing. It is a matter to be established by simple observation that people advocate various educational proposals using arguments that need critical attention and, in particular, using terminology that carries a point by its ambiguity. People *do* talk blandly about 'the educated man', or 'the need for the teacher to be neutral', without thinking very deeply about what an educated man is, or what neutrality involves. If we are going to have any real communication or meaningful debate, we obviously need clarity and precision.

The second argument I find considerably more appealing, if only as an interesting conundrum. There is an obvious and telling rejoinder to the conclusion that the philosopher can make: he is not better at analysing 'democracy' or 'creativity', in the sense that he knows how to arrive at the 'right answer', since the idea of a right answer does not make much sense here. There is not one and only one correct answer to the question 'What does "democracy" mean?'. If there were, there would be none of the confusion that there is, caused by the fact that people use the word in different ways, and there would therefore be no need for clarification. But the philosopher may be better, and in theory should be better, at analysis than other people, in the limited sense that as a result of much practice he is familiar with the business of attempting to clarify complex concepts; and perhaps it may be added that in the case of certain specific concepts he has thought deeply and for a long time about them and made use of the written work of other philosophers on these concepts. Therefore, he may say, he has an important job to do in prompting students to see for themselves just how very obscure many concepts that we tend to take for granted are. It is not sufficient simply to tell people to think about meaning; one has to initiate people into the task. And this is what any philosopher would say.

In my view this defence is legitimate. Most of us pick up fairly quickly the point that 'rationality', for example, may mean different things to different people, and few of us have not at one time or another responded to an argument by saying something like 'It all depends what you mean by such and such'. We have got the hang of the game. But the fact remains that a lot of people do not play it very well: they do not really subject 'rationality' to razor-sharp analysis, pursuing it as far as they can, trying to establish whether there are certain conditions that just have to be met if somebody is to deserve the epithet 'rational', and other conditions that are quite incompatible with it.

Nonetheless, I sympathise with those who question the relative value of devoting necessarily limited time to a full-length course concerned with examining the meaning of a variety of educational concepts. They are hitting an awkward nail right on the head when they point out that, insofar as words have the meanings that men choose to give them, there is a limit to the value of pressing ever onwards with an examination of the meaning of 'rationality', 'creativity', 'teaching' and so on. They are surely right to stress that it is more important to concentrate on understanding the meanings being attached to slippery words by specific people in specific arguments than it is to examine concepts in a vacuum; and they are therefore right to conclude that once the basic point that words can be slippery has been made, what is needed in educational theory courses is more time to examine what is being said by those who are dealing with empirical data, in a broadly philosophical manner, and less time doing philosophy. And finally they have the philosopher neatly cornered on the question as to precisely how and when he is going to distinguish between his role as teacher – when he is presumed to have some expertise that makes him an authority – and his role as a participant in inquiry, when he makes no claim to superior excellence and therefore offers no reason for people to discuss with him, rather than with others.

Philosophy of Education and Moral Philosophy

The argument as I have outlined it in the previous pages is naturally rather stylised. It is worth setting out in this manner only because it draws attention to certain things that the philosophy of education tries to do (clarify terminology and police argument) and the sense of frustration that some people who are called upon to do it undoubtedly feel.

What this argument does not do is draw attention to two other very important tasks that philosophy has to perform in the sphere of education, namely, to draw substantive conclusions from the analysis of certain concepts and to get to grips with the problems involved in the making of value judgements and more particularly moral judgements.

So far, in talking about philosophical analysis, I have concentrated on a range of concepts the precise meaning of which carries little by way of consequence beyond the fact that it becomes clear what we are talking about. But there are some concepts, central to the sphere of education, the analysis of which carries logical consequences for the teaching process. This is particularly true of a cluster of concepts, such as knowledge, understanding and intelligence, which technically belong to the sphere of epistemology or philosophy of mind. What it is to understand is clearly of crucial importance in trying to promote understanding. The nature of knowledge must have an over-riding control over the way in which one sets about planning an education that is concerned to impart knowledge to children. It is thus no accident that a great deal of important work done recently in philosophy of education has centred on the curriculum and its epistemological foundations. It is quite simply a mistake to divorce means and aims in education and to regard the former as a purely empirical matter and the latter as a purely philosophical matter. Quite apart from the question of whether one values, say, intelligence, what one takes it to mean will dictate certain means rather than others of promoting it, and conversely the means that one employs to promote intelligence will dictate the nature of the 'intelligence' promoted. Thus, for example, if Hirst's view that there are something like eight logically distinct forms of knowledge or ways of knowing open to man is correct, then it follows that a curriculum concerned to promote knowledge should initiate children into all these forms of knowledge. Or again, if an integrated curriculum is to be defended on the grounds that knowledge is a unified whole, then it makes a deal of difference first of all whether it is true that all knowledge is one and if so in what sense, and secondly that the curriculum should be integrated in a way that does justice to the sense, if there is one, in which knowledge is one.

I do not, at this stage, want to say any more about this aspect of the philosophy of education, but it should be stressed that here we have an example of the sort of way in which analysis can be far from sterile and is in fact a necessary prerequisite of coherent educational planning.

The second important contribution of philosophy to education is in the sphere of values. When I write of getting to grips with the problems of moral judgements, I do not mean simply learning to recognise a moral value judgement for what it is and to distinguish it from a factual statement nor do I mean simply recognising the fact that different people have different opinions on the subject. That much most of us can do; and unfortunately that much is all that most of us ever bother to do. There is a tendency for people to fight shy of undertaking a rigorous examination of the question of precisely what, if anything, we can positively assert about moral value judgements. Can some views as to what is good be ruled out absolutely? Can anything be in some sense proven to be good? Are some theories about how one can tell whether something is good untenable? Are any such theories demonstrably more sound than others? Does it make sense to talk of moral propositions as being true or false? Getting to grips with the matter means getting to grips with questions like these, as well as examining specific moral claims either on the level of formal principles (for instance, the suggestion that happiness is more important than freedom), or on the level of particular issues (for instance, the suggestion that student teachers ought to design their own courses in colleges of education).

To stress the importance of moral philosophy as an aspect of the philosophy of education is not to deny the value of analysing more specifically educational terminology, nor the notion of philosophy playing the policeman's role. But, quite apart from the frustration that some people feel with a philosophy course that does no more, these activities are not in themselves enough if philosophy is to make the full contribution that it could make to educational theory. It is not enough simply to know that some words are ambiguous, nor even to know precisely how a particular speaker interprets the ambiguous words he uses; it is not enough to appreciate the distinction between a statement of fact and an evaluative statement, or to detect the point at which a speaker moves quietly from 'is' to 'ought'. If there is to be any point in this clarification, if we are to put the empirical facts with which we are presented to any use, we have to have some objectives. It is not very helpful simply to point out that a value-loaded argument *is* value-loaded, unless one can go on to say something about values themselves.

Educational debate does not only revolve around questions as to what is the case and what can be done. It also involves the question of what ought to be done or what it is best to do. We need to reflect on what we want to do, as well as on what we can do.

To approve of an act, to praise or commend it in some way, obviously involves an evaluative assumption. One could only approve of a man's conduct in helping an old lady across the street, for example, if one valued such behaviour. Approving of something means placing a value on it, and it is therefore logically impossible to approve of something without indicating that one holds certain values. But it is not only when we overtly praise an action that we indicate our values. Any freely made decision to act in one way rather than another also involves evaluative assumptions. If I make a positive decision to do this rather than that, the implication must be that in some way, however slight, I value the course of action that I have chosen more than the various alternatives open to me.

Of course, in practice a great deal of our behaviour is not carefully worked out at all; we simply act on habit or in response to various pressures. But it is clear that, whenever we do consider what to do in certain situations, the coping-stone of any decision to act in one way rather than another must be an evaluative assumption. First we need to appreciate the nature of the situation that faces us, then we need to have some view of the likely consequences of various lines of action, but finally we have to have some view as to the relative value of those different consequences. To decide to act in a certain way, assuming that one has a certain amount of freedom in the matter, is to make a choice; and choosing, no less than approving, involves value assumptions.

When spelt out in this way, the point must seem too obvious to need stating. But the extraordinary thing is that so much debate about what should be done in a sphere such as education simply ignores the questions and problems that arise in relation to value assumptions or judgements. It proceeds as if it were enough to clarify what the situation is at present and to point out the consequences of various proposals, and as if there were no problems and no need for inquiry into that vital ingredient of decision-making, the evaluative assumption. We therefore find certain advocates of the grammar schools, for instance, concerned only to establish that as a matter of fact the grammar schools have maintained and are likely to continue maintaining the highest cultural standards. And we find some advocates of the comprehensive system seeking simply to establish that such a system will promote a greater equality. Certainly, if we are to make a decision between two such systems, we shall need to know whether either claim is true (and incidentally before we could know that we should have to be a little more clear as to what is meant by 'highest cultural standards' and 'greater equality'); but even when we know that, we are no nearer being able to make a decision in favour of one system or the other, until we have found a means of weighing these rival evaluative assumptions in the balance. If it comes to the crunch, what matters more – culture or equality? Is there a way of deciding that? In the same way, it is not enough for champions for and against pornography simply to settle whether pornographic books do or do not have some effect on those who read them. Even if it were established that they do, it would be a further question as to whether such literature should, or should not, be prohibited to some extent. And once again the further question would involve consideration of various evaluative assumptions.

This amounts to saying that since decisions to act involve value assumptions, the question of values must be examined as minutely as the facts of the case, if an informed decision is to be made. The values that we are primarily concerned with are moral values, for it is these that are involved in our view of what is acceptable and just, and that govern our behaviour. But if moral values are to be examined at all, they have to be examined in a philosophical manner rather than by any empirical science. That is to say, one has to rely on applying critical thought to arguments that may be put forward in favour of valuing one thing rather than another; one has to probe such arguments as deeply as one can by pressing for a more detailed account of what precisely is meant by, say, happiness or freedom. One cannot turn to empirical tests or rely on observation. Observation will tell us what people do value, historical research will tell us what people have valued, and sociological research will tell us that as a matter of fact different people value different things. But none of this will tell us whether some people are not making a mistake in valuing what they do value. The Romans did not think it wrong to throw Christians to the lions. But it is still open to us to say that it was wrong. To put it simply, we have to consider what it would mean to say such a thing.

One final point should be made about the importance of moral philosophy as part of the philosophy of education. Most of the words that philosophers of education consider need close analysis are normative (i.e. involve an evaluative assumption as well as a descriptive content, as I suggested was the case with 'creative'). The reason for this is not difficult to find. Words that are generally used in a purely descriptive manner (school, classroom, headmaster) do not cause much confusion: we all grow up to use such words in the conventional way and make our value judgements quite clear in respect of them by saying 'I am in favour of schools', or 'I am against schools', or 'There are various types of school; I approve of some and disapprove of others'. It is words that carry some notion of approval or disapproval in their meaning that cause confusion. People who grow up with the idea that to be creative is a good thing, for example, and who know that others feel this, are naturally reluctant to drop this association of desirability with creativeness. Therefore when they find that they do not value what others do value in the name of 'creativity', they tend to want to redefine the descriptive reference of the term. Rather than say 'I'm against creativity' they say '*That* is not creativity'. The result is that over a period of time normative words acquire a variety of different shades of meaning for different people. The word 'indoctrination', for instance, was originally synonymous with 'teaching'; both meant to 'imbue with an idea'. But as some people came to object to the practice of simply implanting beliefs in children they reserved the word 'indoctrination' for it, and reserved 'teaching' to describe a process they approved of. The result is that with an unsuspecting audience, a speaker can dismiss a particular type of teaching of which he disapproves by referring to it as 'indoctrination'.

Clearly then, since normative words involve evaluative assumption in their meaning, a full and acceptable analysis of such words presupposes a moral framework. Whereas with a simple descriptive term such as 'table', analysis of its meaning depends solely on considering the various ways in which the word is used and distinguishing between central uses and what are apparently peripheral or extended uses (mathematics tables; the Table Mountain), analysis of a normative word, such as 'creative', involves attempting to produce a definition that fits both descriptively and evaluatively. One is not being 'creative' if one types out the page of a book, because this is not the sort of activity to which the descriptive content of 'creative' applies; but equally one would not call an original painting a creative piece of work if one thought that it was an utterly worthless daub. When people argue about whether much of what goes on in the classroom under the name of creative work really is creative or not, they are arguing to some extent about values. They are arguing about whether what is being done really is worthwhile.[4]

Similarly, some have maintained that 'to indoctrinate' means to cause people to believe something without giving them proper understanding of what they believe. Those who object to this analysis of the concept of indoctrination do so on the grounds that it is not necessarily a bad thing in all circumstances to do this; therefore, since indoctrination is bad by definition, this activity cannot be indoctrination.

One has to have a value structure before one can analyse such normative terms, and therefore if the analysis is to be meaningful, the value structure itself must come under examination.

To summarise this section: whatever criticisms may be made of the philosophy of education, it can hardly be denied that there is an important philosophical job to be done in relation to education in the sphere of values, particularly moral values. One may sympathise to a greater or lesser extent with those who feel that a seminar devoted to the concept of 'teaching' is time wasted. But the fact remains that there is a need for more conceptual clarity, and more rigorous logical appraisal, in a great deal of educational theory. Whether this will be best achieved in courses of philosophy may be debatable, but what is surely not debatable is that moral philosophy is something that needs to be done.

REFERENCES

1 Hirst, P. H., 'Educational Theory' in Tibble, J. W. (ed.), *The Study of Education* (Routledge & Kegan Paul, 1966), p. 31.
2 Ibid., p. 57.
3 Stenhouse, L. A., reviewing the Open University course on the curriculum, *Journal of Curriculum Studies*, vol. 5, No. 2 (1973), p. 178.
4 Possibly I am begging certain questions here about the concept of creativity. For a full discussion of this concept, see Chapter 10. At this point I am only attempting to illustrate the problem that may arise with normative words.

FURTHER READING

Wilson, John, *Philosophy* (Concept Books, Heinemann Educational Books, 1968) provides a concise introduction to the business of philosophical analysis for those who are entirely unacquainted with philosophy. Hospers, John, *An Introduction to Philosophical Analysis* (Routledge & Kegan Paul, 1973) is considerably more advanced, but is particularly to be recommended.

On the nature of educational theory, see Hirst, P. H., 'Educational Theory' in Tibble, J. W. (ed.) *The Study of Education*, and Woods, R. G., 'Introduction' in Woods, R. G. (ed.) *Education and its Disciplines* (University of London Press, 1972). See also the exchange between O'Connor, D. J., and Hirst, P. H., on 'The Nature of Educational Theory' in *Proceedings of the Philosophy of Education Society of Great Britain*, vol. 6, no. 1 (1972).

Lucas, C. J. (ed.), *What is Philosophy of Education?* (Collier-Macmillan, 1969) is a useful collection of articles which illustrates the great diversity of views amongst philosophers on this question. See also Peters, R. S., 'Philosophy of Education' in Tibble, J. W. (ed.), *The Study of Education*, and Woods, R. G., 'Philosophy of Education' in Woods, R. G. (ed.), *Education and its Disciplines*. Thompson, Keith, 'Philosophy of Education and Educational Practice', in *P.E.S.G.B. Proceedings*, vol. 4 (1970) argues persuasively for the policeman role of philosophy.

Chapter 2

Moral Philosophy

Those philosophers who are content to define philosophy simply as 'thinking about meaning', tend also to stress that philosophy is easy; it is not a mysterious pursuit suitable only for wise gurus and sages. Anybody can do it, and in a sense everybody does do it some of the time, for everybody at one time or another applies his critical powers to some problem of meaning. There are, however, dangers in stressing the ease with which one may philosophise: the implication is that provided one questions, rather than passively accepts, one is doing the job. Even allowing that this is in some sense true, it is a further question as to whether it is easy to do the job well and whether all spheres into which one might choose to inquire by 'thinking about meaning' in them are equally easy to penetrate.

Certainly the techniques of philosophy do not have to be acquired by most people, as the techniques of building might have to be. The techniques of philosophy are no more than one: that critical examination of meaning already referred to. That is *how* philosophers proceed in any sphere; and most of us have this technique to some degree at our finger-tips. It is therefore not difficult for people to settle down to the task of philosophising. There is nothing particularly exalted about being a philosopher. But it would be a mistake to conclude that the going must therefore be easy in any philosophical inquiry. Whether it is or not will depend upon the complexity and difficulty of the sphere of inquiry.

Irritating as it may be to say it, for those who like easy answers or who believe that they have the answers to moral questions, the moral sphere is not particularly easy to inquire into. Here, as in any other sphere, anybody can play the philosopher. Anybody can ask what is meant by saying that something is good, anybody can return an answer to this question, and anybody can reject passive acceptance of some traditional view. But going through the motions of philosophy in this way does not get us far. Hitler did these things, and Hitler was a very bad philosopher, if it is reasonable to call him one at all. It is not so easy to cut a coherent path through the many varied approaches and solutions to moral problems that have been offered at one time or another; it is not so easy to arrive at a satisfactory account of what 'freedom' means and to explain why and in what sense people ought to be free; it is not so easy to establish whether a philosopher such as John Stuart Mill did, or did not, prove what he set out to prove in his essay *Utilitarianism*. It is not even all that easy to establish what he did set out to prove.

It may seem silly of me to emphasise the difficulty of the task at the outset. Those who insist that philosophy is easy, may at least hope to hang on to their readers. But nobody need be intimidated or put off by this emphasis, for it remains true that the way in which we have to proceed, the manner of inquiry, is nothing mysterious and can be handled by virtually everybody. All that I am stressing is that the moral sphere is not an area that admits of easy answers and obvious solutions. And this needs stressing at a time when so many people seem so sure that they know the answers. The fact that something is wrong with this state of affairs should be immediately apparent when one reflects that different people apparently know completely different answers.

The moral sphere is complex precisely in that various people, including professional philosophers, have such different accounts to give of it. There is not only sharp disagreement as to what kind of behaviour is morally acceptable and what kind of actions are good; there is an equally great divergence of opinion as to what it means to call something 'good', or what it is about what somebody regards as morally acceptable behaviour that makes it morally acceptable. If I describe a table as square, there is not much room for doubt about what I am doing: I am attributing a specific quality to the table, namely the quality of squareness. I am telling you its shape, and you are unlikely to be ignorant of what shape the word 'square' signifies. But what am I doing when I describe an action as good? Am I attributing some quality to it? If so, what? What does 'good' signify? All manner of answers have at one time or another been put forward, more or less persuasively, to this kind of question. They range from the view that a thing is good, and can only be good if God approves of it, to the view that to describe something as good is just a way of saying that one likes it – and that is quite a range.

Given the many quite distinct positions that have been adopted in relation to moral values, few of which are so obviously absurd as to merit no consideration, it is at least a possibility that it is going to be very difficult indeed to offer some complete and incontestable explanation of the moral sphere. However, it is not so difficult to understand these different viewpoints, to see how they gain whatever measure of plausibility they have, and hence to understand the nature of the problems that are to be found in this area.

Understanding the problems, understanding where, in what way and why moral philosophers have been perplexed, and why they have failed to agree on convincing answers to questions such as 'What ought we to do?' or 'What does "good" mean?' is an enormous step forward. For in practical terms, the problems surrounding the question of moral values are only of interest and importance because different people have such different values, and often these values are mutually incompatible. It is this fact that gives practical urgency to the demand for all to do moral philosophy.

An integral part of what it means to adopt certain moral values is that one feels strongly that other people ought to adopt those same values. If I have certain aesthetic values, such as an admiration for Wagner's music, it does not necessarily follow that I resent the fact that others do not share my taste. But if I adopt a moral value, such as the view that no man ought to take another's life, then it does follow that it matters a great deal to me when others can be seen by their actions not to share this value.

Insofar, then, as people have different and incompatible values, there is an obvious case for looking into the matter in an attempt to see whether some are more acceptable than others. And insofar as the adoption of a moral viewpoint involves the desire that it should be universally adopted, and insofar as some people's moral values may actually be repugnant to others, the exercise of doing moral philosophy may be extremely important, even if it does not lead to a comprehensive and indisputable right answer. Even if ultimately we feel obliged to conclude that there is no way of distinguishing between the correctness of rival value claims, no way of establishing beyond reasonable doubt that certain things ought to be done and that certain others ought not to be done, as some philosophers would claim, it would at least be beneficial in practical terms that people should appreciate this awkward conclusion, rather than assume that they know that other people are wrong.

One prevalent view held today is that there is no real problem about moral values, because the sort of things a particular society values is simply a matter of choice on the part of that society. A problem, it is claimed, is artificially created by those who try to argue that there is some eternal moral truth and that therefore certain things ought to be regarded as good and others not, at all times and in all places, whatever any particular people may think. People who maintain, for instance, that human sacrifice always was and always must be wrong are simply confusing the issue. All they are entitled to say is that *they* would never approve of it. Our society happens to have adopted this particular value, but it might not have done, and it does not make sense to ask whether it should have done or not. According to this view, various factors may be produced to explain why a particular society values some particular code of behaviour, but these factors will be economic or social. They will explain, but not justify. The notion of justification is out of place. Human sacrifice is not a custom that can be condemned as in some sense always necessarily wrong, any more than a custom such as monogamy or the wearing of long hair can be. All three are similar in that they are culturally induced conventions; the only difference between them in our society is the strength of feeling associated with them. We don't regard length of hair as a moral issue because we don't feel very strongly about it. Conversely we do regard human sacrifice as immoral because we disapprove of it very strongly. Perhaps, it may be felt, the accuracy of this analysis of the situation is indicated by the fact that attitudes to monogamy and related sexual practices are at this moment changing. Fifty years ago, if we may generalise, people felt strongly about marriage and approved of Christian ideals of monogamy and chastity before marriage. They therefore regarded relations between the sexes as a moral issue. Today, many people feel that these ideals are questionable; they do not value them so highly, and therefore the issue ceases to be seen as a moral one.

This relativist view – so called because it stresses that moral values are relative to particular societies – is not new. It was around when philosophy as we know it was born. Many of the fifth-century Athenian sophists seem to have been relativists, and it was precisely this view that Plato tried to combat by arguing that, although different societies might adopt different values, that did not in itself show that they were right to do so, or that the values adopted by some societies were not preferable to those adopted by others.[1] According to Plato, regardless of what some societies chose to value, there were nonetheless some things that just ought to be valued and others that ought not. He was therefore the first recorded absolutist; that is to say he believed in certain absolute moral values that were always and would always be binding on all people at all times and in all places whether they recognised them or not. In semi-mystical language, which in the long run has probably done his argument more harm than good, Plato claimed that there were eternal Forms of such things as Goodness situated somewhere, somehow, beyond the material world. An action could only be good if it partook of the Form of Goodness in some way, and since the Form did not change, so the goodness of actions on earth could not vary. Since most people feel that they have no idea what Plato is talking about, his theory of Forms is not of much help. But it is clear that it represents a metaphorical attempt to state an absolutist position.

Since that time battle has never ceased to rage between relativists and absolutists, two fairly recent champions of either position being Karl Marx and John Stuart Mill. Ignoring a certain inconsistency in his writings, Marx was a relativist. He took the view that moral values were culturally induced conventions and that they reflected the economic structure of a given society: those who had the power, effectively promoted standards of right and wrong that would perpetuate the status quo and therefore their power. For instance, feudal societies tried to maintain the belief that it was morally right for the serf to show loyalty to his overlord. (Marx's view is substantially the same as that attributed to a character named Thrasy-machus in Plato's dialogue, the *Republic*.)

Mill, on the other hand, was a utilitarian, which is to say that he believed that the promotion of happiness was, and must always be, the supreme moral consideration. Rules and conduct in a society were good if, and only if, they contributed to a greater balance of happiness over misery. If one could demonstrate that a particular custom was in fact promoting un-happiness, then it was wrong, and it was wrong whether people regarded it as wrong or not. It is clear that Mill is not committed to the view that certain actions and customs must necessarily always be wrong or right, as some absolutists have been. For people and conditions might change, so that a practice that once promoted happiness might begin to promote unhappiness. Nonetheless he is an absolutist in the sense that his formula for testing whether something is good or not, is supposed to be absolutely binding on all men at all times.

It is worth drawing attention to the long history of the debate between relativists and absolutists, because some people today who adopt a relativist position tend to talk as if their point of view was obviously correct and as if it is only because previous generations lacked the knowledge of the world that we now have that they failed to appreciate this. They sometimes talk as if until very recently all people were some kind of primitive sheep who believed in nonsensical moral absolutes, but that now man is so knowledge-able, so much master of the world, that he can see that in the past he has merely been a victim of superstition. But the matter is not as simple as that.

The case for some kind of relativism certainly looks strong. This is partly because of the indisputable fact to which relativists draw attention that moral values vary in different societies and even change with time within one society. But this in itself will not substantiate their point of view. After all, different societies have had different opinions about other things besides moral values, and some of them have then been shown to have been wrong. Many people have believed that the world is flat. But the world is not flat, and the fact that some people may think it is does not make it so. In the same way, the fact that some societies have thought that it is morally acceptable to practise cannibalism does not show that it is.

What really gives relativism plausibility and what makes the fact that different cultures have different values look significant is the difficulty of seeing how one could ever *know* that any particular moral viewpoint was the one that ought to be adopted. The relativist's caricature of history as a steady line of development from blind superstition to complete knowledge has at least this much truth in it: it is difficult to see how those who have claimed to know what is good could convincingly show that it is.

Imagine some primitive society, all the members of which are convinced that certain things are good and certain ways of behaving are right. They have a rigid code of behaviour and nobody is in any doubt, for example, that paying back one's debts is good and burning one's neighbour's house is bad. In such a society there is no question about *what* is good and no question *that* it is good. Nobody is puzzled about how it was originally discovered that paying back debts was good. Questions such as 'Why is it good?' do not arise. The world is flat and paying your debts is good. Two facts; two truths. And that, as far as the members of this society are concerned, is all there is to it. They know that these two statements are true.

The word 'know' can be used in a number of distinct ways: one can know that something is the case, one can know why something happened, one can know how to do something, or one can simply know someone. We are clearly concerned with 'knowing' in the sense of 'knowing that'. Normally, when we claim to know that something is the case, we are claiming both that it is as a matter of fact the case, and that we can produce, or at least point to, the evidence which shows that it is the case. In other words we claim that the matter is demonstrably true and, by implication, that anybody would have to accept the demonstration or the evidence as convincing.

Thus in theory if I claim to know that my wife is at home, you would expect me to be able to produce evidence to support this claim, such as that I have just rung her up and spoken to her. If I am merely assuming that she is at home because she generally is at this time, it would be more accurate to say that I have strong reason to believe that she is at home. When we say that we know that pearls dissolve in acid, we can back up our claim by an appeal to empirical demonstration. In practice, of course, we may use the word 'know' very loosely, but if we really have knowledge that something is the case, we must have access to the evidence that shows that it is. Otherwise we merely have opinion or belief. Knowledge therefore presupposes generally accepted rules as to what counts as evidence. Most people will accept the evidence of their own eyes that pearls dissolve in acid as convincing; and in normal circumstances people will accept the fact that I have just spoken to my wife on the telephone as good evidence that she is at home.

And so it is that we can show that the members of this primitive society were wrong in their belief that the world is flat. Evidence of various sorts, the most immediately recognisable being aerial photographs, is available to support the claim that we know that it is round. There is no convincing evidence to support the claim that it is flat. But when we turn to the moral claims of this same society the situation is entirely different. It is not simply that they cannot produce the evidence to support their claim that they know that it is wrong to burn one's neighbour's house down. We cannot produce the evidence to show that they are mistaken either. For it is completely unclear what sort of thing is allowed to count as evidence one way or the other.

Claims to knowledge in any sphere do not make sense without generally agreed standards as to what counts as evidence. What are the criteria for claiming moral knowledge? What sort of evidence is one supposed to produce to show that something is good? Statistical surveys would show us what people think is good, but not that it is good. Demonstrations might indicate that a certain type of action invariably has certain consequences that people like, but that would not show that either the action or its consequences were good. To reach that conclusion one would have to show that what people like is good. And how would one do that?

The question arises as to whether the idea of producing evidence that all would have to accept to show that paying debts is good is not as absurd as the idea of producing evidence to show that cake is delicious. Cake neither is, nor is not, delicious. Such statements are absurd. All one can say is that some people find some cake delicious. Whether a cake is delicious or not is a matter of taste, not knowledge. Is the same true of moral values? Are the relativists right? 'Freedom is good' may look like a straightforward factual proposition like 'Pigs are four-legged', but the more one looks, the less obvious is the parallel. 'Pigs are four-legged' causes no problem. We know what is meant by all the words involved and we know how to test the truth of the statement. We line up all the pigs we can find and we look and see whether they do or do not have four legs. Only the blind could seriously question the evidence. But how do we test the truth of the statement that freedom is good? What is freedom? But far more important: what is 'good'? What are we looking for? One certainly could not establish that freedom is good simply by observation, for at the very best one could only demonstrate something such as that freedom produces results that one approves of. But one's normal supposition is that 'good' means something more than 'what I approve of'. Is that merely because, as some would claim, one has been brought up to *assume* that it means more, without having any good reason for so doing?

Once societies, or individuals within them, get as far as questioning their moral beliefs, the temptation to adopt some form of relativism is very great. Once one appreciates the difficulty of talking about knowledge in the moral sphere, what could be more plausible than to say that there is no more to moral values than the adoption of certain rules by a given society that promote consequences that it happens to like? And that, therefore, it makes no sense to talk of certain societies having values that are bad or immoral in any absolute sense?

But in historical terms, the realisation that moral values were open to questioning and that their truth could not simply be taken for granted did not lead to widespread relativism. Once the matter was open to debate, all kinds of solution to the problem were offered. Common to virtually all of them was an attempt to lay down a precise meaning for 'good'. For philosophers rightly saw that if one knew what 'good' meant, if one had a definition of the term, as one has a definition of the term 'bachelor', it would be as easy to distinguish between good and bad as it is to distinguish between bachelors and married men. And so out the definitions tumbled: 'good' meant 'productive of happiness'; 'good' meant 'natural'; 'good' meant 'pleasing to God'; 'good' meant 'contributory to security'.

But none of these solutions achieved very much. In the first place, the definitions themselves were often as ambiguous and obscure as the term 'good'. What, for instance, is natural? Natural behaviour might mean spontaneous behaviour; it might mean the sort of behaviour that is presumed to have gone on in pre-civilised jungle life; it might mean what people regard as normal (as, for example, when people refer to heterosexuality as natural and homosexuality as unnatural). Or how do we know what is pleasing to God – assuming, that is, that we know that God exists in the first place? Even the suggestion that 'good' means 'productive of happiness', which looks a little less complex at first glance, poses the problem of what precisely we mean by 'happiness'.

But secondly, and much more importantly, where would the acceptance of any one of these definitions get us? The assumption of the members of the primitive society had been that if something was morally good, then by definition one ought to do it. And this is the assumption of most of us still. Even if we are relativists, we may accept that insofar as somebody or some society does think that something is morally good, then they must feel that that something ought to be done. But in the case of each of the proposed definitions of good it seems quite reasonable to ask why, in that case, one ought to be good. It seems quite reasonable to ask why one ought to behave naturally, why we ought to promote happiness or security, and even why we ought to please God, assuming he exists. The only way in which one could hope to persuade people that 'good' actually means one of these things is by showing that people must agree that they ought to do one of these things. But it is precisely the possibility of showing that certain things ought to be done that is in doubt.

By the beginning of this century the frustration caused by the apparent impossibility of getting anywhere in the search for moral knowledge was beginning to tell, and impatience beginning to show. G. E. Moore announced shortly, in his book *Principia Ethica*: 'If I am asked "what is good?" my answer is that good is good, and that is the end of the matter. Or if I am asked, "How is good to be defined?" my answer is that it cannot be defined, and that is all I have to say about it.'[2] But Moore was not a relativist. He believed that certain things were good, regardless of whether any particular society recognised them as such or not, but he believed that the only way in which one could know that something was good was by intuition. He was followed by various other philosophers, who modified his view in various ways, and it is these men rather than Moore himself who are usually meant when the intuitionists are referred to.

Intuitionism was really a rather extraordinary ethical theory to have arisen so late in the history of moral philosophy. The point of the theory was that it was supposed to preserve the idea that there were objective moral truths that were not dependent on the changing tastes of society, and the idea that moral knowledge was possible. But whereas scientific knowledge was acquired and substantiated by empirical demonstration, moral knowledge, on this view, was acquired and substantiated by intuition. As many people have pointed out, the difference between claiming to *know* something on the strength of intuition and simply *believing* something is difficult to see. And it is therefore difficult to distinguish between the members of a primitive society who claim to 'know', without being able to produce any publicly acceptable evidence, that 'paying debts is good', and the twentieth-century intuitionists who might claim to 'know' the same thing on the strength of their intuition. Despite the appeal of this theory for those who wished to defend some notion of absolutism against the relativist, it was in effect a completely pointless theory.

This is not to say that it provided a false account of the situation. It is very important to realise at this stage that one cannot necessarily say that the intuitionists were wrong. It may be the case that there are certain things that ought to be done and others that ought not, whatever most people think at any given time. It may yet turn out that it makes sense to say 'This is good, and everybody ought to do it', even though most people object to doing it. And it may be the case that the only way one can know what, as a matter of fact, ought to be done is by intuition. But in practice the theory is quite unhelpful because different people have different intuitions as to what is good. How are we to decide between these different intuitions? By intuition, presumably, but *whose* intuition? In the last resort, intuitionists are indistinguishable from relativists; for in the face of the adoption of different moral values by different societies, the relativist will say there is nothing to choose between them in terms of being right – it is a matter of taste. The intuitionist will claim that it is a matter of knowledge that some societies have adopted the right values, but this 'knowledge' that he claims to have turns out to be his intuitive feeling – which to most of us looks suspiciously like his taste.

As if in answer to this rather feeble last-ditch defence by certain absolutists, a particularly extreme form of relativism was then launched by A. J. Ayer. This was emotivism. The emotivist theory of ethics has subsequently been modified in various ways by Ayer himself and others. But in essence the theory is nothing more than a view that was hinted at above as being a possibility – namely the view that to describe something as good is simply to say 'I like it'. That, according to emotivism, is really all there is to morality. The reason that nobody can find the moral truth, and the reason it is so difficult to agree on what would count as evidence to support a claim to moral knowledge, is that there is no such thing as moral truth and no such thing as moral knowledge. 'Freedom is good' does not resemble 'Pigs are four-legged' in any way at all, beyond the similarity in superficial appearance. The latter proposition makes a factual claim that can be tested; the former does not make a factual claim at all, although it may look as if it does. The expression 'Freedom is good' is just a way of saying that I, the speaker, like freedom.

Emotivism was the straw that broke the camel's back. It was at about the time of the emergence of this theory that most moral philosophers seemed to come to the conclusion that moral values could not be produced out of thin air and convincingly shown to be true. To put it cynically, they lost their nerve. To put it as they would choose to put it, it was appreciated that the moral philosopher's job was not to produce elaborate systems of desirable behaviour nor to prescribe good conduct, but to analyse the way in which we do in fact use moral language, as the emotivists had claimed to be doing. His job was not to discover what was good, so much as to show how people use the word 'good'.

Now this redefinition of the moral philosopher's role – it was not something completely new so much as a decided shift of emphasis – did not arise because all philosophers accepted an emotivist position. As a matter of fact, very few of them accepted it in its original stark form which reduced moral judgements to no more than expressions of personal taste. But they recognised that it represented a possible explanation of all that was involved in morality. So too, however, as they saw and as I have stressed, did intuitionism. So, if it came to that, did many of the other ethical theories that had been produced at one time or another: perhaps happiness is the only ultimate good; perhaps the ten commandments do represent eternally significant injunctions. Philosophers were not necessarily committing themselves to the view either that any of these theories were false or that they were correct. Nor were they denying themselves the right to adopt specific moral values and to attempt to argue in support of the adoption of these values. What, in general, they had effectively concluded was that it was inconceivable that anyone should ever establish one ethical view as the correct view beyond all doubt. Knowledge of ultimate moral principles was impossible. (Belief concerning them, of course, was not therefore illegitimate; nor was knowledge related to specific moral rules ruled out, provided that it was appreciated that one could only talk of 'knowing' that a certain rule was a good one in the light of ultimate moral principles that were accepted on the strength of belief. For example, if we agree to value happiness then we may talk of knowing that certain behaviour is bad because it promotes misery.) Philosophers, in effect, were simply retreating from what they regarded as an insoluble problem.

Unfortunately, to a great extent the view that emotivism was the correct view seeped into the public conscience and won the day for relativism. Some people, of course, clung to specific moral values and continued to claim that they knew that this, that and the other, ought to be done. From a philosophical point of view, as we have seen, this position is extremely suspect: how do they know? Where is the publicly acceptable evidence necessary to substantiate a claim to knowledge? And from a practical point of view, this position may be dangerous: fanaticism is bred of people's conviction that they know what ought to be done and that people who do not agree are just wrong and can therefore be ignored. But many other people adopted, and still adopt, the view that we now know that emotivism, or some other form of relativism, represents the truth about morality. On this view, we *know* that moral values are simply conventional and arbitrary. It should be clear that this view is equally suspect from a philosophical point of view. And, incidentally, from a practical point of view it may be no less dangerous: fanaticism may be bred of the conviction that there is only one right answer, but the equally insidious feelings of apathy and alienation may be born of the conviction that there are no right answers.

Emotivism is not necessarily the correct view of what morality involves. It gains its plausibility because, in common with other relativist views, it lays stress on two aspects of moral language that it would be difficult to deny. When people describe something as 'good' they certainly do indicate their approval of it; and when they are asked how they know that it is good, it seems difficult – and perhaps impossible – to conceive of an answer that everybody would have to accept as convincing. We certainly do not 'know' that 'freedom is good' in the way that we know that bricks fall to the ground when dropped. We do not see what would count as evidence for knowledge in the moral sphere. This much must be conceded. Equally it must be acknowledged that emotivism can explain without difficulty why it is that different people have different views as to what is good.

But even allowing for its plausibility, emotivism is not without its problems. Am I really *only* indicating my approval of freedom when I say that it is good? Is it true, as another emotivist has put it, that the 'major use' of ethical judgements is simply 'to create an influence'? Is the remark that one ought not to steal no more than an indication of my dislike of the practice and an attempt to create an influence designed to promote that dislike? R. M. Hare, in putting forward the ethical theory known as prescriptivism, has suggested two further features of moral judgements. First, he argues that judgements of the form 'You ought to do such and such' do not just attempt to create an influence, they have the more positive function of attempting to guide people's conduct. They are disguised imperatives that amount to the order 'Do this', but they differ from other imperatives in that one expects consistency of a man who says 'You ought to do this', in a way that we do not expect it of a man who says 'Do this'. Moral judgements, on Hare's view, are universalisable. That is to say that if I say that you ought to do this in these circumstances, then I commit myself to the view that I, or anybody else, ought also to do this in the same circumstances. Without going into these suggestions in any detail, is it not possible that they indicate some inadequacy in emotivism? Although prescriptivism does not represent a denunciation of relativist theories, and although it may have its own problems, it surely suggests that emotivism as originally stated was an unconvincingly bald ethical theory.

And then, allowing for such modifications to emotivism as Hare or others might wish to introduce, do we really accept that in saying that Jews ought not to have been treated in the way in which they were treated in Nazi Germany, we are essentially saying no more than that we do not like the fact that they were? Is it totally meaningless to suggest that it was wrong and that it would have been wrong even if we had all decided that we couldn't care less? One can concede all the difficulties already raised in this chapter – the difficulty of showing what it would mean to say that it just was wrong, and the difficulty of seeing how one would set about proving that it was wrong. But all that I ask here is whether we are prepared to accept that 'Exterminating Jews is wrong' *means* simply 'We do not like exterminating Jews'.

To revert to our starting position – the conflict between absolutists and relativists – the point is this: just as absolutist views are suspect because we do not see how people could justify a claim to *know* that something is good, so we do not *know* that a relativist view is the correct one to adopt. To claim that relativism is the correct view to adopt involves claiming that we know that there is no more to moral values than the observable fact that different societies choose to adopt different values. But how do we *know* that this is all there is to the matter in the normal sense of 'know'? Where is the evidence to support the claim that a statement such as 'Gassing Jews is wrong' cannot have any objective validity and cannot be regarded as either true or false? What argument has been produced to show that the intuitionists, for example, were incorrect? The answer is none. The truth is that because we have no agreement (no understanding, perhaps) as to what would count as criteria for claiming moral knowledge, we know absolutely nothing about morality. And that means that we do not know that relativism is more correct than absolutism.

All that we have as a consequence of this brief survey of various ethical views is something akin to a number of possible solutions to a murder mystery. At this stage many of the proposed explanations of the moral mystery may seem plausible. It may be that ultimately this mystery cannot be solved, or at any rate not to everybody's satisfaction. However we cannot simply ignore the mystery. And some explanations may turn out on closer examination to ignore certain important features of the case; some may ultimately be seen to be more plausible than others; and conceivably only one explanation will finally prove acceptable.

When Socrates was told that the Delphic Oracle had pronounced him to be the wisest man in Athens, he was at first puzzled.[3] But as he went the rounds of the various experts in the city – the expert politicians, playwrights, carpenters and so on – and heard them pontificating on every subject imaginable, he came to see that he was perhaps the wisest of them all, in that he knew that he knew nothing. To put it less epigrammatically, he knew the limits of his knowledge. And, of course, the notion of a man wise in his ignorance is more than an ingenious paradox. To distinguish between what one actually knows and what one believes or accepts on the authority of others, to know that to talk of knowledge in certain fields is sometimes inappropriate, is a genuine increase in positive knowledge. To appreciate that one cannot glibly assume that various moral truths are known is to learn something and to learn something important.

Nonetheless many people may feel that to have got this far raises the question of whether it is worth going further in moral philosophy. Absolutists and relativists alike merely have to agree that it would be more accurate, by standards of normal usage, for them to state their positions in terms of belief rather than knowledge. The former believe that certain things are good and ought to be done in any society at any time; the latter believe that this kind of talk is meaningless. And that is all there is to it. If it is a question of belief and if knowledge is out of place in this sphere of inquiry, there is not much point in pursuing the matter. So, at any rate, they may feel.

There are, however, two considerations that give considerable point to inquiring further into the matter. First, whether we like it or not, we are continually faced with the need to make decisions that involve moral assumptions – and this, as suggested in Chapter 1, applies particularly to those involved in education. We have to decide whether this or that ought to take place, ought to be encouraged, or ought to be discouraged. At the very least, we have to decide whether teachers ought to make such decisions on behalf of their pupils or whether children should be left free to do what they choose to do. Given this responsibility and the realisation that there are no easy answers in the moral sphere, it surely becomes all the more important to look again, and in much greater depth, at our own moral assumptions. One consequence of abandoning the idea that some of us 'know' what is good is that all beliefs as to what is good have an equal claim to be taken seriously. The absolutist must ask himself whether his beliefs are based on anything other than the influence of those who brought him up, for example. The relativist must ask himself whether, despite his interpretation of morality, there are not in fact some things that it seems more reasonable to regard as morally desirable than others. The alternative to a more thoroughgoing examination of various moral beliefs is to settle for some form of dogmatism or nihilism – to conclude that, since ultimately no belief as to what is good can be shown to be wrong, we cannot justify condemning anything and should settle for a policy of anything goes, 'anything' presumably including dogmatic fanaticism as well as extreme laissez-faire. Are we prepared to accept that?

Secondly, as indicated in the previous paragraph, the fact that something cannot be known to be true does not necessarily do away with a distinction between reasonable and unreasonable belief. One can think of many areas of history, for example, where our lack of evidence rules out the plausibility of a claim to 'know' what was going on, but where we could nonetheless produce reasons for regarding some suggestions as preposterous and others as possible. There is still a distinction to be made between the sphere of history, where there is not much doubt as to the sort of things that would count as evidence in support of a particular view, and that of morality, where there is even disagreement as to what would count as evidence. But even in the moral sphere there may be a distinction between what we regard as good reasons for adopting certain moral values and what we regard as bad reasons.

As Aristotle pointed out in his *Nicomachean Ethics*, it is the mark of a rather foolish person to expect to find the same degree of certainty in all spheres of human inquiry.[4] Certainly the idea of moral knowledge and the proof of moral propositions conceived of on the scientific model has received a nasty shock. But why should we expect to demonstrate moral propositions in the same way and with the same degree of certainty as we demonstrate simple scientific propositions? After all moral propositions are *not* scientific propositions. But there are all kinds of statements that we may make, that either cannot convincingly be proven or where we are very uncertain as to how we would set about trying to prove them, which may nonetheless be more or less reasonable and even possibly true or false. For example, it might be very difficult to prove that Beethoven was a better composer than I am, because it is very difficult to produce agreed criteria for good music; but he probably was, and not many of us would regard the suggestion that he wasn't as very reasonable. It might be difficult for me to prove that my wife loves me, but I have good reason to suppose that she does. I cannot prove that Athenian democracy in the fifth century was a shambles, if by 'prove' we mean demonstrate to the satisfaction of all who are interested in the demonstration. In this case, of course, the problem is one of incomplete evidence and disagreement as to how to interpret what evidence there is. But what I can do in this case, as in the others, is expand and clarify precisely what it is I am claiming and put forward my reasons for the claim. As a result of doing this, in conjunction with others who are interested in the question at issue, one may hope to approach that degree of certainty that is appropriate to the case.

In the same way we can consider various suggested moral values, clarify their precise meaning, and examine the reasons that may be put forward in favour of and against their adoption. It may be that at the end of the day there will still be a measure of disagreement, but at least the nature of that disagreement will be clear, and when all is said and done there is a difference between agreeing to differ after real consideration of the matter and refusing to agree in blind ignorance.

REFERENCES

1 On Plato and the sophists see Plato, *Gorgias* and *Republic* (Book One). See also Guthrie, W. K. C., *The Sophists* (C.U.P., 1971) for a scholarly examination of the sophists, or Barrow, R., *Athenian Democracy* (Macmillan, 1973) for a very basic introduction.
2 Moore, G. E., *Principia Ethica* (C.U.P., 1962), p. 6.
3 See Plato, *The Apology*, for this story.
4 Aristotle, *Nicomachean Ethics*, 1.3.

FURTHER READING

In this chapter I have not been able to offer a complete history of moral philosophy. See MacIntyre, A. C., *A Short History of Ethics* (Collier-Macmillan, 1966). For a fuller account and critique of the developments in moral philosophy in this century, see either Warnock, G., *Contemporary Moral Philosophy* (Macmillan, 1967), or Warnock, M., *Ethics since 1900* (O.U.P., 1960). An excellent, though long, introduction to the problems of ethics is provided by Hospers, John, *Human Conduct* (Hart-Davis, 1970).

The following books either by or about specific moral philosophers or ethical theories are all fairly short and available in paperback: Kamenka, E., *Marxism and Ethics* (Macmillan, 1969); Hudson, W., *Ethical Intuitionism* (Macmillan, 1967); Moore, G. E., *Ethics* (O.U.P., 1966); Ayer, A. J., *Language, Truth and Logic* (Penguin, 1971); Hare, R. M., *The Language of Morals* (O.U.C., 1964).

The suggestion that one cannot simply derive an evaluative conclusion from a descriptive premiss originates with David Hume in his *A Treatise of Human Nature*. A considerable quantity of literature has grown up around the more complex aspects of this question. See Hudson, W. D. (ed.), *The Is/Ought Question* (Macmillan, 1969).

Part Two

Chapter 3

Reasonable and unreasonable arguments

In view of what has been said in Part One of this book it is obvious that my intention here, in Part Two, is not to pose as a moral expert, who will reveal the answer to the question 'What is morally acceptable behaviour?' as the medical expert might give one the answer to the question 'What sort of factors are conducive to heart failure?'. Nor is it my intention to 'prove' that a particular moral viewpoint is incumbent upon us, if we assume 'prove' to mean 'demonstrate in some incontrovertible manner'. My purpose rather is to put forward an argument for a particular point of view and to appeal to the reader to consider the argument as an argument. Naturally it is my view that the argument is convincing and that it consequently leads us to accept a particular moral viewpoint. But at the same time I am aware, and it is important that the reader should be too, that this argument, which is not in essence original, and this viewpoint, which has been held by various people throughout history, has never yet met with universal acceptance. Some people evidently do not find the argument convincing. All that is asked of the reader is that he should examine it for himself and accept or reject it by reference to the argument rather than by reference to such considerations as whether he happens to like it, whether it leads to conclusions that he has been brought up to accept, or whether it coincides with what most people think.

I shall proceed by examining two concepts that have long been widely valued: 'freedom' and 'equality'. I shall try to argue that regardless of what we may *casually* think about these concepts – what we think they mean, whether we think them morally important and what relative importance we attach to them – if we think *carefully* about what is meant by such claims as that 'Men ought to be free' or 'Men ought to be treated equally' there are certain conclusions that cannot be avoided. To be precise I shall argue that there is a sense in which 'freedom' and 'equality' are to be valued, but that their value is subordinate to the value of happiness. In other words I shall be arguing for a modified form of the utilitarian view of ethics, pioneered most notably by Jeremy Bentham and John Stuart Mill, which claims essentially that the measure of goodness or of the rightness of actions or rules is the extent to which they promote happiness, and the measure of wrongness or badness is the extent to which misery is caused. (See Chapter 6 for a more detailed presentation of utilitarianism.)

Since I shall be arguing that there is good reason to adopt this particular moral viewpoint or that utilitarianism is a more reasonable ethical theory than any other, for the remainder of this chapter I shall make some general comments about the sort of considerations that would lead one to regard a particular view, explanation or argument as relatively reasonable or unreasonable. I shall do this by first considering an example from the sphere of aesthetics.

Suppose that a teacher, who prefers the novels of George Eliot to those of Ian Fleming, and who regards them as superior or better works of art, wishes to justify that value judgement. (This wish to justify is not, of course, simply an academic exercise. If the teacher has no criteria whereby to justify his selection then he has no criteria whereby to select at all, and the teacher generally does need to make some kind of selection.) Why is George Eliot a better writer than Ian Fleming?

The realm of aesthetic value judgements is no less tricky than the realm of moral value judgements, and on many views of aesthetics it is more or less impossible to lay down fixed rules or criteria for assessing the aesthetic value of a work of art. Certainly there is as much disagreement and uncertainty about what criteria count for evaluating works of art as about what criteria count for assessing the goodness or rightness of actions and behaviour. One can, of course, pin-point features of various works. One can say, for example, that George Eliot has an ironic touch, that she is good at developing characters, or that she shows respect for unity of design. To pin-point such features in a particular writer may not be an easy task – for instance, one might argue for a long time about precisely what constituted good character development in a novel, about how one judged whether characters in a particular novel had been well drawn, and whether in point of fact a writer like George Eliot did develop her characters better than a writer like Ian Fleming. But in principle it is not an impossible task, and indeed it would seem to be the sort of thing that most literary criticism is about. However, to say that George Eliot has certain features that Ian Fleming lacks, or that she does some specific thing better than Fleming, is one thing – to say that she is a better writer, or even that she is more worth reading, is quite another.

If one had certain specific ends in view – for instance, if one wanted children to study character development in novels – then, of course, one could say that Eliot was better for that purpose. But then the question of the value of the end or purpose one had in mind would arise, and one could only claim that Eliot was more worth reading than Fleming in some general sense, if one could establish that to study character development was a relatively worthwhile thing to do. And unless one could establish that the features that Eliot's writing was agreed to have were the necessary features of good writing, one obviously could not conclude that Eliot was a better writer than Fleming.

In other words, although in principle we can agree on the features exhibited in the writing of a particular novelist, it is always open for someone to say that he does not see why those particular features are relevant reasons for judging a novelist to be a good novelist. He might say, and it is not obvious that it would be absurd to say, 'Eliot develops character better than Fleming, but Fleming is more exciting, and therefore Fleming is a better writer'. The problem here is that, since it is not clear what count as good reasons for judging a novelist to be a good novelist, since it is not clear that one could rule out 'being exciting' as an irrelevant consideration, it is not clear that one could describe any view as unreasonable, provided that it did offer some kind of reason. Does it follow that, if I were to say that it seemed to me more reasonable to regard George Eliot as a good novelist than to regard Ian Fleming as a good novelist, I would effectively be begging the question and assuming that the sort of reasons I produce for valuing Eliot are good reasons, whereas the sort of reasons that others might produce for valuing Fleming are bad reasons? Yes, I think it does follow: I would be begging the question. What are we to say, then? Is any assessment of any writer as reasonable as any other? Not necessarily.

What is clear is that, insofar as it is agreed that one cannot 'prove' that good novelists must have certain specific qualities, one cannot 'prove' that one novelist is better than another. It follows that, whereas in some spheres such as science one can say that certain theories are unreasonable because they fly in the face of the evidence and can be shown to be false, one cannot simply assert that some value judgements about particular novelists are unreasonable on the grounds that the values appealed to are false values. Nonetheless, although we have to concede that we are not in a position to lay down the law about what count as good reasons for evaluating novels highly, it does not follow that any view is as reasonable as any other. There are at least four ways in which a person's assertion that a particular novelist was a good novelist might be regarded as an unreasonable assertion, even though one might concede that one could not prove that the assertion was false.

1. In the first place a person might simply make such an assertion and refuse to produce any reasons for his judgement. One could scarcely regard it as reasonable for a teacher to insist that Eliot was a brilliant novelist, while refusing to give any reasons for that claim.

2. Secondly, although we may disagree about what sort of reasons count as good reasons for regarding a particular novelist as a good one, it does not follow that *any* reason will do. There are surely *some* reasons that none of us would accept as relevant reasons and which, if somebody were to use them, we should regard as a clear indication that the person in question

had not got the faintest idea of the sort of thing that we were trying to do in evaluating novels. If somebody were to argue, for instance, that Ian Fleming was a better novelist than George Eliot because more of his books had been turned into films, because he wrote more novels, because he was a man, or because his books were more attractively printed, we should just say – and I don't see why we should not say – that he clearly did not grasp the sort of thing that we are trying to do. These kinds of reasons just are irrelevant to the question of whether a novelist is a good one or not. At the very least, reasons put forward in defence of the quality of a novelist must relate in some way to his writing.

3.   But suppose that somebody were to argue that Fleming was a better writer because he was more popular or more generally enjoyable? Would that be an unreasonable criterion? Although most people seriously concerned with literature would probably foam at the mouth at such a suggestion, this seems to me a much more tricky question. It is true that the popularity of a novelist need not be related to anything to do with his style of writing. He might simply hit upon a popular theme, or become a cult figure by whatever mysterious process people become cult figures. But one might argue that the essential criterion of a good book was that it should provide enjoyment, and that, therefore, writers who were popular obviously were good novelists, since by definition they had the talent for writing enjoyable books. We may think it odd to make writing books that people enjoy the sole criterion of good writing. We should probably *feel* that this was unreasonable (and I am sure that most of us would *say* it was). But is it? I don't know. But what does seem to me to be quite clear is that, if somebody were to insist on the claim that this is a good reason for judging a novelist to be a good one, we could not rule his suggestion out as absurd (as we could if he evaluated by reference to the attractiveness of the printing), and we could not prove that he was wrong.

I have introduced the example of someone who proposes the enjoyment a book gives as the sole criterion of literary worth in order to draw attention to the third way in which an argument about the worth of novelists may be unreasonable. Although the claim may not *in itself* be obviously unreasonable, it would be unreasonable of somebody to put forward this argument if they were not prepared to accept the consequences of their argument. If the suggestion is put forward seriously that this is the sole criterion of literary worth, then we should expect the person who put it forward to accept, consistently with his argument, not only that Ian Fleming is a better writer than George Eliot, but that Agatha Christie is better than both of them and, interestingly, that the Bible, being the best seller of all time, is the best book ever written. In the same way, if somebody were to put forward the suggestion that books were better in direct proportion to their length, crazy as this may seem to us, I do not see how one could prove that it was a bad criterion. But we could say that it was an unreasonable suggestion unless the individual concerned was prepared to accept the consequences: for instance, that by and large Victorian novels, written as they generally were in three volumes, were ipso facto better than twentieth-century novels, or that I can turn this into a good book by going on writing for three thousand more pages.

All this may seem pretty absurd, but it has a point. The observation that for a view as to what constitute good reasons in this sphere to be reasonable its consequences must be consistently accepted by the holder of the view, in fact does a great part of our job for us. We may not be able to prove that a particular view is unreasonable in some objective manner, but very often, by pointing out the consequences of the view, by getting its proponent to think more carefully about what he is committing himself to, he will himself come to agree with us and reject his original view as unreasonable. One thing that would clearly be unreasonable would be to claim that such and such was a good reason for valuing a writer in one instance, but then to say that it was not a good reason in another instance.

4.   Finally, and most obviously, a view or an argument might be regarded as unreasonable if the reasoning offered to support it was in some way fallacious or inconsistent. For example, one might encounter some variant of the notorious argument 'All cows are four-legged. This is four-legged, therefore it is a cow'. Thus somebody might try to argue that a particular novel was obviously a good novel on the grounds that it had unity of design and on the assumption that it was agreed that good novels had unity of design. But from the agreed premiss that good novels have a unity of design, it obviously does not follow that all novels that have a unity of design are good novels, unless it is also agreed that unity of design is the *only* criterion of a good novel.

Here, then, are four ways in which arguments about the quality of a writer may be unreasonable, even though we concede that we are not sure precisely what kind of reasons are good reasons for evaluating a writer highly. We shall not regard as reasonable suggestions that are put forward without any attempt at all to back them with reasons, arguments that make use of reasons that seem totally irrelevant to the question at issue, arguments the consequences of which the proposer will not himself accept, and arguments that are inconsistent or fallacious.

These same considerations enable us to distinguish between reasonable and unreasonable arguments in the moral sphere, as I shall now illustrate.

1.   Suppose that somebody were to suggest that everybody ought to commit suicide – that this was the right thing for us all to do. Such a suggestion no doubt seems odd, like most examples that philosophers tend to drag up. But the fact that it seems odd, unlikely, even preposterous, is no objection to it. It is conceivable that somebody might say it, and if we

are really keeping an open mind at this stage about what ought to be done, we cannot simply dismiss suggestions that we would not ourselves propose. The question is, if somebody were to make such a suggestion, could we say that it was unreasonable?

For all we *know* to the contrary, it may in some sense be true that we ought to commit suicide. We certainly cannot dismiss the suggestion as obviously false, simply because we do not like it, we think it silly, or only one in a million people would take it seriously. To do that would be equivalent to arguing that George Eliot is obviously an inferior writer to Ian Fleming, because we prefer Fleming. *We* would be being unreasonable, because the mere fact that we do not like a suggestion is not a good reason for concluding that it is false. So what do we do, when faced with this bizarre suggestion? We take it seriously.

'Right,' we say, 'you suggest that we ought to commit suicide. This does not strike us as either obvious or true. As it stands it is obviously not a particularly reasonable suggestion, since you have offered no reasons whatsoever to support it. But we are willing to listen to your argument for this point of view. What reasons have you for assuming it to be true that it would be a good thing if we all committed suicide?'

Now, the proponent of the view in question might reply simply by saying that he has no reasons to offer – he merely intuits it. Can we say that he is wrong to intuit it? We certainly cannot. But there are a number of things that we can say: we can say that there is no reason to suppose that his intuition is correct. We can say that it would be unreasonable to expect the world to act in accordance with his intuition, when it does not share his intuition. We can say that there seems no reason why we should place the claims of his intuition before the claims of anyone else's intuition. But above all we can point out that if he believes that we ought to act in this way, and, therefore, presumably, wishes to convince us that we ought, he will *have* to produce some kind of convincing reasoning, and that is all there is to it. Proof we do not ask for; but some reason to share his conviction, we naturally demand. If he sticks both with his conviction and with his acknowledgement that he has no reasons to offer in support of it, then the question of whether he is right or wrong in some metaphysical sense becomes in practical terms irrelevant. We cannot be expected to regard as reasonable a point of view for which we have no intuitive sympathy and for which there is apparently no argument. Now, of course, it may be that on closer scrutiny all moral viewpoints will be seen to end up with some fundamental assumption that has to be accepted on intuition and which is, as a matter of fact, only intuited by some. If this turns out to be the case, we are indeed in a mess. The suicide ethic would be no more unreasonable than any other. But at this stage, when we are embarking upon the search for a reasonable moral viewpoint and when it is an open question as to whether there is one or not, we may fairly say that here, at any rate, is one that does not appear to be reasonable.

Of course the man we are concerned with might offer some kind of reason. He might say, for instance, that the reason that we ought to commit suicide is that God demands it. That is certainly a reason, but clearly it does not really escape the problem of the simple intuitive view, for it merely pushes the question of what reasons there are to accept the view one stage back. Instead of asking what reasons there are to accept the claim that we ought to commit suicide, we should naturally ask what reason there was to suppose that God exists, or, more crucially, what reason there was to suppose that a specific idea of a God, who amongst other things made this demand for suicide, corresponded to any reality. How do we know, what reason have we for supposing, that God, even if he does exist, does indeed make this demand? Evidently we shall soon be back with the intuition of the person in question. Even if he could produce some religious texts, allegedly the work of prophets who knew the will of God, we should only have his intuition to support the claim that these texts were indeed the work of people who knew the will of God.

Here then we have an example of a moral view that we can see no reason to accept at all. It involves either a naked assertion, backed by no reasoning whatsoever, or else bases itself on a premiss that is itself merely asserted and is very obviously open to question. This does not stop those who do believe from believing. Contrary to one popular opinion it does not even show that they are wrong or necessarily foolish so to believe. But it does stop anyone from legitimately claiming that it is reasonable to believe and unreasonable not to. It is neither reasonable nor unreasonable; reason does not come into the matter.

2. Consider now an example of a moral viewpoint that does make appeal to reasons but where the reasons given are simply irrelevant. As with the aesthetic sphere, despite the problem of deciding precisely what reasons do count as good reasons in this sphere, there are nonetheless some sorts of reason that evidently do not count at all. Let us assume that somebody claims that it is morally objectionable to spit. We ask him what his reasons are for asserting that we ought not to spit. There are a number of replies that we can imagine that he might give, some of which it would be difficult to dismiss as obviously absurd. He might say that we ought not to spit because spitting was a hazard to public health and we ought to be concerned about maintaining public health. On the assumption that it was empirically true that spitting spread germs, this would be a reasonable *kind* of argument. One cannot dismiss concern for the health of others as obviously irrelevant to the question of how we ought to behave. But suppose instead that he had said that the reason one ought not to spit is that spitting causes one to purse one's lips in an ugly manner. In this case there is no need for

us to quibble about whether or not it is true that spitting is ugly, since, even if it is true, such a consideration seems entirely irrelevant to a moral question. It is the wrong kind of reason.

Again, suppose that a man objects to adultery and claims that it is immoral. Suppose also that we disagree with his judgement, but recognise nonetheless that his point of view deserves to be taken seriously and therefore ask him for the reasons that lie behind his conclusion. He might argue along a number of different lines: that adultery involves deception, that in general it leads to the breakdown of marriage and hence is detrimental to the welfare of children, or that sex is not something that should be indulged in except within wedlock and with a view to procreation. Now these are very different arguments and our attitude to them might well vary from person to person in respect of each argument. Furthermore, if unconvinced by them, we might wish to counter each argument in a quite different way. As against the first argument it might be objected that deception is sometimes justified or, perhaps, that adultery need not necessarily involve deception. As against the second it might be argued that there is no necessary reason for adultery to lead to the breakdown of a marriage, or that, even if it did, it is not true that broken marriages are detrimental to the welfare of children. With regard to the third argument we might simply say that we do not agree with his view of the role of sex, and demand some further argument from him to substantiate his claim.

But what is clear is that, however much we disagree with this man, all these attempted arguments of his are prima facie plausible. That is to say that, although we may not accept his arguments, he is at least appealing to reasons that seem related to the moral sphere: his reasons for condemning adultery are that we should avoid deception, that we should refrain from causing suffering, or that we should not sin, and these are recognisable as moral reasons. He and we are at least talking the same language.

If on the other hand he had argued that we ought not to commit adultery because adultery involves taking off one's clothes and we ought to take off our clothes as little as possible, we should regard him with bewildered astonishment. A man who argues in this way clearly does not have the first idea of what morality is about. Such reasoning would not simply be silly and unbelievable – it would be absurd and irrelevant, because a consideration such as that people take off their clothes just is not a moral consideration. He is not offering the sort of reason that could count as a moral reason. And despite all that has been said about the difficulty of 'knowing' anything in the moral sphere, we all *know* that.

It may be felt that the point that I am making here is a small one, since surely nobody actually would offer reasons of this sort. But it is a crucial point. For if the reader accepts that making ugly faces and taking off one's clothes, however fanciful such examples may be, cannot in themselves constitute moral reasons for acting or refraining from acting in various ways, then he has conceded that only some reasons count as moral reasons. If that is so, then clearly moral rules or moral commands must be backed by *moral reasons*, and our job is to discover in more detail what reasons do count as moral reasons. I shall be arguing in Chapter 6 that ultimately there is only one kind of reason that can count as a moral reason.

3.   Thirdly, we may regard it as unreasonable for somebody to claim commitment to a particular moral viewpoint unless he is prepared to accept all the consequences of that viewpoint. In my view a number of those who commit themselves to emotivism as the correct view of ethics, when first introduced to it, may be regarded as unreasonable on these grounds. For, as we have seen, if one accepts emotivism (at least in one form) one commits oneself to the view, in Ayer's words, that in saying '"Stealing money is wrong" I produce a sentence which has no factual meaning – that is, expresses no proposition which can be either true or false . . . I am simply evincing my moral disapproval of it'.[1] To which we may add that, in saying it, I am trying to 'create an influence' of disapproval amongst my audience. But if this were so, if this was all there was to be said, it would follow that I could not meaningfully make the remark 'Stealing money is wrong' in the company of people who shared my disapproval (for how could I be trying to create what already exists?); that one could not meaningfully distinguish between making this remark and making a propaganda film to discourage stealing (for both would involve evincing one's own feeling and attempting to create an influence); that the way to assess the quality of a moral argument would be in terms of how effective it was in creating an influence; and above all that there would be no recognisable distinction between a remark such as 'Bullfights – ugh!' and 'Concentration camps are wicked'.

My point here is not that these consequences are unacceptable, although I believe that they are, but that some people who might claim to be emotivists will nonetheless be found saying that stealing is wrong, even in the company of those who agree with them, assessing moral arguments by criteria other than their persuasive power, and even distinguishing between what they merely do not like and what they regard as morally wrong. In other words their practice is inconsistent with their preaching. They do not give evidence of accepting the consequences of their view. And *that* is unreasonable.

4.   Finally, there is the most common way in which a moral viewpoint may be unreasonable, namely when the argument for it is fallacious. Obviously arguments may be fallacious in a number of different ways, and we cannot review all the various forms of fallacious reasoning here, but perhaps the single most dangerous form of fallacy in the moral sphere is the assumption that the fact that something is the case constitutes a good

argument for concluding that it ought to be the case, to which attention has already been drawn in Chapter 2. Another kind of fallacy that has to be guarded against is the use of reasoning to support a particular viewpoint that is prima facie relevant reasoning, and that is not in itself inconsistent, but which is not obviously sufficient to establish its conclusion; reasoning, in other words, that is not strong enough to do the job required of it. It seems to me that the standard argument for a relativist theory of ethics is of this kind. It is, of course, absolutely true that different societies have had and have now different moral values – some societies have even lacked a concept of morality, as we should understand it, altogether; furthermore, it is true that this is a pertinent consideration for the individual trying to inquire into the problem of morality to take into account. But this consideration is not sufficient to establish the validity of a relativist position. It is not true that it proves that morality is a purely conventional game and that there is no more to be said on the matter. It is unreasonable to assume the truth of a conclusion based on the strength of such a selective consideration alone.

Perhaps the most notorious (and anyway an excellent) example of an argument riddled with fallacy is provided by Hitler's argument in *Mein Kampf* for Aryan supremacy, which is well worth exposing once again. Hitler wrote:

'In opposition to the bourgeois and the Marxist-Jewish worlds the folkish philosophy finds the importance of mankind in its basic racial elements . . . It by no means believes in an equality of races, but along with their difference it recognises their higher or lesser value and feels itself obligated to promote the victory of the better and the stronger, and demand the subordination of the inferior and weaker in accordance with the eternal will that dominates this universe. It serves the basic aristocratic idea of nature and believes in the validity of this law down to the last individual . . .

All the human culture, all the results of art, science and technology that we see before us today, are almost exclusively the creative product of the Aryan. This very fact admits of the not unfounded inference that he alone was the founder of all higher humanity . . . For the formation of higher cultures the existence of lower human types was one of the most essential preconditions . . . The Aryan gave up the purity of his blood and therefore lost his sojourn in paradise: blood mixture and the resultant drop in the racial level is the sole cause of the dying out of old cultures.'[2]

Notice the different kinds of suspect argument that Hitler manages to pack into these brief extracts that serve so admirably as a text for fallacious reasoning. First the simple falsehood (or stupidity) of asserting as fact what is palpably not fact, namely the assertion that 'all ... human culture' is 'almost exclusively the creative product of the Aryan' or that 'blood mixture' is the 'sole cause of the dying out of old cultures'. Secondly, what on earth is meant by the phrase 'the founder of all higher humanity' and why would the fact, if it were a fact, that the Aryan was responsible for 'human culture' imply the inference that is drawn that he is the founder of all higher humanity? Thirdly, where is the link between this claim about cultural superiority and the conclusion that the Aryan is therefore superior in some general sense? Even if it were true that the Aryan was culturally superior and the founder of all higher humanity, why would it follow that the Aryan counts for more, as Hitler evidently assumes. But above all on what grounds does Hitler identify the better with the stronger? Could there be a more glaring instance of fallacy than to argue that, because the strong dominate the weak as a matter of fact (an observation dressed up by Hitler as the product of an eternal will and a law of nature), it is right and proper that they should?

One might worry the less if this type of argument were confined to the brain of a Hitler. But unfortunately it is not. Quite apart from the fact that thousands accepted this particular argument, this type of argument is still to be found, as it has been since the time of the ancient Greeks. Plato, for instance, put almost the same argument into the mouth of Callicles:

'Nature demonstrates that it is right that the stronger should prevail over the weaker ... Right consists in the superior having the upper hand. By what right did Xerxes invade Greece? By right of his natural superiority ... just as Hercules drove off the cattle of Geryon without paying for them or being given them, because this was natural justice: that all the possessions of those who are weaker and inferior belong to the man who is better and superior. That is the truth of the matter, Socrates, and perhaps you would realise it, if you wasted less time toying about with philosophy and turned to something more important.'[3]

I imagine that the reader does not require me to point out in detail the arguments used by certain modern states to justify racial discrimination that essentially merely repeat this fallacious argument of Callicles.

My conclusion is that there are various ways in which a point of view may be classified as unreasonable even if it is not known to be false. We have looked briefly at some of these ways and some ethical positions that apparently are unreasonable. We are looking for a reasonable ethical view, which is to say one that is argued for, that is not fallaciously, irrelevantly or inadequately substantiated, and that above all is supported by reasons that count as moral reasons. Now it may turn out to be the case that several views are equally reasonable, or that no view is ultimately more reasonable than any other. But my contention is that utilitarianism is reasonable, that no other view is, and that utilitarianism incidentally reveals to us what it is that makes a reason a moral reason.

REFERENCES

1   Ayer, A. J., *Language, Truth and Logic* (Penguin, 1971), p. 142.
2   Hitler, A., *Mein Kampf* (Hutchinson, 1972), p. 348.
3   Plato, *Gorgias*, 483.

FURTHER READING

The central claim of this chapter, that only certain kinds of reason can count as moral reasons, has been most fully argued by Warnock, G., in *The Object of Morality* (Methuen, 1971). Peters, R. S., also uses this argument in 'Form and Content in Moral Education' in *Authority, Responsibility and Education* (Allen & Unwin, 1973).

On the concept of 'reasonableness' and other associated concepts, see the articles collected in Part Two of Dearden, R. F., Hirst, P. H., and Peters, R. S. (eds), *Education and the Development of Reason* (Routledge & Kegan Paul, 1972).

Chapter 4

Freedom

People have valued freedom highly for a long time. Amongst the earliest references to it as an ideal are the writings of various Athenians of the fifth century BC. And this is no accident, for Athens gave birth to democracy, and traditionally freedom and democracy go closely in hand. Pericles is made to dwell upon the freedom of the Athenians in a famous panegyric on the city recorded by Thucydides.[1]

Herodotus goes so far as to attribute Athens' sudden increase in power in the fifth century to her new-found freedom. 'Proof,' he suggests, 'if proof were needed, of how noble a thing freedom is, not in one respect only, but in all respects.'

This is good stirring stuff, and it could be paralleled by extracts from a number of political speeches, plays and novels throughout history. But what does it all mean? What precisely are we to make of remarks such as this one from Mick Jagger:

> 'I'm against anything that interferes with individual freedom. As a nonconformist I won't accept what other people say is right. And there are hundreds like me, thousands.'[2]

Are these remarks supposed to be connected? Is a conformist necessarily opposed to individual freedom? Does a nonconformist have to reject everything that anybody else says is right in any sphere? What kind of a nonconformist is surrounded by thousands of people like himself? Above all, what is this thing called 'individual freedom' which Jagger alone (with thousands of other people) is in favour of? As it stands the remark quoted seems as unhelpful as Eric Burdon's point, quoted in the same volume, that Zappa must be 'very important' because 'he'll be photographed sitting on a toilet with a bunch of flowers, if he believes it will wake people up'.

In this chapter I want to suggest that a great deal of talk about freedom amounts to meaningless or incomprehensible slogan-shouting. Just to say that one is in favour of 'freedom' or that 'freedom' is a good thing does not get us anywhere. But I am not trying to argue that freedom is a *bad* thing or that people ought *not* to be free, for such remarks would be as obscure as their opposites. Rather, I want to suggest that it is misleading to proceed as if there was some thing, individual freedom, which is either good or bad in itself. We have to be more specific.

Two interesting and important points may be noticed straightaway about the way in which people tend to talk about freedom. Both are evident right from the moment that it first became important to the Athenians. First, it was not only the democratic Athenians who were proud of their freedom. The Spartans also prided themselves on being a free people. Now this is really rather extraordinary, because Sparta was a rigid authoritarian state, far more controlled or conditioned than most of those modern states that we tend to regard as totalitarian, or undemocratic and lacking in individual freedom. How could the Spartans reasonably claim to be free? How, if it comes to that, can the Russians claim to be free? And yet they do. 'Freedom', one suspects, is too emotive a term for anyone to dare openly to dismiss it as relatively unimportant.

This brings us on to the second point. Not only has the word 'freedom' such powerful overtones of desirability (not only is it 'prescriptive', to use the technical phrase), so that apparently incompatible types of government are eager to claim that they are 'for' freedom, but the ambiguity of the term, the uncertainty as to what it means descriptively, makes it easy for an able mind effectively to turn the notion on its head. Again the Greeks provide a vivid illustration of this. Plato had this to say about democratic government and its emphasis on freedom:

> 'In a democracy people are free . . . Anyone is allowed to do what he likes . . . That being so, every man arranges his own manner of life to suit his pleasure. The result is a greater variety of behaviour than you will find under any other form of constitution. So perhaps democracy is the finest type of government, with its variegated pattern of all sorts of characters. Certainly many people may think that it is best, just as women and children tend to admire those dresses that have many-coloured patterns. At any rate, if we are in search of a constitution, here is a good place to look for one. A democracy is so free that it contains a sample of every kind. You are not obliged to exercise responsibility, however competent you may be, or to submit to authority, if you don't like it . . . you may have no right to hold office or to sit on juries, but you will do so, if the spirit moves you. Indeed, a free and easy life.'[3]

But Plato did not simply content himself with ironic and sarcastic jibes at democratic freedom. Instead he argued at great length that people were not *really* free in a democracy. Being able to do what you like is not being free. Rather, he argues, the truly free man is the self-controlled man – one whose passions, impulses and desires are controlled by reason. Laws in a community ideally uphold reasonable ends, and therefore law is a necessary condition of the free society. Thus one can say that Plato's social objective was freedom, but 'by this he meant personal liberty not in the sense of being allowed to do what one likes, but in a sense including freedom from arbitrary arrest and, in general, subordination only to laws devised in the general interest'.[2] This view of freedom led him to advocate an authoritarian form of government, which, though it may plausibly be argued is demanded by his premisses, is clearly not exactly what democratic advocates of freedom had in mind. Plato may plausibly argue that his Republic provides 'real freedom', but somebody like Mick Jagger might reasonably respond that it is not what he means by 'individual freedom'. Certainly one doubts whether Jagger would fit easily into the Republic.

I do not intend to pursue Plato's argument here, though it is not dissimilar to attempts to formulate what is called a positive conception of freedom which I shall consider below. But his example should serve to warn us that 'freedom' is a tricky concept that can be taken over for their own purposes by the proponents of a wide variety of views.

What, then, can we say about freedom?

A good starting point, as well as a fine rallying cry, is provided by Rousseau's remark at the beginning of his Social Contract that 'Man is born free; yet everywhere he is in chains'. Rousseau's thesis is that just as he was born free, so man ought to remain free through life. Unfortunately the thesis is riddled with problems. What exactly does the claim that man is born free mean? In what sense is man born free? Inasmuch as man is born more or less helpless – far more helpless than most other animals are at birth – he is not born free to do very much, for surely it only makes sense to say that somebody is free to do such and such, if, amongst other things, he is *able* to do such and such. Nor as a matter of fact is man born free from all restrictions; nor would he be in a state of nature (as opposed to a civilised community), since various natural phenomena would presumably serve as restrictions on his freedom. Nor is it even true that all men are born free in the limited sense of free from the restrictions arbitrarily imposed upon them by other people: one may deplore it, but the fact remains that plenty of people have been born directly into slavery. Furthermore, even if we allow that in some sense it is true that man is born free, it would not follow logically that man ought to be free. Such an argument would involve the fallacy of moving from 'is' to 'ought' – from the statement that something is the case to the conclusion that it ought to be – without any reasoning being given to justify the transition. That this move is fallacious can easily be illustrated: from the fact, if it is a fact, that man tends to behave selfishly, we would not conclude that it is right that he should be selfish; from the fact that a human being is born heavily dependent upon the mother, we do not conclude that he ought to remain so through life. It may be true in some sense that man ought to be free, but if it is true, it is not true *because* he was born free, even if it were true in some sense that he was born free.

Given these considerations, nobody can really doubt after a moment's reflection that Rousseau is simply asserting his opinion that men ought to be free. He is not offering us any reason to share his view. A remark such as 'Man is born free; yet everywhere he is in chains' does not constitute part of an argument at all. It is an emotive remark designed to win over sentiment, like a political catch phrase. It is an appeal for freedom.

However it is an appeal that many of us would automatically respond to. Many of us, like Rousseau, value freedom, although it might be worth bearing in mind that we were brought up in, and live in, a society that places considerable stress on freedom, and which consequently may to some extent have contributed to the formation of that evaluation in our minds. From the fact that by and large we do value freedom, it obviously does not follow either that man *has* to value it or that we are right to do so. But for the moment let us accept our immediate feeling that freedom is valuable, and ask the obvious question: What is freedom? For we cannot come on to the question of how valuable it is, until we have clarified what we mean by it.

Certain philosophers have tried to argue for what is termed a positive conception of freedom. They point out, correctly, that one can be 'free from' various restrictions and impositions, but that one can also be 'free to' do various things. They then suggest that if, in advocating freedom, we have in mind freedom from various restrictions (a negative conception of freedom, as it is called), we are putting forward a dull and uninspiring ideal and will run into the problem that some restrictions may seem to be desirable. They therefore argue that what freedom really means is the freedom to do something like 'develop one's potential', 'realise one's personality', or 'set up the rule of reason over one's desires and passions'. (This is the positive conception of freedom, which can be traced back to Plato and to Aristotle, who thought that the negative conception of freedom was 'mean-spirited'.) If we think of freedom in this way, it obviously follows that restraints and restrictions may actually be necessary in order to promote freedom. Thus Bantock writes: 'What the attainment of "true" freedom involves is some measure of restraint; it is, in fact, something to be realised, not something to be accepted.'[5]

It is no accident, I think, that one of the foremost advocates of the positive conception of freedom, Bantock, should be an educationalist. For it is in relation to children, whose talents, intellect, character and abilities are not yet fully formed, that it seems most immediately persuasive to suggest that just removing all restrictions from them is not much of an ideal, and that by actually imposing on them in various ways we can positively contribute to their development and ultimately their freedom. By forcing the child to attend school (I deliberately use strong language here), by compelling him to learn to read and write, by making him study literature, we may undoubtedly open up avenues for him in later life that would otherwise have remained closed; he will thus, as an adult, be free to do things that he would not otherwise have been free to do.

However to suggest that at least in some instances it is justifiable or desirable to place restrictions on people is one thing. To claim that freedom necessarily involves 'some measure of restraint', which seems tantamount to saying that 'some measure of restraint' is part of the *meaning* of 'freedom', is quite another.

I am not at this point concerned to take sides on the issue of whether it is or is not desirable to impose certain restrictions on either children or adults. (I shall consider that question below and in Part Three.) Here I merely wish to suggest that the positive conception of freedom is a piece of verbal jugglery that does not help and that runs counter to the obvious meaning of 'freedom'. If we were to accept the idea of a positive conception, we should still be faced with the question of precisely what positive conception we ought to adopt as our ideal. Ought we, for instance, to aim at 'realising the personality' or 'setting up the rule of reason'? Are these two phrases synonymous, perhaps? What does 'realising the personality' mean? Do we want all personalities 'realised'? And then how important is the distinction between 'freedom from' and 'freedom to' on which this conception is based? Not very important, I suggest, since one can always rephrase a specific 'freedom from' in terms of 'freedom to', and vice versa. If a child is free to realise his personality, then he is free from restrictions that might have prevented him doing so.

But the central objection is that the positive conception of freedom confuses the issue by moving away from the obvious meaning of freedom, which is surely an 'absence of restraint'. It should be stressed that my claim here is that that is what *freedom* means, but it does not follow that it is sufficient to say that a *free man* is simply a man who is not subject to restraint. The matter is a great deal more complex than that, essentially because if freedom means an absence of restraint then it follows that there are various different kinds of freedom. To be precise there are as many kinds of freedom as there are kinds of restraint. We may talk of physical freedom (i.e. the absence of physical restraints), psychological freedom (the absence of psychological restraints), moral freedom, legal freedom, and so on. Now clearly it is conceivable that a man should be physically free but not psychologically free, or legally free but not morally free. And given that this is so it is plainly insufficient to say that a free man is one who is subject to no restraints. No man is literally free from all restraints. The question of whether a man is free or not is to some extent at least a question of degree.

To arrive at a view of what constitutes being a free man therefore involves making a selection amongst the various kinds of restraint that a man might be subject to, but which it is logically possible for him not to be subject to, and arguing that a man is to be regarded as free insofar as he has a particu- lar kind of freedom or freedoms (i.e. insofar as he is not subject to par- ticular kinds of restraint).

But the matter is further complicated by the fact that in order to give an individual the opportunity for freedom at a later stage it may be necessary to curb his freedom in various ways now. For example, John White has recently argued that ideally people should be free to choose for themselves what activities they wish to partake in and regard as worthwhile. But, as he rightly observes, if people are to be free to choose for themselves, then they must be able to choose for themselves. This means that they must at least have some understanding of what is involved in various activities. For I could not really be said to have *chosen* not to write poetry, if I haven't the first idea of what is involved in writing poetry. The upshot of this particular argument is that education must therefore place various restraints on the child by way of demanding that he gains some experience of activities that he would not otherwise be in a position to make a choice about. 'We are right,' White concludes, 'to make [the child] unfree now so as to give him as much autonomy as possible later on.'[6]

It is necessary, however, to simplify the complex task of elucidating the problem of individual freedom by concentrating on one question at a time. I therefore propose to pursue the question of what I shall call social free- dom. This is the question of the extent to which people should be subject to restrictions imposed upon them by others, either directly or indirectly by way of law or convention. Some appear to hold the view that there should be no such restrictions on the individual's freedom to do what he is capable of doing and chooses to do. I shall begin by attempting to show that this is a pretty silly sort of view.

First consider the consequences of this demand. One has already been referred to (in a different context) when we considered the reasoning behind attempts to formulate a positive conception of freedom. If nobody ought to impose restrictions or restraints on anybody else, then nobody ought to make any demands on children. That is to say, nobody should insist that they have any education, and nobody should impose any specific restraints on them such as the demand that they take exercise, eat healthy food, or learn to count and read. Now, of course, we know that a number of educa- tionalists *do* argue for such things as deschooling and question the worth- whileness of making children learn to read. But we should distinguish between those who think that as a matter of fact there are more effective ways of helping children to learn than forcing them to attend classes, and those who think that we ought not to make children do anything or prevent them from doing anything they choose to do. We should distinguish between those who question the value of learning to read in the television age, and those who question the right of adults to place any restraints on children at all. The demand that we are considering here is *not* the demand that specific restraints should be removed from children, but that *all* should be. Surely we cannot accept this. If we were to do so, it would follow that we accepted that, if a child showed signs of developing into a bully and a philistine, this, though perhaps unfortunate, should not be guarded against. It would follow that we agreed to refrain from *any* short-term imposition on the child designed to provide him with long-term benefit. Ironically, since the demand seems so radical, it would in practice inevitably lead to gross inequality and stratification of society, since some with natural flair and curiosity would rapidly develop skills, knowledge and abilities, through their own choice, which would drastically mark them off from the weak and the dull. Surely, in the case of children at least, there must be *some* curtailment of freedom.

Secondly, if no restraints are legitimate, then even amongst adults we shall perpetuate a situation that works to the advantage of the strong and the 'haves' against the weak and the 'have-nots'. For, as has often been pointed out, restraints and restrictions very often work to the advantage of various individuals. Restrictions on people's freedom to steal my property, beat me up or kill me, are restrictions that I, for one, am pleased to benefit from. A world in which there were no restrictions would be a world in which only the strong survived.

So much for the consequences of advocating absolute freedom (i.e. an absence of all restraint). In my view contemplation of them is alone quite sufficient to indicate that this unqualified demand for freedom is unacceptable. But perhaps I am just faint-hearted and cowardly – frightened of being on the losing end. How can we demonstrate to those who hope to end up on top that this call for absolute freedom is unacceptable? It is not difficult to show that the claim that people ought to be free to do anything they want to do constitutes both an impossible and an absurd ideal.

The reason that the ideal is impossible to realise is simply this: if every individual is literally free to do as he chooses and is subject to no restrictions from his fellow citizens, either directly or indirectly through the process of law, then presumably nobody is entitled to stop him doing things like making a noise late at night, doing no work, paying visits to people, killing or stealing. It is not only the prima facie wrong acts, such as killing or stealing, that should raise an eyebrow here. The point is that, if we take the demand that people should be free to do what they choose to do at its face value, we run into difficulties even with innocent acts like visiting people. For visiting people, like most human activities, impinges on other people. If I visit you, then I impinge on your freedom, unless you either choose to be visited by me at the same time or have the freedom to say 'Go away' and to close the door on me. But if you choose the latter course of action then you are impinging on my freedom: it is no longer true to say that I am free to pay you a visit. In other words the notion of everybody being literally free to do as they choose is a logical impossibility, unless as a matter of fact everybody's choices happened to coincide all the time.

Is the ideal also absurd, as I have maintained? One might reasonably claim that any ideal that involved logical impossibility was pretty absurd, but another objection to the ideal is that the consequence of committing oneself to it would be that anything was all right, any action was acceptable, provided that it was done freely. If ideally people ought to be free to do what they choose to do – if, in other words, no qualifications are added about the sort of things that they ought to be free to choose to do – then it follows that, ideally, it does not matter what they do, provided that they freely choose to do it. That is to say that bullying, eating sweets, committing suicide, killing, stealing, having sex, reading Shakespeare, sitting on the lavatory holding a bunch of flowers, wasting away one's talents – would all be acceptable activities. Once again note that I deliberately do not confine myself to prima facie objectionable activities. I do not at this stage want to beg the question by saying that there are certain specific things that people ought not to be free to do. The point here is that, if our ideal is absolute freedom of choice, if that is what ultimately matters, then we are effectively saying that there is no moral distinction to be made between any of the activities listed – or indeed any other activities. Now what reason is there to accept this extraordinary conclusion that there is no moral distinction to be drawn between any actions, and that the supreme moral question is whether they are performed freely or not? I can see no reason at all. The fact that I cannot see a reason to accept it does not of course constitute a proof that it is unacceptable. But I now appeal to the reader: can one accept the consequences of this view? Can one accept that there is no distinction to be drawn between the moral worth of *any* acts? If the reader agrees with me in feeling that he cannot accept the consequences, then it follows that it would be unreasonable for him to make use of the formula 'People ought to be free to do what they choose to do', or either to object to specific restrictions of freedom simply on the grounds that they are restrictions, or, conversely, to defend specific freedoms simply on the grounds that people ought to be free.

If we accept that we can conceive of things that people ought not to be free to do, even though at this stage each one of us may have very different ideas as to what these things are, it becomes incumbent upon us to do more than simply assert that 'freedom', without qualification, is good, or that people ought to be free to do what they choose to do. For it appears that it is not the case that we think freedom is good, or that it is good that people should be free, but rather that we think it good that people should be free in certain specific, though as yet unspecified, respects or that we

think that people ought to be free to do as they choose with certain qualifications.

If my argument so far is accepted, then clearly the next step would be to
consider in what specific respects people should be free or what qualifications should be added to the basic claim that people should be free to do
what they choose to do. I shall not in fact take that step until Chapter 6,
for this reason: to decide what limits to set upon people's freedom, we
have to take into account our other values. For example, if I wish to argue
that no employer ought to be free to pay a wage as low as £3 a week, even
if he could find somebody desperate enough to accept it, then, to substantiate my case, I should obviously have to argue that something was more
important than the employer's freedom to do this. Similarly, in all other
cases where one wishes to consider whether people should be free to do
something (or free from something) one needs to weigh up the value of
people being free against one's other values. Since this is so, we obviously
cannot be very precise about what people should be free to do until we have
considered those other values. We cannot, for example, assert that the
claims of equality may over-ride the claims of freedom, until we have looked
at the concept of equality, come to some conclusion as to what is involved
in it, and formed some view as to its relative importance compared with
freedom, should the two clash.

But before bringing this chapter to a close I shall look at two attempts
to specify the limits that need to be set on freedom that do not seem to
involve any reference to other values.

One view is that the only limitation that should be set on people's freedom
to do what they choose to do is the limit set by freedom itself. In other
words everybody should be free to do what they want provided that they
do not act in any way that impinges on the freedom of others. This formula
is attractive to many: it seems clear enough and it looks as if it will guaran-
tee a fair amount of freedom in practice. But closer inspection makes one
extremely doubtful whether it would in fact result in much freedom and
indicates that the formula is not satisfactory.

As we have already seen, a great deal of quite innocent human activity
automatically impinges upon the freedom of others. Given that this is so,
either we have to deny people the freedom to do all sorts of things that none
of us would seriously suggest denying them, or else we are confronted with
a problem similar to that of deciding which came first, the chicken or the
egg. For when we are trying to decide on desirable freedoms, using this
formula, what comes first: my freedom to do what does not interfere with
your freedom, or your freedom to do things that might interfere with my
freedom? To take an example: do we say that you ought not to be allowed
to play your trumpet during the evening in the flat adjoining mine, because,
if you do play it, you effectively deny me the freedom to study in my flat.

Or do we say that I ought not to be guaranteed the freedom to study, because that interferes with your freedom to play the trumpet? Before we could make effective use of this formula we would *already* have to have decided, *by some other means,* that some freedoms counted more than others. Thus we might argue that freedom to get a good night's sleep was not of supreme importance, and that therefore haulage contractors should have freedom to drive ten-ton lorries past houses at night. The demand that lorries should not be driven through residential areas at night could then be interpreted as an illegitimate attempt to interfere with the freedom of haulage contractors. But on what grounds, in this case, was it originally decided that the freedom of sleep, which is being interfered with, is relatively unimportant?

One might modify this formula, in an attempt to make it more common-sensical and to avoid the examples I have selected (which may seem trivial to some, though not, I would guess, to those who live next door to trumpet-players or haulage contractors), by saying that people should be free to do whatever does not involve physical limitations on the freedom of others. Thus it may be said that I should not be free to assault you, because that impinges on your freedom in an obvious physical sense. But such a modification will not make the formula satisfactory. In the first place, to make it usable, we should need a much more precise definition of what constituted 'physical restriction' on someone else's freedom. In the second place it seems likely that, once we had arrived at a more precise definition, there would be numerous activities that did not involve physical limitation of other people's freedom, which would therefore be activities that people ought to be free to indulge in, on this view of how one limits the claims of freedom, but which would nonetheless be activities that few of us would be prepared to tolerate, such as blackmail. Besides which, we should still be faced with the chicken/egg problem: if you are free to physically exclude me from your house, I am not free, physically, to enter it. If I am free to enter it, you are not free to keep me out. How do we decide between these two freedoms? Evidently not by appealing to the principle that people should be free to do that which does not physically limit the freedom of others.

A second way of attempting to define the limits of freedom, without making any reference to other values, is to draw a distinction between 'licence' and 'liberty'. This approach has been exposed many times by philosophers for the muddle it is. However, it seems necessary briefly to consider it yet again, since it has been resurrected by such educationalists as A. S. Neill. On this view 'liberty' is desirable freedom, whereas 'licence' is undesirable freedom. The problem of freedom is thus very simple to solve and the limits easy to define. We should ideally provide unlimited liberty and no licence.

It will be seen at once by the reader that this is a verbal and meaningless trick. For although in theory we no longer have to ask 'What freedom should people have?' or 'How do we decide which freedoms to grant people?', since the answer to both these questions is that we should give people 'liberty' but not 'licence', we have to ask instead how we are to distinguish 'liberty' from 'licence'. Clearly that is exactly the same question. Since 'liberty' is defined as 'desirable freedom', the question 'What freedom is liberty as opposed to licence?' is exactly the same as the question 'What is desirable freedom?'. But there is absolutely nothing in this approach to the problem of freedom that helps us to answer the question, whichever way it is phrased.

If the reader cares to turn to Neill's *Summerhill* he will find some stirring denunciations of people who fail to appreciate that in advocating freedom he is not advocating a policy of total non-interference with children. 'It is this distinction between freedom and licence that many parents cannot grasp,' he asserts.[7] But, however diligently one reads the book, one will find no guidance as to how one is supposed to distinguish between the two. All that can be found are various examples of freedoms that Neill allows, which must by definition be 'liberties', and freedoms that he does not allow, which are by definition 'licence'. It is not explained *why* they are respectively categorised in this way, and sometimes it is difficult to see what is essentially different about two freedoms one of which is allowed (liberty) and one of which is not (licence). For instance, on what grounds does Neill regard it as acceptable that children should play with their mother's valuable ornaments even if they break them, but regard it as unacceptable that they should kick the study door? It should be stressed that the question here is not do we agree or disagree with Neill's particular judgements, but by what criteria does he distinguish between these two, or any other, examples of freedom?

The argument of this chapter has been as follows: 'freedom' is a highly emotive concept, such that throughout history people have attempted to interpret it in any way that suited their policy. Nonetheless it seems reasonable to avoid attempts to formulate a positive conception of freedom, and to accept that 'freedom' means an 'absence of restraint'. We start with a prima facie conviction that people ought not to be subject to restrictions from their fellow men or pushed around against their wishes. But it quickly becomes apparent that we cannot accept that there should be *no* restrictions or restraints on people. This is partly because it is unavoidable that there should be some, and partly because we feel that there are in any case some things that people ought not to be free to do. There is also the further consideration that restraints and restrictions can, from a long-term point of view, actually lead to an increase in freedom.

82 / *Moral Philosophy for Education*

The suggestion that people should be 'free to do anything that does not interfere with the freedom of others' was rejected, on the grounds that it would be impossible to arrive at any conclusions as to what people ought to be free to do on the basis of this formula alone. The suggestion that the problem is solved by granting 'freedom' but no 'licence' was dismissed as an absurd misunderstanding of the nature of the problem.

What is required is some account of the circumstances in which the claims of other values may over-ride the claims of freedom. Such an account presupposes some view of various other possible values; no answer to the question 'What are the limits of freedom?'. therefore, can be given until a later chapter.

But what is already clear, if the argument of this chapter is accepted, is that there must be *some* consideration (or considerations) that *can* over-ride the claims of freedom. There comes a point at which the claims of freedom are not of paramount importance. If this is so, it can never be sufficient to object to a specific restriction simply on the grounds that it *is* (by definition) a curtailment of freedom. It is never enough to simply say 'But that is objectionable because it restricts freedom'; one would need to continue the argument by explaining why this particular restriction on freedom is objectionable, whereas others are not.

REFERENCES

1 Thucydides, *The Peloponnesian War*, 2.35 ff.
2 *The Permissive Society*, The Guardian Inquiry (Panther, 1969), Vox Pop, p. 15.
3 Plato, *The Republic*, 557 (adapted).
4 Crombie, I., *An Examination of Plato's Doctrines*, vol. 1 (Routledge & Kegan Paul, 1962), p. 161.
5 Bantock, G. H., *Education and Values* (Faber & Faber, 1965), p. 99.
6 White, J. P., *Towards a Compulsory Curriculum* (Routledge & Kegan Paul, 1973).
7 Neill, A. S., *Summerhill* (Penguin, 1968), p. 105.

FURTHER READING

For a basic philosophical discussion of the problems relating to freedom, see Benn, S. I., and Peters, R. S., *Social Principles and the Democratic State* (Allen & Unwin, 1959). Peters, R. S., *Ethics and Education* (Allen & Unwin, 1966) covers essentially the same ground in less detail.

Classic texts relating to freedom are Mill, J. S., 'On Liberty' in Warnock, M. (ed.), *Utilitarianism* (Fontana, 1962) and Locke, J., *A Letter Concerning Toleration* (Bobbs-Merrill, 1950).

Chapter 5

Equality

The American Declaration of Independence states at one point: 'We hold these truths to be self-evident, that all men are created equal [and] that they are endowed by their Creator with certain unalienable rights.' Obviously, far from all Americans now believe in a Creator and, as we have already indicated in remarking briefly on intuitionist theories of ethics (Chapter 2), the claim that these are self-evident truths is not particularly helpful, since they are only self-evident to those who believe in them. Nonetheless most of us do claim to believe in equality. The question is what it means to say that one believes in equality. What is equality? Can any reasons be produced for valuing it?

Remarks such as 'All men are born or created equal' or simply 'All men are equal' obviously cannot be taken as straightforward statements of descriptive fact. Those who say that all men are equal cannot be understood to be making a statement parallel to 'All men have blood in their veins' or 'Most men have two legs'. All men are *not* equal as a matter of descriptive truth. They are unequal in size, intelligence, sensitivity and a variety of other ways. It seems that 'All men are equal' must be understood as a way of saying that, in the speaker's opinion, 'All men ought to be equal'. But what does the claim that all men ought to be equal mean? There is not much point in saying that all men ought to be equal in height, weight, intelligence and so on, since it seems clear that all men *cannot* be equal in these respects, and anyway the question of whether they shall be or not is not in our hands. Surely what is meant by the claim that all men ought to be equal is that all men ought to be treated equally, or regarded as equally important and having an equal claim to consideration of their interests. Bald statements such as that all men are equal thus serve as a way of saying, to take an extreme example, that some men should not be enslaved to others, since to divide the world into slaves and masters obviously involves unequal treatment and giving unequal consideration to the interests of one group.

But a problem now arises. Slavery is an uncontentious example of unequal treatment in our own times. But what in fact is involved in equal treatment? If enslaving some people is treating them unequally, what about domestic servants? Are they being unequally treated? Are coal miners or school teachers getting unequal treatment? Is a society unequal insofar as it pays different wages, insofar as it provides different kinds of jobs, insofar as it provides different kinds of schooling, or insofar as its members live in different kinds of houses and have different kinds of life-styles? Would an equal society, for instance, demand that everybody lived in identical houses, or at least, as in Poland, that each individual had exactly the same maximum limit of living space? Some anti-egalitarians have tried to suggest that 'to treat people equally' means 'treating them in exactly the same way,' and that an egalitarian society would be a society of more or less identical beings, lacking all individuality, rather like a flock of seals, and that there- fore equality is of dubious value. But *is* this what is meant by an equal society or a society in which people are treated equally?

Although many people may happen to desire a society in which there is considerably less difference between a number of aspects of individuals' lives than there is in our society, there are surely very few people who would mean by 'equal treatment' literally the same treatment for all, in all respects. For to advocate this would be to advocate, amongst other things, no special medical treatment for the sick, no pensions for the elderly, the same amount of food for new-born babies and adults, and exactly the same education for everybody from the mentally defective to the child prodigy. So, although some might conclude that equal treatment for all as an ideal led to certain specific consequences, such as the same wage for all, they could not *mean* by 'equal treatment', 'the same treatment'. The question we have to ask, therefore, is what does 'equal treatment' mean, such that providing special medical attention for the sick does not seem prima facie incompatible with it, and yet such that specific demands such as the same rate of pay for all seem prima facie to be plausibly demanded by it? How can 'equal treat- ment' involve the same treatment in some respects, and different treatment in other respects?

Imagine that somebody were to object that providing medical attention only for the sick was an example of unequal treatment. What would one say in reply? Something like this, I suggest: 'There is no point in wasting money in distributing drugs and medicines in equal quantities to all people, regardless of whether they are sick or not, and it would be absurd to give operations to all people regardless of their physical conditions. We give medical attention to those who need it. The fact that somebody is sick is a *relevant reason* for giving him, rather than other people, medical atten- tion.' In the same way, if someone wished to argue that all men ought to receive the same wage regardless of the nature of their work, he would presumably proceed somewhat as follows: 'Why do we pay the managers of companies more than the workers? Because they exercise more respon- sibility, because they work harder, because they are cleverer? But these claims are either untrue, or else they do not provide *relevant reasons* for receiving a higher wage. Why should the fact that a man is academically more qualified, or in some sense cleverer, be regarded as a *relevant reason* for giving him more money?' Whether such an argument is convincing or not is irrelevant to the point being made here, which is that, when we consider whether a specific example of different treatment is or is not acceptable in the name of equality, the way we proceed is to ask whether there are differences between groups of people that constitute *relevant reasons* for differential treatment. In other words we may say that equal treatment involves the same treatment except where differences between people constitute relevant reasons for differential treatment.

This is to say that the principle of equality or the claim that all men should be treated equally is identical to the principle of impartiality or the claim that all people should be treated impartially. To be impartial is not to treat all people in the same way; that would rather be indiscriminate. An impartial person is one who discriminates only with good reason. For example, an impartial film critic is one who distinguishes between films, praising some, scoffing at some and condemning others, on relevant grounds, which is to say on grounds that are relevant to the nature of the job that he is doing. But a critic who enthused over all films would be indiscriminate: the notion that there might be reasons relevant to the task of distinguishing between these films (for instance the quality of the acting, the camera-work, the direction and so on) would mean nothing to him. A partial critic would be one who *did* discriminate between films, but whose reasons for so doing were bad reasons or reasons that were irrelevant to the nature of his job. For instance, he might praise all those films that were made by his friends, simply because they *were* made by his friends.

Is there then any argument to support the contention that we ought to be impartial? There is a peculiar argument that one sometimes comes across nowadays to the effect that there is such a thing as 'justified partiality', or that it is sometimes a good thing to be partial. This view seems to arise out of a misunderstanding of what is meant by 'impartiality', and the consequent assumption that an impartial man is an uncommitted neutral. The view thus arises that the plea for impartial teachers, for example, is a plea for woolly liberals: men who refrain from taking sides and from standing up for any particular point of view in front of the children whom they teach, and therefore (the implication seems to be) from criticising the status quo, and strenuously arguing against the injustices of our society. But, of course, as already indicated, an impartial teacher is not necessarily uncommitted. If we understand 'neutral' to mean 'poised between two points of view or two sides', or 'uncommitted to either of two opposing viewpoints' and 'refraining from helping one side or the other', which seems an acceptable working definition, then there is no necessary reason why an impartial man should be neutral in any specific instance. The impartial film critic is very far from neutral when it comes to judging the films that he has to see. He is 'for' those that he judges to be better, and 'against' those that he judges to be worse. A truly impartial man will only be neutral, in the sense of uncommitted, in those situations where he can see no good reasons for taking up one side rather than another. If there are good reasons for adopting one viewpoint rather than another, or for actively supporting it, he will do so. Since the demand for impartiality is no more than the demand that one should have good reason for discrimination or taking sides, it is logically impossible to have good reason for being partial, for that would mean having good reason to discriminate or take sides without good reason.

In this book the notion of having good reason plays an important part, and it therefore seems only fair to consider briefly a question that is sometimes sincerely raised today: 'Why should I worry about having good reason for my beliefs, my attitudes and the way I behave? Is this stress upon reason not part of a particular tradition, and is it not being used to maintain a particular way of life, a particular way of looking at things, and a particular set of values? After all human reason is fallible, why should we not rely on our instinctive feelings instead?' (The crucial question of how one decides upon what represents a 'good reason' will be examined in the next chapter.)

Such questions seem recently to have been raised more frequently than ever before, perhaps as a result of an increased disillusionment with the results of the rational tradition. Men have stressed reason for centuries, but they have not come up with reasonable answers. The problems of the world seem no nearer solution than ever, and what could be more irritating to the dedicated and passionate social reformer than the quibbling of those who cling to an insistence on faultless reasoning? If one is incensed at social injustice and committed to a specific solution, it is tiresome, to say the least, to be held at bay by criticisms and exposures of flaws in the detail of one's argument.

At the risk of irritating such anti-rationalists yet further, it must be insisted that we distinguish between the view that reason has not solved the world's problems, and the view that we can formally dispense with the ideal of having good reason for beliefs and actions. Not only must it be conceded that reason has not produced heaven on earth, it may also be conceded both that it probably never will, and that over the years the rational tradition has built up a number of assumptions that are *presumed* to be reasonable, but which may in fact not be so. But it is one thing to argue that a number of people who put the stress on reason are not in fact particularly reasonable and that in practice there may be a tendency on the part of some to identify being reasonable with seeing things their way, and quite another to argue that it is not important to be reasonable.

There has been repeated criticism lately (from students and educationalists) of schools and universities, on the grounds that the teachers in such institutions do, in fact, not only demand an emphasis on reason, but also decide themselves what counts as reasonable, and thus the status quo is preserved. To what extent it is true that the status quo is taking cover behind the emphasis on reason, I do not know. Nor do I intend here to go into the question of the extent to which the status quo should be dismantled. My concern is to point out that, though we may properly criticise individuals on the grounds that their view of what is reasonable is not itself reasonable, we cannot commit ourselves to the view that having good reason is in principle unimportant. If it were, on what grounds would we be criticising those whom we regard as upholding an unreasonable view? If a position does not need to be backed by good reasons, then why should anyone feel that it is an outrage that some people, to retain the example, should be concerned to maintain the status quo? It surely only makes sense to feel indignant if one feels that those who do this are mistaken in some way. But if there is no distinction to be made between adopting a position with good reason and adopting one without good reason, how can anyone be 'mistaken' in the view they adopt?

The point to stress is that, in insisting that the notion of having good reason is important, one is not insisting that people should agree that specific reasons are good. That is a separate question. And it is difficult to see how anybody, once he understands that it is only the formal principle of having good reason that is being upheld, could deny that it was important. To ask why it is important, for instance, is already to indicate that one does value the notion, for one is asking for a good reason to value it. Furthermore, what would be the point of asking the sort of questions that we are concerned with in this book, if we were not concerned with whether the answers were reasonable or not? If the notion of having good reasons is abandoned as an ideal, it is difficult to see how we could continue to communicate. 'I do not like you because you have five fingers' would be indistinguishable, in respect of its acceptability, from 'I do not like you because you keep beating me up'.

I take it then that we are committed to the principle of impartiality or the principle of equality understood in this way, but of course the fact that it is only a formal principle does make it of limited practical value. It tells us the manner in which we should proceed if we wish to treat people equally, but it does not tell us what equal treatment in any specific instance would actually involve. It tells us that we must only differentiate between people when there are good reasons for so doing, but it does not tell us what reasons *are* good reasons for discrimination, and it does not even tell us how to set about judging whether a reason is good or not. On the assumption that we agree, for instance, that medical treatment should be freely available for all when they need it, it is not the principle of equality itself which gives us this specific injunction. Rather it is our judgement of what are relevant considerations to the distribution of medical attention; and that has to be decided by reference to whatever our objectives may be, the varying needs of people in relation to those objectives, and the nature of medical attention. Medical care is a way of preventing or curing sickness, our object is to keep people healthy, and therefore we provide medical care to those who are sick. All the principle of equality does is to tell us to adopt this kind of approach. But, of course, when people disagree as to whether reasons are relevant or not to a particular distributional problem, as seems to be the case with such suggestions as that responsibility or intellectual ability are relevant criteria for different wages, the principle of equality does not help us. Those who advocate equal wages have to do more than simply say that equality demands equal pay, for that would only be obviously so if we understood equal treatment to mean identical treatment in all cases; in which case we should be back to square one, faced with the conclusion that all people in all cases should be treated exactly the same. It is necessary for them to explain why no proposed criteria for differentiating between people in respect of wages are relevant. Conversely, it is necessary for those who maintain that there are relevant reasons for paying different wages to explain why such reasons are relevant. In neither case will the principle of equality itself be of any help.

Because it is purely formal, and so vague and unhelpful in itself when it comes to answering specific questions about distribution, some people wish to dismiss this formulation of the principle of equality. But one cannot dismiss something simply because one does not like it, or it does not answer to one's purpose. The question is simply: first, do we accept that it can be justifiable to treat people differently in some respects? Secondly, assuming that we do accept that, is it possible to say anything more positive about certain respects in which there are felt to be no conceivable good reasons for differential treatment? If it is, then one will acquire a more substantial view of what equality involves, but the fact remains that one can only do this by appealing beyond the principle of equality itself.

Nonetheless the principle of equality has at least two strong teeth. First, the demand that people shall only be treated differently if good reasons can be given for so doing puts the onus on those who wish to treat various people differently to produce a good argument for so doing. The principle embodies a presumption in favour of treating people in the same way that can only be set aside for good reason. Secondly, it involves the assumption that all people have to be considered as of equal importance, or that the claims of all people have to be taken equally seriously. It therefore rules out from the beginning an argument of the form 'Well, I don't need to consider whether there are good reasons for distributing wages equally to blacks or Jews as well as Aryans, because blacks and Jews don't count'.

The presumption is that all men count, though in specific instances there may be differences between them that warrant different treatment.

But what if a man argues, not that some people don't enter into consideration, but that the fact that a man is a Jew, or coloured, or red-haired, or short, *is a relevant reason* for giving him no freedom, or no pay, or whatever? Well, of course, philosophy cannot prevent the existence of people who think in this way. All it can do is strenuously deny that such factors are relevant reasons for a differential distribution of anything. The onus remains on those who wish to assert that they are to convince us. We are all aware that some people would like to convince us of this, but, in the view of most of us, they fail. The obvious example to take is the one we have already considered: Hitler attempted to show that there was good reason to ignore Jews. But even he did not dare stick at the simple assertion that Jews can be ignored *because they are Jews*. Instead he tried to invoke considerations of cultural and physical superiority. But the argument was manifestly unreasonable. In default of any convincing argument – or even the beginnings of one – to the effect that some group of people, be they Jewish, red-haired, long-haired, communist or whatever, for that reason do not count, we shall continue to assert firmly that everybody counts.

As with freedom, my central concern in considering equality in this chapter has not been to answer specific questions about distribution and treatment, but to indicate the way in which the question of equality needs to be approached. In particular I have attempted to bring out one important point, and that is that to decide what is equal treatment in any specific situation, one is going to have to appeal to some other value beyond equality. We have seen that there is reason to treat people impartially. We have also seen that in specific instances this may demand either that we should treat people the same or that we should treat them differently. But, in order to substantiate any specific demand for similar or dissimilar treatment, it is necessary to produce good reason for so doing. What constitutes a good reason obviously has to be decided to some extent by the context: a good reason must relate to the matter in hand, as sickness relates to medicine and as responsibility relates to wages. But this is not in itself enough; although the responsibility that a man has is obviously prima facie related to the question of what wages he should receive, in a way that the colour of his hair is not, we can still argue about whether it provides a *good reason* for a man to receive more wages than others. Similarly, although as a matter of fact we probably would not disagree about the suggestion that sickness constituted a good reason for receiving medical attention, it is not in fact merely because medicine and sickness are related that it is a good reason. (One can think of situations in which the fact that a man was sick did not constitute a good reason for giving him medical attention.) In both these cases, and in all other examples, we can only finally accept that a reason is a good one in the light of some further assumption. There must be some higher value or goal in the light of which we can assess whether the fact that a man is sick or that he exercises responsibility constitutes a good reason for receiving, respectively, medicine or higher wages. What is the assumption (or assumptions) in the light of which we are to decide? What is the value (or values) that finally determine whether a reason that relates to the distributional problem at hand is a good reason?

FURTHER READING

See Wilson, J., *Equality* (Hutchinson, 1966), Benn, S. I., and Peters, R. S., *Social Principles and the Democratic State* (Allen & Unwin, 1959) and Peters, R. S., *Ethics and Education* (Allen & Unwin, 1966).

Chapter 6

Utilitarianism

The examination of the concepts of 'freedom' and 'equality' in the preceding chapters has been brief. A lot more could have been said about most of the points raised, and many other points might have been raised. But I have made the point that I regard as all-important: in the case of both freedom and equality it seemed clear that there was something – possibly more than one thing – in the light of which assessments had to be made. There is something in the light of which freedom may be restricted. This 'something' might in practice be such that certain specific freedoms would never be interfered with. But clearly there can be good reason to stop people doing certain things. Likewise, although treating some people as if they were not deserving of consideration seemed objectionable, it is clear that in principle good reason can be given for treating people differently in specific circumstances.

The question that is forced upon us is where are the good reasons going to come from? What value or values are more important than freedom? What value or values should give substance to the formal principle of impartiality? What makes a reason a good one? The reader will note that we have arrived back at the point in Chapter 3 where it was suggested that the trouble with the moral sphere is that there is disagreement about what count as moral reasons. The suggestion of this chapter is that there is one consideration that constitutes an essentially moral reason, and that this consideration provides a good reason, in some instances, for curbing freedom and treating people differently. This consideration is the utilitarian one of promoting happiness. Happiness is the sole ultimate value. It is in the light of happiness that everything is to be judged good or bad. Reasons that relate to happiness are moral reasons. Considerations of happiness provide the reason, and the *only* legitimate reason, for restricting freedom or treating people differently. The formal principle of fairness (or justice or impartiality as it is variously called) has to be filled out with content by the principle of happiness. That is my contention.

I have so far referred to 'the utilitarians', as if the theory of any one utilitarian was indistinguishable from that of any other. This is not in fact the case. In the first place there is a distinction to be made between 'ideal utilitarians' and 'hedonistic utilitarians'. The former, however, although they take the view that the rightness of actions is to be assessed by considering their consequences, do not accept that happiness is the sole ultimate value, and do not concern us here. But there are distinctions to be drawn even between hedonistic utilitarians.

Jeremy Bentham, for example, regarded 'happiness' as something to be assessed solely in terms of the *quantity* of pleasure experienced. A man was happy insofar as he experienced pleasure, unhappy insofar as he experienced pain, and no distinction was to be drawn between different kinds or qualities of pleasure. Various factors, such as the intensity and duration of a particular experience of pleasure, had to be taken into account in assessing the quantity, but Bentham resisted the suggestion that one experience might be regarded as more pleasurable than another because it was of a superior sort. Hence his celebrated dictum that '*quantity* of pleasure being equal, pushpin is as good as poetry'.

The uncompromising nature of Bentham's theory proved an embarrassment for some of his supporters. It was one thing to suggest that the avoidance of pain and the promotion of pleasure was all that mattered, quite another to suggest that, since there was no distinction to be drawn between qualities of pleasure, a life devoted to Bingo, sex and pop records (in modern terms) might in principle be a worthwhile life. John Stuart Mill therefore attempted to bring in the notion that a distinction might also be made between the *quality* of various pleasures, and he offered another now-famous dictum, which may be seen as a counterweight to Bentham's on pushpin: 'Better a Socrates dissatisfied, than a fool satisfied'.

Mill's attempt to bring in the notion of quality, if successful, would probably result in a far wider acceptance of utilitarianism (at least amongst that segment of society that regards itself as cultured) than Bentham's view could command. But the attempt is not successful; so clearly not, that many doubt that Mill was actually making the attempt. The obvious problem for Mill is that, if pleasure is really the only criterion of good, it is difficult to see how he is going to establish that one pleasure is qualitatively better than another. To say that the pleasure derived from poetry is superior to that derived from pushpin, even when the quantity is the same, is surely tantamount to saying that something is more valuable than pleasure. How is one supposed to assess the quality of pleasure, except either by quantity (i.e. the more the better, as Bentham wanted to do), or by introducing some new criterion, which would strike a blow at the essence of utilitarianism, namely that pleasure and hence happiness is what matters? Mill argues in effect that those pleasures are superior which those people who have experience of various types of pleasure deem to be preferable. He continues by claiming that those people who have experience of both what may be termed the animal pleasures (e.g. sex, eating) and those pleasures dependent on the higher faculties (e.g. reading, poetry) prefer the latter. This is not a very convincing argument. Is it even true that all people capable of experiencing both what Mill terms 'lower' and 'higher' pleasures regard the latter as superior? And, in any case, it is not at all clear that all such people would mean is not that the 'higher' pleasures are *more* pleasurable to them personally. The inescapable point is that, if I say that the pleasure I get from reading poetry is less than that that I get from listening to pop music, but that the former is *better* pleasure, I am saying that something is more important (more valuable) than pleasure. This the utilitarian cannot consistently say.

In other words, the final conclusion must be either that what Mill meant by qualitatively superior pleasures were pleasures that as a matter of fact gave more or deeper pleasure, or that he was not a consistent hedonistic utilitarian. One might, for instance, try to argue that as a matter of fact people who can appreciate poetry get more pleasure out of it than people who take pleasure in eating, and conclude that the pleasure from appreciating poetry was superior to that from eating. But this use of 'superior' would not in fact mark out a qualitative difference between the two pleasures: in referring to the pleasure of poetry as 'superior' one would only be making the claim that it was more pleasurable. If on the other hand one argued that the pleasure from appreciating poetry was in itself a better kind of pleasure than the pleasure to be found in eating, one would cease to argue as a hedonistic utilitarian.

I shall therefore be arguing for a Benthamite position which involves denying that any pleasure can be judged to be *in itself* more valuable, more worthwhile or qualitatively superior to any other pleasure, assuming that they are quantitatively equal. If my pleasure in listening to pop records is as great as my pleasure in listening to classical records, neither pleasure is *in itself* superior to the other. But, of course, Bentham was not simply arguing that all was well provided that the individual took great pleasure in whatever he was doing: central to his ethical theory is the principle of utility or the greatest happiness principle, which now needs explaining.

Bentham's premiss is that 'Nature has placed mankind under the governance of two sovereign masters, pain and pleasure. It is for them alone to point out what we ought to do'.[1] But we do not live in isolation, and Bentham was committed to the distributive principle of impartiality such that ideally every individual's pleasure ought to count equally. Furthermore, since he regards pleasure as a good, he naturally desires that there should be as much pleasure and as little pain in the world as possible. The principle of utility therefore becomes the basis of the utilitarian theory, for by it is meant 'that principle which approves or disapproves of every action whatsoever, according to the tendency which it appears to have to augment or diminish [or promote or oppose] the happiness of the party whose interest is in question'.[2] And it is crucial to realise that 'the party whose interest is in question' refers to anybody and everybody who is affected either directly or indirectly. Thus Bentham is arguing that the question of whether some practice such as, let us say, imprisoning criminals is morally justifiable is to be answered by considering whether the practice tends to promote or oppose the happiness of those interested, which in this case will include all members of the community.

At this point something must be said about the concept of 'happiness', for we obviously cannot begin to assess this theory if we do not know what is meant by 'happiness'. Since for most of us 'happiness' is a vague and appealing notion, it sounds well enough to say that happiness is the supreme consideration; but it may well be that when we attempt to delineate the term more precisely some support will be lost for the utilitarian theory. For example, some might claim that happiness is a specific and rare emotion associated with such terms as ecstasy or joy, in which case it might seem dubious whether this emotion really was the supreme moral consideration. Conversely, if one associates 'happiness' with 'contentment' some may feel that this is a rather colourless and unworthy goal.

The utilitarians' greatest mistake from a tactical point of view may well have been their choice of the terms 'pleasure' and 'happiness' as the key to their theory, for these concepts are obscure, and philosophers can happily spend hours redefining them. But it would be a mistake to imagine at this juncture that the acceptability of utilitarianism rests entirely on the question of whether they have understood the true meaning of happiness, even assuming that it makes sense to talk of the true meaning of such a concept. What we obviously require now is some account of what the utilitarians as a matter of fact meant by happiness, or some conception of happiness that suits their theory, so that we can understand that theory. And here there is no great problem.

'What happiness consists of,' writes Bentham, is 'enjoyment of pleasures, security from pains.'[3] Now clearly this does not involve identifying pleasure and happiness or claiming that they are one and the same thing, which really would be most implausible. We can certainly say that a man, though experiencing some pleasure, is not happy. On the other hand we could hardly claim that a man might be happy while taking no pleasure in life at all. Bentham's view takes account of these points, and it does involve the claim that happiness is *dependent on* the satisfaction of pleasures and the avoidance of pains: happiness is that feeling which arises out of the satisfaction of desires or the experience of pleasures.

But here we have to note that all talk about happiness is in danger of being confused by the fact that, although we tend to talk as if people are either completely happy or completely unhappy, the truth is that happiness is a matter of degree and what we usually mean by referring to someone as a happy man is that he is relatively or generally happy. So what Bentham may be taken to be saying is that people's happiness is diminished to the extent that they are pained and increased to the extent that they find pleasure in life. Clearly in practice some pleasures will be more important for happiness than others, since some pleasures will mean more to people than others. But since Bentham does not distinguish between qualities of pleasure, he cannot distinguish between qualities of happiness either. Thus Bentham at least is committed to the view that if a man were to take great pleasure in all aspects of his life, then he would be a happy man, regardless of the nature of the things he took pleasure in. And, although we might disapprove of the way in which a particular individual found his happiness, what we cannot do on this view is deny that somebody is happy just because we don't think much of the sort of things that give him pleasure.

I must stress that whether this view of happiness strikes us as convincing or not is not the important question here. What is important is that this is what Bentham is talking about when he refers to happiness. It is happiness understood in this way that we are going on to discuss. But we can add that this conception of happiness fits in well with a point that we would surely all accept, namely that there are a number of concepts that are logically incompatible with happiness. For example: anxiety, frustration, disappointment, depression, guilt, insecurity, alienation, anomie and envy. In saying that these terms are logically incompatible with happiness, I am claiming that it does not make sense to say that a man is 'anxious and happy', 'envious and happy' and so on. It is of course meaningful to say that someone is 'happy, but anxious' if we mean by that that he is *generally* happy, but anxious about some specific thing or at this particular moment. But it is not possible to be happy in general but anxious in general, or happy in respect of some specific thing but anxious in respect of the same thing at the same time.

Therefore we may say that a utilitarian such as Bentham is aiming at the ideal of a world in which all people are entirely satisfied or in which they experience only pleasure. The ideal involves no preference for one kind of pleasure over another except insofar as one kind of pleasure involves more pleasure all told than another. This means that in practice utilitarianism faces the problem of how one is to quantify pleasure, which will be considered below. But it must not be forgotten that when it comes to estimating quantity of pleasure the utilitarian is concerned to take into account not simply the pleasure to the agent but also the pleasure or pain that may come about for others as the result of an agent's action. In particular, in accepting a distributive principle of impartiality, the utilitarian has committed himself to the view that no man's claim to happiness can be simply ignored.

When he is writing about actions Bentham refers to their 'tendency' to promote pleasure or pain. This brings us on to another important distinction between utilitarians, for some are what are called act-utilitarians and some rule-utilitarians. Philosophers are not always in agreement as to how Bentham himself should be classified, which for our purposes is perhaps not particularly important. But the distinction itself is as follows: an act-utilitarian is one who believes that every single act should be assessed on utilitarian principles, whereas the rule-utilitarian believes that in assessing any individual act one should consider whether it is desirable – on utilitarian principles – that such an act should be generally performed; if it seems that it would not be desirable that it should generally be performed, then it should not be performed, even if in particular circumstances it might promote happiness. In an imperfect world the practical difference between the two types of theory may be considerable. A rule-utilitarian, for example, might argue that, although one can conceive of situations in which it would contribute more to the general happiness to kill a politician than to do anything else, it is preferable to adopt the general rule that politicians ought not to be killed, on the grounds that such a rule contributes more to the general happiness than a situation in which there was no such rule would do. An act-utilitarian, on the other hand, would wish to assess the rightness or wrongness of each proposal to kill a specific politician on its own merits.

There is surely little room for doubt that rule-utilitarianism is to be preferred to act-utilitarianism on utilitarian grounds. That is to say that it contributes more to the general happiness for society to adopt various moral rules (on utilitarian principles) than to leave individuals to assess for themselves every situation on its own merits. Suppose, for example, we accept act-utilitarianism, and therefore say in respect of killing that people should refrain from killing except in circumstances where to kill would contribute to the general happiness; then we have to face the consequence that in practice some people will kill, either because they sincerly, but mistakenly, believe that a particular killing will promote happiness, or because they malevolently recognise that, though a particular killing may not be justified, they may nonetheless be able to get away with pretending that they sincerely thought it was. Thus some individuals may be tempted to rationalise their immediate impulses (e.g. consumed by jealousy, I kill my wife's lover, persuading myself that he would ruin other marriages if left alive, and that I can make my wife happier in the future); sincerely committed communists will feel justified in killing the members of right-wing governments and vice versa; and the ruthless may be tempted to calculate whether to kill those whom they want out of the way or not, solely by reference to whether they expect to be able to convince a jury that it was their sincere intention to promote happiness. The likely increase in the number of actual killings, and the inevitable increase in the uncertainty that we shall all have as to whether we are going to live out the day or be killed by some sincere but misguided individual, will obviously lead to considerably less happiness in general than the adoption of a rule against killing would do.

Furthermore, rule-utilitarianism is not open to the objection that it might lead to the conclusion that certain acts that we find it very difficult to accept could ever be justified, *are* justified, in the way that act-utilitarianism is. For example, suppose that I have been caught red-handed breaking and entering a house by a policeman. I offer him a bribe. Now it is quite conceivable that for me to offer the bribe, and for him to accept it, will contribute more to happiness than any other course of action in the circumstances, provided, at least, that nobody else ever knows about it. (If others came to hear of it, it is unlikely that it would contribute more to happiness in general than the policeman's refusing the bribe would do, since people's faith in the police force would be undermined, and their hope that their property is safe weakened.) But if nobody gets to know about the bribe, why then, surely *they* are neither more nor less happy than before, whereas I am very happy at avoiding conviction, and the policeman is happy because he has some money – in which case the act-utilitarian would seem to be forced to conclude that the policeman did right in accepting the bribe. But the rule-utilitarian is not forced into accepting this conclusion, because he will argue that it is not contributory to the general happiness to have a situation in which bribery may sometimes be justified, and he will therefore argue that a rule of the form 'Never bribe' should be adopted.

I should add that rule-utilitarians do not have to accept rules that absolutely forbid (or demand) actions only. The rule may contain specific qualifications. Thus a rule-utilitarian does not have to accept the rule 'Never kill', if he feels that killing can sometimes be justified. His rule might take the form 'Never kill, except in self-defence', for instance.

Now it is sometimes suggested that this admission destroys rule-utilitarianism, on the grounds that it leads to rule-utilitarianism cascading into act-utilitarianism. The argument for this view appears to be that if the rule is to be qualified then surely it must be qualified by reference to considerations of happiness. Thus if the rule 'Never kill' is modified to become 'Never kill except in self-defence', this must be because there is reason to suppose that killing in self-defence may be justified by appeal to considerations of happiness. The conclusion is then drawn that this amounts to saying 'Never kill except where to do so would contribute more to the sum of happiness than not to do so', which obviously amounts to advocating act-utilitarianism.

But this conclusion surely does not follow and the argument as a whole fails to note a crucial distinction between act and rule utilitarianism. For there is clearly a difference between saying 'Adopt the rule that one should always act in a specific situation in that way which promotes most happiness' and saying 'Adopt those rules which will promote most happiness if they are adopted as rules'. Thus there is a distinction between 'Don't kill except in self-defence' and 'Don't kill except where to do so would promote more happiness than not doing so'. For the latter demands that each individual should attempt to judge each case on its merits, so that sometimes it might be justifiable to kill, whether in self-defence or not, and sometimes not. But the former demands not that each act be judged on its merits, but that the rule be judged on its merits. If the rule is judged to be a good one on balance then it should always be obeyed. The rule-utilitarian who accepts that one should never kill except in self-defence would do so on the grounds that it is on balance more conducive to happiness to have a firm rule in society to this effect than not to have one, notwithstanding the fact that on a particular occasion it might contribute more to happiness to kill when it is not a case of self-defence or not to kill when it is. Thus there is an irreducible difference between act- and rule-utilitarianism, and, as already stated, there seems good reason to prefer the latter.

Rule-utilitarianism, then, holds that ideally one should always act in that way which, if it were adopted as a general rule of conduct by mankind, would contribute more to the happiness of mankind than any alternative way of acting that is open to one in the circumstances. In practice, of course, this will lead only to the adoption of a limited number of moral rules which seem clearly to be necessary for the happiness of the community. This is because very often there is apparently nothing to choose between various ways of behaving, in respect of happiness, and one may reasonably argue that to multiply rules that are at best only *possibly* demanded would itself contribute to diminishing happiness.

I shall now consider nine standard objections to this straightforward ethical theory. None of the objections strikes me as damaging to the theory, but perhaps the reader will think otherwise.

1.   The reaction of some people to utilitarianism is one of horror. It seems so crude and philistine. If it were accepted that the only consideration in organising a society and framing rules, laws and codes of conduct was the promotion of the greatest happiness of the greatest number, would it not follow that in principle it might be legitimate, in fact right, to limit all manner of freedoms, to accept a tasteless and vulgar culture, to employ deceit and useful lies on occasion, and to make no effort, via education, to distinguish between some activities as more worthwhile than others, regardless of the quantity of pleasure involved? Could not a ruthless commitment to utilitarianism lead in principle to a totalitarian state, in which all were carefully manipulated to the end of ensuring happiness? Could not Hitler have made out a plausible case for claiming to be aiming at the greatest happiness of the greatest number?

The answer to the last question is certainly no, even if, for the sake of argument, we were to allow that the majority of Germans were more happy under Nazi domination than they had been before (incidentally an enormous, even preposterous, allowance). In the first place, aiming at the greatest happiness of the greatest number does not mean simply making the majority as happy as possible at the expense of the minority. It means, ideally, aiming at full happiness for all, and, in practice, at as much happiness as possible for as many as possible. This does, of course, raise the problem of how, in practice, one calculates what will produce the most happiness for the largest number of people possible (see below). But the suggestion that the misery involved in the dispatch of 6 million Jews might be offset by the benefits accruing to non-Jews, and hence justified on utilitarian lines, is as absurd as it is obnoxious. Secondly, whatever the difficulties of calculating the happiness value of various courses of action, written into utilitarianism is the assumption that nobody's claim to a share of happiness can simply be written off.

But the answer to the other questions – and I may as well admit it – is surely, in principle, yes. But the stress is on 'in principle'; that is to say that, if it were the case that preserving a specific freedom or attempting to foster a high level of culture was causing more misery than restricting that freedom or jettisoning that culture would do, then on utilitarian principles it would be justifiable to restrict that freedom and to cease to foster that culture. If it were the case that for a government to tell the whole truth and nothing but the truth in a specific instance would lead to more suffering than maintaining a judicious silence would do, then it might be justifiable to suppress the truth. But why should we be intimidated by these theoretical flights of fancy? If, as a matter of fact, we were all miserable because television churned out High Culture all night rather than popular entertainment, why would it be so outrageous to stop it? The point is that in practice there is absolutely no reason to suppose that we *would* be happier on the sort of scaremongering terms envisaged. In fact, it seems far more plausible to argue that there are many, many specific freedoms that positively contribute to happiness in the long term, that by and large the practice of deceit by governments is detrimental, and that an educational concern (or a television preoccupation) with the trivial is relatively unrewarding.

Does this last point not attempt to smuggle in Mill's claim that some pleasures are more worthwhile than others, regardless of the degree of pleasure involved? No, it does not. For what a utilitarian may quite consistently argue is that the pleasure derived from reading Shakespeare with understanding is greater than that derived from Bingo, for those who can be brought to take pleasure in it at all. Furthermore he may argue (although to work out this argument in detail would obviously be a complex business) that a society that cannot do more than take pleasure in things like Bingo, that has no appreciation of any literature, is liable to have other features that will not contribute to a maximisation of happiness. Such considerations avoid Mill's inconsistency of introducing qualitative differences between pleasures, and make it quite clear that there is no obvious reason to assume that utilitarianism leads to vulgarity and triviality.

All that a utilitarian is necessarily committed to is the conditional clause that, if some activity is promoting suffering, it ought to be stopped, provided that ruling that it must be stopped does not cause an even greater diminution of happiness.

2. It may be suggested that there must be something wrong with utilitarianism as an ethical theory because it places all the stress on the consequences of actions. Actions are good if they have certain consequences. Don't people's *intentions* matter? Was Aristotle wrong to suggest that people should not be blamed for whatever they do, if they could not help doing it, or if they did not foresee the consequences? Ought we to punish the child who steals, regardless of why he did so? Of course not. Aristotle was quite right to draw attention to the reasons that people have for their actions and to their intentions, because he was concerned with the question of what deserves praise or blame. Similarly Kant (whom we shall consider in more detail in Chapter 7) was quite right to say that what we mean by acting morally is acting from a sense of duty. But we are not here concerned with the question of praising and blaming people, nor with what distinguishes an act done morally from the same act done, say, prudentially. We are concerned with how to evaluate various practices, how to assess what ought to be done.

What the utilitarian will not accept is that the mere fact that you could not help doing something, that you did it from a sense of duty, that you intended different consequences or that you meant well by it, makes it a good thing to have done. Would *you* accept such claims?

3. A third objection is related to the first. It argues that all this talk of 'the greatest number' is very impersonal, and that the individual is sacrificed to some 'whole', some abstraction, the State. 'The greatest number' is, of course, an abstraction, but it clearly means the greatest number of individuals. What *is* true is that, again in principle, it is conceivable that some individuals in a perfectly organised utilitarian state might gain less happiness than they could have acquired in another state. But this objection obviously applies to *any* system, in *any* society where people have different aspirations, interests and sources of pleasure. Any society that for whatever reason forbids something, thereby irritates and curbs the happiness of those who want to do it – and there must be some people who want to do it, whatever it is, otherwise there would be no need for a restriction on the activity. An objection that applies equally to every ethical theory is no objection to a specific theory.

4. Then it is objected that the notion of assessing what will promote the greatest happiness raises insuperable difficulties.

How does one measure quantity of pleasure? The first point to remember is that one does not only take into account the pleasure to be obtained by the individual agent in any situation. Because the ideal is to promote as much pleasure as possible for as many people as possible, bearing in mind that no individual's claim to happiness can just be ignored, we obviously must also take into account various other factors. The essential factors to be considered are: (i) The *intensity* of pleasure experienced by the agent. (ii) The *duration* of the pleasure experienced by the agent. (iii) The propensity of an action to be followed by further experience of pleasure rather than pain. (Bentham referred to this factor as *fecundity*. An example of what he had in mind might be that drug-taking or drinking heavily, while they may give pleasure to the agent at the time, may be followed by painful experiences.) (iv) The *extent* of pleasure caused by an action, which is to the pleasure that it may bring to people other than the agent either directly or indirectly.

The rule-utilitarian is therefore committed to the view that rules of behaviour should be adopted if their adoption would contribute more to the pleasure of the community than their non-adoption would do, taking these four factors into account. Thus, to stick for the moment with our relatively simple example: although it is very possibly true that some individuals might gain pleasure of some intensity and duration from killing, it is nonetheless reasonable to suppose that the extent of pleasure brought about by a rule that forbids killing would be so great as to lead to the conclusion that such a rule would promote more pleasure than the absence of such a rule. The extent of pain caused by a situation in which people kill when they feel like it would outweigh the pleasure experienced by the killers; whereas the intensity of pain experienced by would-be killers who are prevented from so doing would be outweighed by the pleasure gained in general.

It should also be added that, because his concern is simply to produce as great a balance of pleasure over pain as possible, the utilitarian is constrained to look beyond the immediate present and to take the long-term view into account. Thus it is conceivable that at a given point in time to impose some restriction upon people might cause them considerable immediate pain, but nonetheless contribute to an increase in pleasure in the long term. A painful half-hour at the dentist, for instance, may obviously contribute more to pleasure in the long term than a painless half-hour avoiding the dentist.

Now in all this there is admittedly a problem. I suggested that it is 'reasonable to suppose' that a rule against killing is justified on utilitarian terms. And I might have added that taking the long-term view this would be so even if at a given point in time a number of people took great pleasure in being free to kill if they felt like it. But how long is the long term and can one in fact measure the pleasure potential of various courses of action?

To take the first question first, there is clearly a danger of the utilitarian putting himself into a position in which 'the long-term' consideration serves as a vague blanket term that renders any actual calculations vacuous. That is to say he could advocate a specific rule on the grounds that it will promote happiness and when it is pointed out to him that the rule is not apparently promoting happiness, he might reply that it is still possible that it will in the long term. Provided that he makes 'the long term' sufficiently long, he can, if he chooses, continue to maintain that the rule in question might be justified. But this is evidently absurd. If utilitarianism is prepared to defend rules that are patently misery-provoking at the moment, on the grounds that in, say, a thousand years' time they might promote happiness, it surely does lose any claim it has to being a plausible and workable theory.

At the very least 'the long term' must be interpreted to mean the foreseeable future. The phrase serves essentially to remind us that it is not only the immediate pleasure that arises out of a course of action that needs to be taken into account, rather than as the impossible demand that the consequences for all time be taken into account. Thus, it is perhaps conceivable that a thousand years from now the world and people in it will be so changed that everybody on balance gains greater pleasure from a situation in which the law of the jungle once more obtains. But this kind of hypothesis we cannot take into account. What we can do is assess the desirability of, say, some proposed legislation to limit the number of children that people have, by taking into account considerations such as the likely population figures for fifty years ahead if no such legislation is passed, the likely extent of resources such as food and the likely consequences for people's happiness in the future of such considerations. It is the need to take this kind of consideration into account as well as the immediate pain or pleasure that might be occasioned by the imposition of some rule that utilitarianism is stressing when it refers to the need to take the long-term view.

But can one in fact make these measurements? Can one in fact *measure* the relative intensity, duration, fecundity and extent of the pleasure arising from various couses of action? The answer must be 'no' in the sense that we cannot compare the quantity of pleasure arising from a rule against killing with the quantity of pleasure arising from no such rule, as we can compare the quantity of sugar in two sugar bowls. It is impossible, for instance, to compare literally the *intensity* of pleasure that you experience in a situation with the *intensity* of pleasure that someone else experiences. And it is extremely difficult, if not impossible, to assess accurately the comparative *duration*, *fecundity* and *extent* of two pleasures. Thirdly there is the problem of how one weighs, say, the claims of the *intensity* of one pleasure for the agent against the *extent* of another pleasure, for there is no common unit of measurement. Whatever else it is, Bentham's pleasure calculus is certainly no ready-reckoner.

But do these considerations constitute the devastating objection to utilitarianism that some imagine? Surely not. We have to distinguish two distinct objections that seem to some to arise out of this problem of how one can compare the quantity of pleasure involved in various ways of behaving.

The first is the claim that it is impossible to proceed at all. But this is plainly false. The fact that we cannot prove that one rule of conduct will lead to greater happiness than another does not mean that it cannot be true that it will, and it does not stop us making reasonable estimates. As Quinton observes, 'the use of the "calculus" [of pleasures] is to remind us of what we must take into consideration if our assessment of the alternative possibilities is to be complete'.[5] One cannot literally weigh the *intensity* of one pleasure against the *extent* of another, 'but to deny that pleasure and pain can be appraised by numerical calculus is not to deny that they can be compared in a more total and impressionistic way and any such comparison will be rational just to the extent that it takes relevant factors other than intensity into account'.[6]

In other words, it is a misunderstanding to see Bentham's so-called pleasure calculus as a calculus. It is rather a pointer to factors relevant to the estimation of the pleasure potential of a rule. And as Stace says, we do not need a calculus in the literal sense:

'I cannot conceive why any philosopher should want to have one . . . It is said that if you cannot make a calculation of the relative amounts of pleasure and pain which your actions will produce in the world, you cannot know which actions are good which bad. This, however is a very shallow argument. In the first place, even if you cannot measure pleasures and pains, this does not prevent you from knowing that some pleasures or pains are greater than others. A man does not need a thermometer to know that he is being frozen to death or boiled alive . . . So too a man knows that some pains are terrible, some slight; that some pleasures are great, some small; although he cannot measure either the pleasures or the pains.'[7]

Clearly, then, it is possible to proceed. One can compare things in respect of the quantity of pleasure they will provide, and one may make such estimates more or less reasonably.

The second objection is that, although such estimates can in principle be made, it will be difficult to make them and one will never know that they have been made accurately. As observations these claims contain some truth, but that is not to say that they are valid objections to utilitarianism.

It is true that such estimates will sometimes be difficult to make and furthermore that finally they depend on the question of what does as a matter of fact give people pleasure which may vary from individual to individual and which is in the last resort a subjective matter. It is not for me to tell you what will give you most pleasure, still less to lay down as an alleged fact the claim that such and such just is very pleasurable for every-body. But the fact that this is undoubtedly true should not blind us to the fact that it is also true that the individual may sometimes be mistaken about whether something will in fact bring him pleasure. The pursuit of pleasure is therefore not simply a question of doing what you choose to do. Further-more, although the individual must be the final arbiter of whether he *has* gained any pleasure from something, that does not mean that it is absurd for us to make predictions about other people. On the basis of our know-ledge about people and circumstances it is possible to form generalisations that may be important and that are eminently reasonable. Thus, although only you could know how much pain you would experience if your posses-sions were stolen or how much painful anxiety you would experience in a situation in which stealing was not outlawed, and, indeed, although no one can incontestably prove that the incidence of stealing is diminished by declaring it to be a criminal act, it is not only not difficult to estimate that a rule against stealing is justifiable on utilitarian terms, but it would be manifestly unreasonable to pretend otherwise.

Similarly it is strictly speaking true that we cannot know what will produce the greatest happiness. To 'know', it would be necessary to make accurate predictions of all the consequences of every conceivable course of action. This we are not in a position to do. We can never be sure that we have done right until we have done it, and even then we cannot be entirely sure, since if we have opted for one course of action we have no real way of knowing what the consequences would have been if we had done some-thing else. But, as we have already seen, it would be quite unreasonable to pretend that the fact that we cannot 'know' what will produce the greatest happiness in this strict sense leads to the conclusion that estimation as to what will is just a case of making random stabs in the dark. Although there are undoubtedly many specific moral problems that are difficult to resolve on utilitarian terms, there are, equally, many that are fairly easy.

However, the real objection to these objections is that they do not in fact constitute objections to the utilitarian theory as such. For to draw attention to difficulties involved in the application of a theory is not at all the same thing as to indicate that the theory is false or invalid. Some philosophers seem to be under the misapprehension that utilitarianism was devised and introduced in order to produce clear and incontestable answers to every specific moral question. They therefore conclude that since it cannot do this, it fails and is to be rejected. But utilitarianism was not 'invented' to *do* anything. It *is* an account of what is involved in morality. It arises be-cause some people see good reason to interpret morality in this way. It seeks to outline the conditions on which a rule would be a morally sound rule: it is an entirely separate question as to how often one can be how certain a rule is morally sound on these conditions.

Of course, if someone proposed a moral theory that was such that one had no way at all of actually deciding between various proposals, then, although it might in fact still be a theory that hit upon the truth, it would not be of much use. Intuitionism is an example of such a theory. But utilitarianism is not. So the conclusion here must be that (a) difficulties in applying utilitarianism have nothing to do with the question of its validity, (b) some questions are not difficult to resolve on utilitarian principles, and (c) the fact that some are need come as no surprise. Morality *is* difficult.

5. Another objection, interestingly, contradicts the previous one. This is the view that if we accept utilitarianism, everything becomes rather boring: there is no problem in principle about what we ought to do. 'There is no such subject as ethics.' Evidently this is a rather peculiar objection. After all we do not inquire into ethics simply for the academic interest of the job. But in any case the objection does not stand up, as the reply to the previous objection indicates. Utilitarianism gives us a clear principle from which to work; it tells us how to set about evaluating specific activities in specific situations – namely, by considering their pleasure potential; it puts an end to the deadlock produced by those who say that nothing can be known, or that there are various moral principles which are equally important and which one cannot decide between, should they clash in practice. But it certainly does not make the actual answers to specific questions easy to come by, as we shall see in Part Three.

6. The next objection is a continuation of the fourth objection. Not only can we not know what is actually best (i.e. most productive of happiness) in specific instances, but it is also difficult, sometimes impossible, to make the sort of calculations that would be necessary to determine what should be done, before we act.

It was considering this kind of objection that caused Mill to exclaim that no ethical theory would work if it were 'conjoined with universal idiocy'.[8] Once again, patiently, it is necessary to say that *of course* the individual does not have time to calculate before every act, that *of course* it is difficult to do it, that *of course* it is sometimes, perhaps often, impossible to know that one's calculations are accurate. But none of this has any bearing on the question of whether or not this is the right kind of approach. As Mill also pointed out, those who believe in a Christian ethic do not presume that before performing any action the Christian will run through in his mind the contents of the Bible. Most actions are habitual and performed in response to value judgements that have long since been internalised. Utilitarians, particularly rule-utilitarians, are not committed to a world in which nobody acts until he has succeeded in accurate calculation in respect of everybody's happiness. All that they are committed to is the view that, faced with a specific rule or a question as to whether we ought to act in a certain way, the question to be examined is to what extent this rule or this way of behaving promotes happiness compared with alternative rules or ways of behaving. And, despite the emphasis of this paragraph, it is in fact very often very easy to answer that question. Let's put it this way: when all is said and done, which of you is actually going to deny that a rule against killing is more productive of happiness than the absence of such a rule?

7. But, it may be suggested, one man's meat is another's poison. Plans for the happiness of the greatest number involve large-scale assumptions about what people need for their happiness, and there will be a tendency to assume that a particular rule or custom suits more people than it in fact does. Since there is obviously truth in the adage that one man's meat is another's poison, we have to take account of it. The solution is simple: give the meat to those who do not find it poisonous. What I mean by this is that utilitarianism does not demand large-scale uniformity, and it will in fact demand the maintenance of various minority interests, provided that those interests do not actually cause a great increase of misery for the majority. Thus a utilitarian would not argue that, since more people like pop music than like classical music, it follows that we ought only to promote pop music. On the contrary he would say that since some derive great pleasure from one and some from the other, and since no fanatic could plausibly argue that the existence of classical concerts caused him more suffering than it caused pleasure for others (or vice versa), the greatest happiness of the greatest number is promoted by a society welcoming the existence of both. On the other hand, he would say that, although a few people may take pleasure in committing murder, that pleasure is insignificant compared with the pleasure occasioned by establishing laws against this activity. The aim of promoting the greatest happiness of the greatest number will lead only to restrictions on those practices that cause more misery than their suppression would do. It does not involve an attempt to suppress all minority interests.

8. There is an oddity that is not really an objection to the theory but which has to be mentioned because some treat it as if it were. Thus Dearden, considering happiness as an aim of education, concludes that, although it is an important aim, it cannot be the over-riding consideration or the supreme aim, because there are other values, such as autonomy, that may conflict with it.[9] Clearly this is not a *reasoned* objection at all. It simply begs the question by asserting that there are other values that are equally important. That is precisely what the utilitarian denies and produces reasons for denying. (For the argument establishing that happiness is the supreme consideration, see below. On autonomy, see Chapter 8.) Nonetheless this would be a good point at which to consider what the utilitarian would say about a situation that appears to land him in difficulties. Suppose that an individual is faced with the choice of rescuing either an eminent scientist

or his father from a blazing building.[10] We will assume that (a) only one of the two can possible be saved, (b) the scientist is working on something, such as a device that will automatically neutralise all nuclear warheads, which it is agreed will contribute positively and greatly to the sum of human happiness, and (c) the father is a fairly useless sort of fellow. Does it not seem clear that on utilitarian terms the individual in question should rescue the scientist rather than his father, since the benefit of the scientist's work to mankind in terms of happiness obviously outweighs the happiness of father and son if the father is saved? And yet do we not feel that it would be right for the man to save his father rather than the scientist, if a choice has to be made? Does this not show that something is wrong with utilitarianism?

I don't think that it does. The utilitarian may respond in two ways:

(i)   He can argue that it would be right on utilitarian terms to rescue the scientist, and go on to say that, although many people may feel that the father should be rescued, they are just wrong. In other words he would say that merely pointing to the fact that some people have some values that run counter to the utilitarian thesis is not an argument. Our sentiment in favour of rescuing the father is an emotional response that has no bearing on the question of what actually ought to be done. He might reinforce this by pointing out that it is inconsistent to justify some ways of behaving on utilitarian grounds and not others. Only people who never attempted to justify any behaviour by appeal to the principle of happiness would be in a reasonable position to continue the argument.

(ii)   But he might argue that in point of fact on utilitarian terms the father should be rescued. Why? Because, he might reasonably claim, filial or family loyalties are in general of great importance to the happiness of people. Therefore a general presumption to the effect that sons should care for their fathers and act accordingly is desirable. It is better (i.e. more productive of happiness), he might conclude, that people should be like this than that they should not, in general, even if this means that in some specific situations the consequence of such ties of affection will be actions that in themselves are not necessarily more productive of happiness than alternative actions that could have been performed.

Such an example, then, certainly does not show that there must be something wrong with utilitarianism.

9.   The only plausible exception to the claim that no other value may override the claims of happiness is truth. Now I have already indicated that, if by reference to 'truth' we mean to pick out the business of telling the truth, then it is conceivable that in specific circumstances the principle of happiness will justify one in not telling the truth. As against this it may be plausibly argued that for a rule-utilitarian there is good reason to suppose that one ought to accept the moral rule that one should never tell lies. This

is merely to say that it seems reasonable to maintain that in the long run the greatest happiness of the greatest number will be enhanced by observation of this rule.

But is this enough? Do we not value truth regardless of whether a rule in favour of it promotes happiness or not? Clearly a person who writes a book like this, even though he nails his colours firmly to the mast of utilitarianism, *does* value truth, since what gives him his impetus is the conviction that what he has to say approaches the truth. One is a utilitarian, not simply because utilitarianism is concerned with happiness, but because one believes that it is true that one ought to be concerned with happiness. Does it not follow that one values truth quite independently of happiness, and that therefore happiness is not the sole supreme value?

This, to me, is the most interesting objection. My reply to it is that we must distinguish between telling the truth and pursuing the truth. The former I have already dealt with. Pursuing the truth is by definition a value that any philosopher is committed to. Consequently, if the occasion ever arose in which it was suggested that in the interests of happiness people ought to be prevented from pursuing the truth, no philosopher, not even a utilitarian philosopher, could accept this. All I can say, and I stress that I think it is rather a weak thing to say, is that I cannot really conceive of a situation in which it could be plausibly maintained that it *would* be in the interests of the long-term happiness of the greatest number to issue a blanket restriction on the pursuit of truth per se. (I can conceive of situations in which, on utilitarian principles, it might be necessary to restrict specific research, but that would be quite different.) In the meantime I can only say that allegiance to truth demands that we should only act on utilitarian principles so long as we are convinced of their truth, and that therefore even the ideal utilitarian state must welcome and encourage further debate as to the validity of utilitarianism. But so long as we believe that the theory is acceptable to reason, we should act on it, since, if it is acceptable to reason, it is not apparently false, and there is therefore no conflict in practice between the values of truth and happiness.

These, then, are the objections that have been raised against utilitarianism and that fail to shake it. But we still have to ask what reason there is to accept this ethical theory. Ought we to be concerned to promote happiness?

To recapitulate: I am arguing that in the face of any specific question about the sort of conduct that ought to be allowed, the sort of rules that are necessary in society, the sort of practice that is objectionable, the sort of issue that should be left to the discretion of the individual, the sort of freedom people should have, and the respects in which they should be treated in exactly the same way, the way to approach it is quite simply to ask which proposed course of action will promote the least suffering. It is *not* to ask 'Well, what is the accepted practice?'; it is *not* to ask 'What do we feel like doing?'; it is *not* to ask authority figures such as priest or schoolmaster what they think ought to be done; it is *not* to inquire into the practice of the animal kingdom and take one's cue from there; it is *not* to counsel despair and assert that nobody knows anything.

I hope that some readers at least are saying to themselves: 'Is this philosophy? It seems more like common sense.' Thank God, if it does. A little common sense is perhaps what is needed.

But now, is this true? Is there any reason to agree that this is the way in which we ought to proceed?

Mill offered a 'proof', although he was careful to say (far more succinctly) all that I have tried to say in Chapters 2 and 3 – namely that it was a 'proof' in the widest sense of the term. It runs as follows:

> 'The only proof capable of being given that an object is visible, is that people actually see it. The only proof that a sound is audible, is that people hear it: and so of the other sources of our experience. In like manner, I apprehend, the sole evidence it is possible to produce that anything is desirable, is that people do actually desire it. If the end which the utilitarian doctrine proposes to itself were not, in theory and in practice, acknowledged to be an end, nothing could ever convince any person that it was so. No reason can be given why the general happiness is desirable, except that each person, so far as he believes it to be attainable, desires his own happiness.'[11]

This consideration, Mill argues, is 'all the proof it is possible to require that happiness is *a* good'. He then goes on to argue that it must be the sole ultimate good, because not only do people desire happiness, but 'they never desire anything else' in the final analysis. (Mill would argue that when people *think* that they act for some other end – to be virtuous, for instance – what is actually happening is that the person is of such a sort that he feels the need to act in this way, if he is not to feel unhappy about his behaviour.)

This argument has been subjected to severe criticism on several counts: some maintain that it simply is not true that people only pursue their happiness; others that, even if they do, it does not follow that the general happiness is shown to be a good. The most powerful objections have been raised against the first steps in the argument: he has failed to realise, it is claimed, that, whereas 'visible' can only mean 'capable of being seen', 'desirable' can mean either 'capable of being desired' or 'ought to be desired'. It is true that, if people do desire something, that shows that it is capable of being desired; but to conclude that because people do desire it, it *ought* to be desired is to make the illegitimate move from 'is' to 'ought'.

My view is that these criticisms are largely misplaced, and that all Mill was trying to argue was that, as a matter of fact, if we think about the matter carefully and if we understand precisely what the utilitarians are claiming, then we shall see that we do all agree that happiness is the only ultimate good. This would not prove conclusively that we were *right* to agree on this, but if we do all agree on it, and if we also agree that ultimate moral principles cannot be proved in the conventional sense of incontestably demonstrated to be true, it would seem odd to persist in suggesting that other ends, which we do not actually value as ends, might be morally desirable ends. They *might* be – but what reason could we have either for supposing that they were or wanting to assert that they were?

However, I shall leave the reader to pursue Mill's arguments and the objections to them for himself, and instead turn to consideration of four reasons which I regard as quite sufficient to cause us to accept the utilitarian contention as reasonable.

1. In taking up moral philosophy one approaches the question of how people ought to behave, and how they ought to be treated. In essence one asks what does a question like 'How ought people to be treated?' *mean* and how does one set about answering it. But obviously one takes the question of how people should be treated seriously. Now, how could one take a question like 'How ought I to treat people?' *seriously*, without some prior notion of what it means to suffer, and an assumption that it *matters* if people suffer? If there were no such thing as suffering (of whatever sort) or if it were agreed to be quite unimportant whether people suffered or not, what would be the point of worrying about how people behaved? A man who had no conception of suffering – a man from Mars, perhaps – would he not lack precisely what we mean by moral sentiment? For is not moral sentiment none other than that sense of concern for other people's suffering? Moral codes may differ fundamentally in their view of what specific sufferings are relatively significant, but a moral code that purported to be completely unconcerned about any suffering would not be a moral code at all.

2. Argument has ranged for a long time over the question of whether the individual must necessarily pursue his own happiness, as Mill maintained, or not, and, if so, in what sense he necessarily does this. That argument I shall not pursue here. But it is surely clear that it is very difficult to conceive of an individual *ultimately* wanting to suffer. ('Ultimately' is important, since nobody would deny that individuals often opt to suffer in the short term, or in specific instances, nor that they often mistakenly choose to act in ways that as a matter of fact bring them suffering.)

The nearest examples to people who ultimately wanted to suffer would be people with enormous guilt complexes or extreme religious convictions. The religious man may choose to endure various experiences that cause him to suffer through life, but he presumably does so in the conviction that ultimately, in heaven, he will suffer the less. The guilty man presumably believes that he must chastise himself and suffer in various ways, to atone for whatever he feels guilty about, because he could not suffer to live with himself if he did not try to expiate his guilt. He would be more miserable if he ignored his guilt than if attempted to atone for it. Or so he feels.

If we accept that certainly for most of us, and probably for all of us, our ultimate happiness – absence of anxiety, depression, alienation and so on – *matters*, given that we want it, can we think of a good reason why we should not strive for it, on the assumption that we have not already committed ourselves to some moral principle or principles that might stand in our way? (This is a quite reasonable assumption at this point since we are inquiring into the question of moral principles. There is not much point in making the inquiry, if we have already committed ourselves to various principles.) Surely there is no good reason. But if there is no good reason why I should not pursue my ultimate happiness, since I want it, is there any good reason why other people, who want theirs, should not also strive for it? In other words is there any good reason for discriminating between people in respect of happiness? We have already decided that the answer to this question is 'no', for to say that it did not matter if certain people were prevented from pursuing their happiness would be tantamount to saying that some people do not count. We thus arrive at the conclusion that we all want our happiness and that there is no good reason, in principle, why we should not all have it.

3.   Consider now the examples that were used to illustrate what is involved in equal or impartial treatment. Impartiality demands more medical provision for the sick than the healthy, more food for adults than for children, greater tax concessions for the poor than the rich, special schooling for the physically disabled and the mentally subnormal. What is the implication of these examples? What exactly are we saying when we accept them as just? We are saying that in each case there is *good reason* for the differential treatment. What those reasons are in each case is clear (sickness, size, poverty and disabilities); it is also clear that they are *relevant*. Being sick is a *relevant* consideration in respect of distribution of medicine, in a way that size is not. Size is *relevant* to the distribution of food, in a way that wealth is not. And so on. But *why* in fact are these reasons *good* reasons? They dare only so *on the assumption that we wish to minimise suffering*. If this were not so, if suffering were unimportant or irrelevant, then why should we bother to give medicine to the sick? They would only be ill if we did not. Why should that matter? They would only be suffering.

4.   The same kind of argument can be applied to freedom. Compare an example of a freedom that most of us would agree should be restricted with one that we should not be willing to restrict: why is it that we place a

restriction on the freedom to kill, but not on the freedom to play Bingo, regardless of our attitude to Bingo? Because no special pleading could persuade us that there would be less suffering if killing were not restricted, and, however trivial we think Bingo may be, we would take some persuading that in the long term there would be less suffering in the community if Bingo were forbidden than if it were played.

In other words, the answer to the questions left hanging at the end of Chapters 4 and 5 ('In the light of what may we legitimately curb freedom?' and 'In the light of what do we decide whether a reason is a relevant reason for discrimination?') is the same in each case: in the light of happiness. The sort of reason that counts as a moral reason, the sort of reason that counts as a good reason in the moral sphere, is a happiness-reason: a reason that relates to the ultimate concern to minimise suffering. Moral injunctions or commands must be backed by moral reasons. We are committed to being moral, we are therefore committed to injunctions backed by moral reasons, and we are therefore committed to promoting the greatest happiness of the greatest number. We have not 'proved' that happiness is what ultimately matters. We have revealed that the assumption that it does is implicit in the sort of way we conduct moral discourse, and suggested that there is good reason to accept and act on this assumption.

It is still open to any individual to say that he has no intention of promoting happiness or supporting courses of action that do, and that he would rather promote other values, such as freedom, even at the expense of happiness. But if he took up this position and wished to impress us with its validity, we should expect him to be consistent. That would mean that he could not, for instance, approve of anything *simply* on the grounds that it promoted happiness. He obviously could not consistently argue, on the one hand, that freedom should not be subordinated to the claims of happiness, and, on the other, that people should not be free to kill, since if they were there would be a great increase in suffering. He would need to produce some other reason for restricting the freedom to kill, or else to demand that people should be free to kill. The onus would also fall on such a man to produce some good reason for ignoring the fact that everybody wants their own happiness.

It does not follow from anything that I have said either that it is odd that different societies have very different moral codes or that they necessarily ought not to have. It is not odd, because the fact that this is a rational view does not mean that people have always seen that it is. Perhaps I should add that the fact that I insist that it is a rational view does not mean that it is! And in any case different circumstances in different societies may dictate different practices under the same principles. In fact we may go so far as to say that many so-called moral rules in a society are not really moral rules at all: they are merely rules of conduct that gain their point from being universally adopted. This is the case, I would suggest, with all sexual morality. Monogamy or chastity before marriage, for example, are not in themselves morally right. But what is morally demanded is some degree of uniformity and stability in this important area. That is to say that in a society the ultimate consideration of happiness will demand some fairly determined attitude to sex – so that people do not feel anxious or shocked at the antics of others, so that children do not suddenly appear on the scene with no one to care for them, so that people do not find themselves deserted in a society that makes no allowance for them – but what that attitude is, within broad terms, is not a moral matter and different societies may quite reasonably adopt different attitudes. Taking this point a stage further, I should argue in response to a specific question such as 'Ought people to sleep together when not married?' that there can be no question that this is not immoral in itself, but what may well be immoral are obvious considerations such as producing unwanted children, and also slightly less obvious considerations such as flaunting this style of living in the face of those who happen to be upset by it.

Nor does the utilitarian ethic imply that people ought simply to aim at and have whatever they want. Ideally it might mean this, but in practice it certainly does not. Morality arises as an attempt to regulate human life; it arises precisely because human beings do not spontaneously consider each other's well-being. The object of the whole exercise is to find that formula or theory which one believes should truly be the measure of right and wrong, and hence the yardstick against which to judge the organisation and rules that society needs. Consequently, although one of the arguments for utilitarianism is based on the suggestion that it is reasonable for people to strive for what they want, once utilitarianism has been accepted, it leads to the immediate attempt to regulate each individual's actual wants in a way that does justice to the over-riding aim of equal concern for everybody's wants.

This last point should be extended to make an equally important general point in relation to education. Commitment to utilitarianism does not mean commitment to the ideal of everybody pursuing their own pleasure as they see fit, and it therefore does not necessarily lead to a view of education that makes the child's wishes the ultimate criterion of what should be done. If what matters is a world so organised that the greatest happiness of the greatest number is achieved, what matters in education is that this end should be served. One may have grave doubts as to whether it would be served by abandoning education to the principle of 'Let the child do what the child wants to do'.

Finally there is one more point to be made about freedom. If we accept that considerations of happiness should over-ride the claims of freedom, we should surely go further with Mill and distinguish between those sorts of activities that may sometimes be restricted, and those which never may be. Mill built up this distinction in two ways: first he separated the sphere of activity from that of thought, and argued that freedom of thought ought never to be restricted. (The question of free expression is left occupying a midway position between thought and action, since it is part and parcel of thought, and yet may be compared to action in that a man, by expressing himself publicly, may incite action.) Secondly he distinguished within the sphere of activity between other-regarding acts (those that impinge on others) and self-regarding acts (those that do not); again, the latter class of activities ought never to be restricted.

This distinction between self- and other-regarding activities is open to criticism on the grounds that virtually any action can be regarded as other-regarding, since it will at least indirectly impinge on other people. Thus Mill's view that to be drunk in the privacy of one's own home is a self-regarding act may be objected to on the grounds that, even if one is not married and is not directly affecting anyone else, nonetheless the mere fact of being a man who gets drunk in his room must have indirect consequences for other people, since it means that one is not doing something else that one might have been doing.

This line of argument seems to me to be logically sound, but it is an interesting example of the way in which sticking to the letter of logic can blind one to the spirit of an argument. If we really want to pursue this line of reasoning to the bitter end we are forced to the conclusion that over-sleeping or spending too long in the bath are other-regarding activities because 'one is not doing something else that one might have been doing'. But though this is strictly speaking true, Mill was nonetheless surely right to draw a distinction between actions that positively affect other people and those that affect them only negatively or in that they involve one in not doing something else that one might have been doing. I thus incline to the view that, while the notion of a purely self-regarding activity may be strictly speaking a misnomer, there is nonetheless an important difference between actions that directly affect other people and those that do not. To get drunk on duty is quite obviously to be distinguished from getting drunk in the privacy of one's home. And insofar as actions are what Mill has chosen to call self-regarding, they are surely not a fit subject for restriction.

But does it not run completely counter to utilitarianism to announce at the finish that some freedoms may never be interfered with even in the interests of happiness? It obviously runs counter to any form of act-utilitarianism, but not to rule-utilitarianism. For the argument here is that freedom of thought and freedom of action, in cases where other people are not directly affected, positively contribute to and increase the sum total of human happiness in the long run; so much so that we must have a rule guaranteeing such freedom. For if we did not have a rule, if we merely said that people could be free to think provided that their thoughts did not militate against happiness, although we would thereby give ourselves the right to suppress particular examples of unambiguously pernicious thought, we should lose more than we gained. Thought that always walks in fear of suppression is not really free at all, and people who live in a society in which they can never be sure whether today's freedom will be there tomorrow are not likely to be particularly happy. The argument, then, is simply that we gain more than we lose in the long term, in respect of happiness, by demanding a fixed rule that thought should always be free and that certain types of action, which Mill called self-regarding, but which in fact still need a more precise definition, should always be free.

What is important is the conclusion that when we say that 'people ought to be free to do X' or 'free from X', or that 'they should be treated the same in respect of X' or 'given equal amounts of X' such remarks are true, if they are true, only because the injunction in each case, if followed, would contribute more to the greatest happiness of the greatest number than any alternative procedure. That is what utilitarianism is all about.

REFERENCES

1 Bentham, J., *The Principles of Morals and Legislation* (Hafner, New York, 1948), p. 1.
2 Ibid., p. 2.
3 Ibid., p. 70.
4 Ibid., p. 2 ff.
5 Quinton, A., *Utilitarian Ethics* (Macmillan, 1973), p. 34.
6 Ibid., p. 43.
7 Stace, W. T., *The Concept of Morals* (Macmillan, New York, 1937), pp. 131–2.
8 Mill, J. S., *Utilitarianism*, Chapter 2.
9 Dearden, R. F., 'Happiness and Education' in Dearden, R. F., Hirst, P. H., and Peters, R. S. (eds), *Education and the Development of Reason* (Routledge & Kegan Paul, 1972).
10 This example is based upon one introduced by Hospers in his *Human Conduct*. See Further Reading.
11 Mill, J. S., *Utilitarianism*, Chapter 4. For a discussion of Mill's attempt at a proof see Warnock, M., in her introduction to the Fontana edition of Utilitarianism.

FURTHER READING

In view of the significance of this chapter in the scheme of this book, I shall offer a longer list of relevant material than usual. Particularly important are a few references that are more or less positively hostile to hedonistic utilitarianism:

Moore, G. E., *Ethics* (O.U.P., 1966); Williams, B., 'A Critique of Utilitarianism' in Smart, J. J. C., and Williams, B. (eds), *Utilitarianism For and Against* (C.U.P., 1973); MacIntyre, A. C., 'Against Utilitarianism' in Hollins, T. H. B. (ed.), *Aims in Education* (Manchester University Press, 1964) is specifically concerned with objection to a utilitarian approach to education. As against his paper it might be argued that he has not fully understood what a utilitarian approach to education would involve.

Relatively neutral expositions of utilitarianism are contained in: Hospers, John, *Human Conduct* (Hart-Davis, 1970) and Quinton, A., *Utilitarian Ethics* (Macmillan, 1973). See also Mabbot, J. D., *An Introduction to Ethics* (Hutchinson, 1966) and Hudson, W. D., *Modern Moral Philosophy* (Macmillan, 1970).

The classic texts are Bentham, J., *The Principles of Morals and Legislation* and Mill, J. S., *Utilitarianism*.

In Barrow, R., *Plato, Utilitarianism and Education* (Routledge & Kegan Paul, 1975) I have considered the concept of happiness in considerably greater detail than I have here. Smart, J. J. C., and Williams, B., *For and Against Utilitarianism* contains an invaluable bibliography of specialist works relating to such issues as act- versus rule-utilitarianism, as well as a generous summary of the more important work relating to utilitarianism in general.

Part Three

Part Three

Chapter 7

Kant and Respect for Persons

Perhaps the most glaring inadequacy in this book so far is its failure to consider the ethical philosophy of Kant. There are two reasons in particular why he should be mentioned. (1) His influence has been considerable, particularly on the work of many philosophers concerned with education. (2) His ethical position stands in contrast to the utilitarian view. However, I shall argue, despite the first point, that there is a difficulty in Kant's position so great as to lead one to the conclusion that he is in some respects plainly wrong, and that what is important in his view is also to be found, under another name, in utilitarianism.

The utilitarians and Kant had at any rate one thing in common: both were looking for something that could be said that was unequivocally true about morality; both were resisting any temptation to adopt a relativist or subjectivist position. Kant proceeded, however, in a quite distinctive manner. He asked himself what the nature of a moral, as opposed to a non-moral, act was. He was not concerned with listing whatever he or anyone else happened to regard as examples of morally good acts; he was not, as a starting point, trying to distinguish between moral and immoral acts. He was concerned with pin-pointing the distinguishing features of actions that prima facie belong to the moral sphere as opposed to morally neutral spheres of human experience. He was not asking such questions as 'Is helping your neighbours morally good?', but rather 'Under what circumstances or on what conditions would helping your neighbours count as moral, as opposed to selfish, prudential, ignorant, random, etc., behaviour?'. In other words, he asked not 'What behaviour is moral?' but 'What do we mean by *moral* behaviour?'.

His answer was that 'a moral act is an act done from duty'. Acting 'from duty' is obviously to be distinguished from acting under compulsion, out of fear, on inclination and a number of other things. But Kant was also careful to distinguish between merely acting *in accordance* with duty, which is not necessarily moral behaviour, and acting *from* duty, which is. Thus a man is not behaving morally simply because he does what he and we happen to regard as the right thing to do; he is only being moral if he acts in a certain way because he freely decides to do so as a result of sensing an obligation to do so. A moral act is an act done because one senses that one ought to do it. Helping your neighbour get his children to school is not a moral act if you do it because you hope that he will return the favour or simply because you like doing it.

Now clearly we cannot accept that *any* action done from a sense of duty is a morally good action. One might, after all, decide to burn one's neighbour rather than help him, and do it from a sense of duty. Without doubt, that is precisely what a number of those who burnt people as witches were doing. We surely cannot accept that burning witches is morally good if people do it from a sense of duty. The consequence of this observation is that acting from a sense of duty has to be seen as at best a necessary condition of morally good behaviour, but not a sufficient condition: to be morally good it is (perhaps) necessary to act from a sense of duty, but it is not in itself enough.

Accordingly Kant's next step is to attempt to delineate the sort of actions that ought to be done or that are morally good. If this can be done then we shall be able to say that the moral man is one who performs these acts from a sense of duty, and he is to be distinguished both from the man who does not perform these actions at all, and from the man who does, but who does so for some reason other than that he senses an obligation to do so.

Man is rational. That is to say that man can and does act in accord with various principles and general rules. Kant calls such principles 'maxims'. (A maxim is 'a general rule' which an individual 'would formulate in explaining his actions'.) And he points out that any action can be explained by reference to some maxim. For instance, in particular circumstances I tell somebody the truth, although it hurts them to hear it. Why did I do it? Perhaps simply because 'I always tell the truth', or because 'I tell the truth when it hurts in the short term, if I believe that it will benefit in the long term', or because 'I always hurt people if I can'. Each of these explanations, and any other that you care to think of, constitutes a maxim. Of course the agent may not consciously formulate a maxim, a maxim may be a great deal more complex than any of my examples, and an agent may not consistently abide by a maxim – he may say 'I told the truth because I always tell the truth', but in fact fail always to tell the truth. None of these considerations affects Kant's point here, which is simply that we, being reflective creatures rather than automatons, do have subjective principles of action, even if we do not always consciously formulate them.

Maxims are in themselves non-moral. But, says Kant, and this is a crucial phase of his argument, a maxim becomes a moral maxim if the individual can will that the maxim should be universally adopted or acted upon by everybody. (Unfortunately, I have to interrupt the flow of this exposition to mention that critics of Kant are not in agreement as to whether he claims that on these terms a maxim *is* moral or merely that it *may* be. I shall return to this point.) For example, I help my neighbour in distress because 'I help anybody in distress'. That is my maxim. Clearly I can universalize this maxim; I can will that everybody should adopt it or commit myself to the formula 'Let everybody always help anybody in distress'. Therefore, since the maxim can be universalized, it is (or alternatively may be) a moral maxim.

Whether we take Kant to be saying that universalizable maxims 'are' or 'may be' moral, it is evident that on his view a maxim that cannot be universalized is not and cannot be moral. Suppose that I borrow some money from a friend, promising to pay him back, but not in fact having any intention to do so. My maxim, let us suppose, is 'When short of money, I will borrow, promising, but not intending, to pay it back'. This maxim, according to Kant, could not be universalized. One could not *will* anything to the effect of 'Let all people, when short of money, borrow, promising, but not intending, to pay it back'. The reason that one could not will this, again according to Kant, is that, if this formula were universally acted upon, it would make nonsense of the notion of promising in respect of paying back loans. If everybody promised, but nobody ever kept their promise, the promises would be, and would be seen to be, valueless. But, if the promises were valueless, they would be pointless and would not achieve their object of securing a loan. No loans would be made. It would be quite inconsistent with the desire to secure a loan, to will something that could be seen to lead logically to a situation in which no one would lend. I cannot consistently seek to gain money in this way and will that everybody else should as a matter of course behave in the same way; therefore, if I am behaving in this way on this maxim, I cannot will that the maxim be universally adopted. Therefore the maxim 'When short of money, I will borrow, promising, but not intending, to pay it back' is not a moral maxim. So, at any rate, says Kant, as far as I can understand him. It must be stressed that Kant claims to be making a logical and not a psychological point. He is not saying 'no man could really want this state of affairs', but 'it is a logical nonsense to will it'.

Kant thus arrives at what he calls the Categorical Imperative. It is 'categorical' because, unlike normal imperatives – 'Do this', 'Shut the door', which imply some further condition such as 'assuming that you want to get home' or 'given that you want to please me', this imperative is absolute: it is a command without qualifications or conditions. The Categorical Imperative is: 'Act only on that maxim whereby you canst at the same time will that it should become universal law.' This is the bedrock of morality. The true moral code should consist of those maxims that can thus be universalized; and Kant, besides maintaining that only some maxims can be universalized, offers examples of those that he thinks can be and that are moral. These are such that he concludes specifically that one ought never to tell a lie, never commit suicide, never neglect one's natural gifts and their development for the sake of pleasure, never break promises, and never ignore others in distress. The truly moral man is thus one who refrains from such activities (and in other respects obeys the Categorical Imperative) from a sense of duty.

There is one important point that Kant is making that is surely correct. That is that we will not accept that a principle of action is morally acceptable unless it is universalizable. It is a feature of what we mean by a moral principle that it should apply universally and not simply consist of special pleading for the agent in question. If I want to convince other people that my action in certain circumstances is moral, then the very least that I must do is concede that others, faced with the same circumstances, may also act in the same way. Thus, if I finally punch a man in the face because he has been taunting me, and if I wish to claim that my action was morally justified, I must at least concede that, if our positions had been reversed, he would have been justified in hitting me.

But the important phrases in the previous paragraph are 'a feature', 'the very least', 'at least'. It will be remembered that I drew attention to the question of whether Kant meant only that a maxim must be universalizable to be moral, or that any universatisable maxim was *ipso facto* moral. What I wish to say here is that, whatever Kant intended to say, only the former suggestion is plausible. The fact that a maxim can be universalized is not sufficient to show that it is moral. The fact that one could will something such as that 'all men, when taunted, should hit the person taunting them' will not persuade most of us that this shows that the action is moral. On the other hand, it is a necessary feature of a truly moral maxim that it should be universalizable, and *one* of the things that we would demand of someone, before we were prepared to regard his behaviour as moral, is that he should act in accordance with principles that he regarded as universally binding. We would not regard him as moral if he ignored principles that he maintained were binding on everyone else or acted on principles which he maintained applied only to him – and this is so regardless of what the principles in question might be.

However one does not have to accept the rest of Kant's argument because one accepts this, and one does not have to arrive at this conclusion by following Kant. Indeed this point about universalizability has already been made in a different way in Chapter 5. For the claim that we ought to act on universalizable principles is one and the same thing as the claim that we ought to be impartial, on the assumption that it is agreed that it is conceivable that differences between people might sometimes be such, in specific situations, as to constitute different circumstances. Kant in fact would not allow that differences between people could ever have any bearing on the question. But they obviously could: the fact that a man was known to be homicidal, for instance, might in some situations be a relevant reason for dealing with him in a way that one would not normally deal with people. If this is accepted, then the claim that a maxim or principle ought to be universalizable becomes equivalent to the claim that people ought to be treated in the same way – and hence allowed to behave in the same way – except where relevant reasons for differential treatment are present, which is to say except where there are differences between people or in circumstances which justify different treatment. If I claim the right to hit people who taunt me, then the principle of impartiality demands that others should be entitled to hit me when I taunt them.

But what is there to be said about the rest of Kant's ethical theory? I have four criticisms to make.

1. Once it is agreed that the claim that a truly moral maxim must be universalizable is only a necessary condition of a moral maxim, it follows that Kant's theory is incomplete. We have no way of deciding which of the various universalizable maxims we can think of are moral, for he has provided no other criteria whereby to decide. For all that Kant has to say on the subject, the maxim 'I hit people when they taunt me' might be moral, since it can be universalized. To take a more extreme, but possibly more realistic example, why should I not (logically) will, what it seems to me many people *have* willed, some such maxim as 'In all circumstances I will put my own interests before anyone else's'? It is obviously quite feasible to universalize this into 'Let every man always put his own interests first and the devil take the hindmost'. What use is an ethical theory that has nothing to say about the distinction between this maxim, which Kant no less than I would certainly have regarded as immoral, and a maxim such as 'I will always tell the truth'?

2. Although Kant fails to tell us how to distinguish between those universalizable maxims that are moral and those that are not, he does, as we have seen, by chance give us some examples of behaviour that he regards as immoral. The most damning objection to his whole approach is that, although we may happen to agree with him that these (or some of these) activities are objectionable, his argument totally fails to show that they are. For at least some of his examples involve maxims, which, despite his spirited denial, one *could* will that they become universal law. Take the case of suicide. Why is it logically impossible for me to act on the maxim 'When I feel like it I will commit suicide'; why shouldn't I will this as a universal law? Again, on what grounds does Kant claim that nobody could will a universal law to the effect that nobody should help anybody in distress? Of course, most of us would *not* will this, and of course most of us agree with Kant in feeling that it would be immoral to will it. But that is not the point, which is that according to Kant it is logically

impossible to will this as a universal law. To which my reply is that it patently is not.

3. A third objection to Kant's ethics is that for some reason he insisted that those positive basic rules that he did produce were absolute and could admit of no exceptions. Thus, it is always wrong to tell a lie; it is always wrong to break promises, and so on. It is not clear why Kant insisted on this, since it does not seem to be a necessary consequence of his theory. And for that reason I do not wish to make too much of it. But, quite apart from the fact that most of us would probably feel that there are circumstances in which a lie might be justified, the interesting question is what would Kant expect us to do when two of his absolute principles clash? If I ought never to tell a lie and ought never to break a promise, what am I supposed to do when asked whether something that I have been told in confidence, and that I have promised not to reveal is true?

4. My final objection takes us back to the beginning. Kant argues that a decision to act can only be morally good if it is made for the sake of doing one's duty. Now if he meant by this simply that a man would not deserve moral credit if he performed good acts but did so for selfish or prudential reasons, I do not in fact have any objection. It is obviously true that if you act kindly, but do so to enhance your popularity or prestige, you do not deserve praise for being moral.

But Kant may have meant, and some people have certainly taken him to mean, that an *act* only has moral value if it is done from a sense of duty. And a distinction is often drawn between utilitarianism, which is described as an ethical theory that puts all the stress on the consequences of actions, and Kantian ethics that puts the stress on intention. This distinction is obviously there, but only because the two ethical arguments are concerned with different questions: utilitarianism is concerned with the question 'What ways of behaving are desirable and how do we decide?'; whereas Kant, when he talks about duty, is concerned with the question 'How does a man have to perform whatever acts are good, if he is to deserve moral credit?'. The suggestion that an *act* only has moral value if the agent has certain intentions is surely preposterous. If we agree, for the sake of example, that one ought to keep promises, then the act of keeping promises is good whenever it is performed and for whatever reason it is performed. There may be nothing good about the *man* who helps an old lady across the street because he knows that he is being watched by somebody whom he wishes to impress, but that does not mean that his action is not good.

Furthermore I am not at all willing to accept even that the man, to be moral, *must* act from a sense of duty. Suppose that he does not have a sense of duty, because no one has ever talked in these terms to him and he has never in his life known what it means to feel a sense of obligation. He just *likes* helping old ladies across the street or what have you. He just has an innate tendency to do the sort of things that we regard as moral. Well, surely, he is moral; he is a naturally moral man. Likewise the man who performs good acts out of habit, without ever having asked himself why he does them and without ever feeling any sense of duty, would, I suggest, be moral. In practice I do not imagine that there are many, if any, people who do completely lack a sense of duty in this way. But it is logically conceivable that they should exist, and that is sufficient to discredit the idea that to be moral one must act from a sense of duty (if it is accepted that such people would be correctly described as moral).

I have my doubts, then, about Kant's approach to ethics and some of his conclusions. I see nothing here that causes one to question the utilitarian approach. But it is not only because one cannot ignore a figure of Kant's stature, and not only to help the reader assess Kant's approach for himself, that I have included this brief summary and criticism. There are two concepts that seem to be of particular interest to educational philosophers today that Kant was one of the first to draw attention to: 'respect for persons' and 'autonomy'.

Kant offered various other formulations of the Categorical Imperative besides that given above, including this one: 'So act as to treat humanity, whether in thine own person or in that of any other, in every case as an end, never as a means only.' Philosophers have argued for a long time over whether this formulation is or is not equivalent to the one I gave above. I shall bypass that problem by observing that, even if it is not equivalent, this formulation would at any rate seem to follow from the previous one. For if we accept the idea that moral principles must apply without distinction to all men, if we accept that all men count equally, then, since nobody would choose to be treated 'as a means only' by other people, it follows that we are all committed to the idea of treating nobody as a means only.

Kant also talks specifically of the need for 'reverence for a person' which 'is properly only reverence for the [moral] law of which that person gives us an example'. I shall ignore the term 'reverence' and the complex view that the individual is an example of the moral law, and concentrate instead on the modern concept of 'respect for persons'. What I wish to argue is that this concept is intolerably vague, that it consequently can only be taken to be making Kant's broad point that nobody should be treated as a means only, and that therefore, although it is certainly important, it is of extremely limited significance.

'Respect for persons' sounds nice and it obviously rules out some ways of behaving: to use people for target practice (i.e. as a means whereby one may improve one's skill at shooting) is patently not to show respect for them. But what about some more uncertain examples: does a man who resorts to prostitutes necessarily fail to show respect for them? Does a commander in time of war necessarily fail to show respect for the soldiers he sends into battle? What *is* respect? And what is a person? Is every human being a person and therefore deserving of respect? Is a vicious torturing thug a person? If so, in what respect should I respect him? Is a new-born baby a person? I may love, care for, be concerned about a new-born baby, but in what sense can I respect him?

The essence of what most of those who are concerned with respect for persons seem to mean by a 'person' is as follows. The concept of a person picks out man's distinctive characteristic of having a determining role to play in life. Persons, as opposed to animals for instance, control their environment. They plan and shape their lives in accordance with wishes, calculations, predictions and so on. They have points of view. A man is a person, and is being treated as such, in proportion to the extent that he takes himself, and is taken by others, seriously as a source of values, decisions, points of view and choices. In other words, as Hirst and Peters put it:

> 'this use of "person" is connected conceptually with having what might be called an assertive point of view, with evaluation, decision and choice, and with being, to a certain extent, an individual who determines his own destiny by his choices'.[1]

I have three immediate observations to make:
1. 'Person' seems to me to be the wrong word here. That is to say it seems an unwarranted departure from normal usage to confine the use of person to this specialized sense. Most of us would naturally refer to all human beings as persons, even when they do not, for whatever reason, to any marked extent 'determine their own destinies by their choices'.
2. This specific sense of 'person' seems at least to run the risk of leading to the conclusion that some human beings, such as very young children or some mentally ill people, are not persons.
3. It raises the question of whether some people *ought* to be persons. Perhaps the vicious torturer mentioned above ought not to be allowed to determine his own destiny at all, in view of the ways in which he might attempt to do so. To deny him the opportunity to determine his own destiny to any extent, would on this view, be to deny him the opportunity to be a person.

However these observations need not stand in our way. The important thing is to understand what those who stress the need for respect for persons mean by 'person', even if we feel, as I do, that they are using the term in a rather odd way. What we are obviously being asked to do is to respect people as independent sources of desire, choice and so on. We are being asked to take the point of view of those who have points of view seriously. We are being asked to respect other people's claims rather than simply to impose our own.

This really answers the question of what is meant by 'respect' here. In another context one might have a great deal of fun parading examples of the use of the term 'respect' and inquiring into which uses seemed central and which peripheral, in an attempt to get close to what really lies at the heart of the concept. (Does 'respect' involve being in awe of someone, letting them do what they choose, listening to their point of view, doffing one's cap, liking them, loving them, having some kind of relationship with them, taking their argument seriously when it seems to be nonsense, and so on?)

But the fact that we are being asked to respect people as persons, in this specific sense of person, shows that we are simply being asked to take into consideration other people's points of view 'with a measure of seriousness sufficient to entertain the possibility of changing one's own opinions or plans in the light of it'.[2] We are not being asked, for instance, actually to like everybody else or to admire them. But we are being asked to bear in mind that other people have their ways of looking at things and to take these seriously rather than to dismiss or ignore them because they do not happen to correspond to our way of looking at things, or because we do not happen to have any liking for the people in question.

Thus the demand for 'respect for persons' is virtually synonymous with the demand that we treat people as ends and not simply as means. For to treat somebody simply as a means is precisely to ignore the fact that he is an independent being who may have his own distinctive objectives. What those who stress the need for respect for persons are saying is: do not regard other people as generally inferior or not deserving of equal consideration (although, of course, different people may well be inferior in specific respects; they may be inferior cricketers or inferior mathematicians, for instance). Do not proceed as if other people do not count.

'To feel respect for persons . . . is to be moved by the thought that another, is, after all, a person like oneself (i.e. a centre of consciousness) and that as such he is to be accorded certain rights and to be treated with consideration.'[3] 'Insofar as we think of an individual as having a point of view, and insofar as this is not a matter of indifference to us, we respect him as a person. To show lack of respect for persons, is, for instance, to ignore his point of view when we use him purely for our own purposes or to settle his destiny for him without taking account of his views about it.'[4]

I do not want to dispute that respect for persons, in this sense, is important. Indeed I have already committed myself to this value in arguing that we ought to be concerned equally about the happiness of all, which obviously involves both regarding people as ends and taking into account their desires and choices. Furthermore, Peters is obviously right in arguing that it is a presupposition of any serious debate about what ought to be done that one formally commits oneself to the idea of taking other people seriously as sources of claims and points of view. What is the point in my discussing with you, if I work on the assumption that you have nothing to contribute to the discussion? The trouble is that this does not get us far. The concept of respect for persons tells us not to ignore others or ride roughshod over them. It does not tell us at what point we may legitimately ignore somebody else's point of view. It does not really tell us what is involved in seriously 'taking account of' someone's point of view.

As Hirst and Peters point out, one cannot allow one's approval of the idea of respect for persons to lead one to accept *any* point of view or to stand by while *any* claim is put into practice. What is the teacher, committed to this ideal, actually supposed *to do*? Clearly he must not proceed as if he is the final authority on everything under the sun and refuse to take any account of what the children with him want or regard as important. He must not simply refuse to listen to their point of view and their argument. But at what point does he in practice ignore their point of view?

Some would say never. This, I suggest, is absurd. 'Respect for persons' is not so important as to lead to the conclusion that if a group of children have a particular point of view and even after discussion maintain it, that point of view should be acted on, no matter what the point of view is and no matter what the age, intelligence or ignorance of the children in question. Taking account of somebody's point of view cannot be taken to mean standing aside and letting it be put into practice regardless of what it is. But if taking account of somebody's point of view does not mean this, if it is quite consistent with taking account of children's views for a teacher nonetheless to ignore them in practice, at least in some instances, how are we actually to proceed? Hirst and Peters write, for instance: the teacher 'must not be so overwhelmed with awe at the thought of another expressing his innermost thoughts that he omits to point out that they are not very clearly expressed or scarcely relevant to the matter under discussion'.[5] Now I happen to agree entirely with this, but nonetheless we surely have to recognize the force of the objection, made for instance by Postman and Weingartner, that to say something like this involves the teacher in being the final determiner of what points of view or what arguments count.[6]

Postman and Weingartner argue that anything the child says in any discussion is relevant because it is relevant to him (otherwise he wouldn't say it). Now surely it is ridiculous to conclude from this line of argument that the teacher ought not to be the final determiner of what counts as a good argument or what behaviour is going to be permitted in schools. That is to say, we are surely not prepared to accept that because a child offers as a reason for bullying his neighbour the fact that the neighbour is black, and because this reason is 'relevant to him', whatever that means, it is therefore a good reason and the teacher should allow the bullying to take place. Nonetheless Postman and Weingartner have uncovered a problem: how does the teacher, in practice, distinguish between points of view that he *thinks* are unacceptable and those that *are* unacceptable? Surely, in practice, despite the formal implications of respect for persons – that children are persons with points of view that count for as much as anybody else's – all that we are being asked to do is to listen to other people's points of view. But in practice, especially in the case of children, we are not being asked to attach as much importance to them as we do to our own points of view, unless they happen to convince us to change our minds.

This amounts to saying that those critics who feel that the notion of 'respect for persons' obscures the point that the teacher, while having this respect, nonetheless remains the final arbiter of various points of view, are correct. That is why I claim that the concept is of limited significance. Really it involves no more than the demand that, while being the final arbiter, the teacher should remain open to alternative viewpoints and in particular should listen to those of the children he teaches and should remember that they do have feelings and ideals that are their own. This, I repeat, seems to me important. But it is very difficult to see how from this principle one can derive any significant observations about what the teacher should in practice do.

REFERENCES

1 Hirst, P. H., and Peters, R. S., *The Logic of Education* (Routledge & Kegan Paul, 1970), p. 53.
2 Ibid., p. 54.
3 Ibid., p. 91.
4 Ibid., p. 92.
5 Ibid., p. 92.
6 See Postman, N., and Weingartner, C., *Teaching as a Subversive Activity* (Penguin, 1971). For further discussion of the view of Postman and Weingartner, see Chapter 11.

FURTHER READING

Kant is not an easy philosopher to get to grips with. Helpful expositions of his moral philosophy will be found in Acton, H. B., *Kant's Moral Philosophy* (Macmillan, 1970) and Korner, S., *Kant* (Penguin, 1955). Paton, H. I., *The*

Moral Law (Hutchinson, 1948) and Kemp, J., *The Philosophy of Kant* (O.U.P., 1968) are perhaps more demanding.

'Respect for persons' is a central theme in Peters, R. S., *Ethics and Education* (Allen & Unwin, 1966) and in Hirst, P. H. and Peters, R. S., *The Logic of Education* (Routledge & Kegan Paul, 1970). See also Downie, R. S., and Telfer, E., *Respect for Persons* (Allen & Unwin, 1969).

Chapter 8

Autonomy

Autonomy literally means self-government or self-legislation. A Greek city state such as Athens, which was independent, had autonomy, whereas the member states of the Athenian Empire sacrificed a degree of autonomy to Athens in return for protection. The Athenians held back the threat of Persian domination, but they made certain political demands of the states that they protected. They had a say in the government of these states and hence these states were not truly autonomous. Universities in this country are autonomous in that they themselves are responsible for their own organization. Although they have access to public funds they are not directly subject to the control of any external body such as the government or the ratepayers' association. There is then a perfectly familiar and straightforward use of the word autonomy, in which to be autonomous is to be free from external interference or control. It is to be master of one's own fate rather than subject to other individuals or other groups of people.

However when we look more closely at the notion of *personal* autonomy or the autonomy of the individual, the situation is complicated by the fact that a person is not necessarily master of his own fate in any real sense just because there is nobody else giving him orders. It seems natural enough to refer to a state as autonomous if what goes on in the state is decided entirely by the members of that state, regardless of the various factors such as ignorance, prejudice, or poverty that may effectively dictate what those members decide. But when we consider the personal autonomy of those individuals, it seems considerably less clear that it makes much sense to regard them as autonomous, in the sense of masters of their own fate, if their freedom of manoeuvre is considerably restricted by such factors. This at any rate is the reasoning that lies behind the attempt of philosophers such as Dearden to produce a more specific and more positive concept of personal autonomy.[1]

The general view has been that to have personal autonomy presupposes three things besides simply being free from the control of other people. The autonomous person must be subject to his reason, rather than, for instance, his emotions. The reasoning that he acts in accordance with must be authentic, which is to say briefly that it must be reasoning to which he is sincerely committed rather than simply a line of argument that he has picked up and now trots out without any real sincerity or understanding. And he must have the strength of will to act as his reason dictates. This last condition is, of course, closely related to the first, as will become clear as we examine each of these conditions in turn.

1.   The first condition writes into the notion of an autonomous agent the demand that his reasoning should control his behaviour. To talk of somebody being master of his fate implies that he directs or controls his behaviour rather than simply that he blows aimlessly in whichever direction the wind blows. And direction implies planning of some sort or some degree of systematic thinking. If a man never thought about what he was going to do, what consequences would follow from various alternative actions, what ends he desired and what means would serve those ends, it would seem rather odd to call him master of anything. He would rather be the plaything of caprice. If a man is to be described as master of his fate, then we should expect him to organize and govern his behaviour in such a way that his actions could be seen to be the product of his judgement, his reflection, calculation and decision-taking. And all these concepts are associated with the notion of reason.

This point can be illustrated by consideration of the alcoholic. In principle an alcoholic may be left to look after himself so that he is not subject to the control of any other people, either directly or through legal restrictions. But it would still seem peculiar to describe him as having any great degree of autonomy, if we stick to the fundamental idea that an autonomous person is master of his own fate. This man is no more master of his own fate than he would be if somebody were pointing a gun at his head. His craving for drink is so strong that it controls him and dictates to him. Relatively speaking he lacks freedom of manoeuvre: he has to do whatever action will get him a drink, and having had his drinks he is further limited in respect of what he is free to do. Similarly the man consumed by jealously is relatively lacking in autonomy. On the assumption that his jealousy is so strong as to distort his judgement, so that, for example, he convinces himself that an old friend who is offering him a desirable job is really after his wife, with the result that he cannot bring himself to accept the job, his freedom to control his life is considerably impaired.

Now one might argue that having a broken leg or believing in God or disliking Irishmen also restricted autonomy, and go on to ask whether one could meaningfully distinguish between the extent to which different people had autonomy and why being an alcoholic should impair one's autonomy any more than any assumption or belief that one had. After all, if a man believes in God this will presumably involve restrictions on his freedom of manoeuvre. The reply to this has to be that to have a belief does not preclude the possibility of rejecting it. So long as one believes in God one's behaviour will thereby be restricted to some extent, but one is still master of one's fate, because it is still open to one to reject the belief and if one does not choose to reject it then it is merely one aspect of one's life that one has selected for oneself. If on the other hand one had been indoctrinated into believing in God, if one had been made to believe in God in such a way that one was incapable of reasoning about the matter and coming to any other conclusion, one's autonomy would indeed be to that extent restricted. In other words one's beliefs and assumptions, although of course in practice they limit one's freedom of manoeuvre, do not curb one's autonomy so long as they themselves are open to question. They do curb one's autonomy when they become unalterable factors determining one's behaviour, factors – like the drink in the case of the alcoholic – of which one is not master. Factors like a broken leg differ from factors like a craving for drink not in that they are alterable – they are obviously not – but in this case they are simply beyond our control; there is nothing we can do about it. In other words the ideal of personal autonomy is the ideal that the individual shall be as much master of his own fate as it is possible for him to be, which will mean in practice that he shall be as free as possible to plan his own actions and way of life in the way that his reason determines, unhampered by such things as unalterable cravings or prejudices that themselves limit his freedom to reason.

The notion of personal autonomy as something rather more precise than simply freedom from the control of other people thus begins to take some shape, and the first condition does not appear to be entirely arbitrary or unduly to stretch the ordinary language use of the term autonomy. If we imagine a man about to make his vote at a general election, it is clear that his action in voting will not be autonomous if he is compelled to vote for a particular candidate by somebody else, if he fails to vote at all because he is drunk, or if his hatred of one of the candidates is so strong as to cause him to vote against him despite the fact that, if his reasoning had control, he would admit to himself that the hated candidate was the one he preferred to support. For his voting to be an autonomous activity it is necessary for him to vote in accordance with his own reasoning. If therefore he votes for a particular party simply because he has been brought up to assume that this is the party to vote for, and if he has never considered the arguments for or against voting for this party, once again he will not be acting as an autonomous agent.

2. At this point we have to consider the second proposed condition of personal autonomy. The notion of acting in accordance with one's own reasoning is rather vague. In practice very few people would vote for a particular party and, when asked why they did so, respond by saying 'That's a good question. I never thought about it. I just was brought up to do so'. It is far more likely that they would produce some kind of an argument in support of what they were doing. They would produce some reasoning, and in one sense any reasoning that anybody produces is their

own: it does not become any the less their own because it is reasoning that others might also employ or even because it is reasoning that they originally picked up from other people. It is in order to distinguish between the man who explains his actions by reasoning that is his own in the sense of understood by him and sincerely believed in by him, from the man who explains his actions by reasoning that he merely repeats parrot-fashion, that the notion of authenticity is introduced.

(a)   For the reasoning that I produce in explanation of an action to be authentic it must, first, genuinely be the explanation of the action. Insofar as a man deceives himself, he is to that extent lacking in autonomy. For instance it is conceivable that a man should explain his refusal to give money to a certain charity by propounding a theory about the degradation involved in people's accepting charity, while in fact the true explanation is simply that he does not like giving anything away. Insofar as this man is lacking in self-knowledge and is deluding himself, he is to that extent not really master of his own fate. His reasoning is not entirely authentic and this affects his ability to control.

(b)   Secondly the reasons that are given, besides being the true explanation of the action, must be reasons that the agent really believes in. In other words it is not enough that the argument that I propound for voting for a particular political party shall indeed provide the reasons for my voting for that party. If this reasoning is to be authentic I must care about it.

(c)   Thirdly the reasoning must make sense in relation to other aspects of my life and other examples of my thinking. My participation in a student demonstration is only prompted by authentic reasoning, and is therefore only autonomous, if I understand my true motivation and if that motivation involves reasoning to which I am sincerely committed. If I really think that the demonstration provides a useful means to an end that I really want, or that it will provide the fun that I really want, then it is autonomous behaviour. If on the other hand I think that I am doing it to register protest, but in fact I am doing it because I dare not deny peer group pressure, it is unauthentic.

3.   Thirdly, a man may lack autonomy in that although his actions are governed by authentic reasoning at the planning stage, in practice he lacks the strength of will to put them into practice. Thus a man sees that from his point of view, given all that he believes in, all that he desires and soon, a certain course of action is dictated, but he may lack the resolution to make the effort. In other words just as craving for drink or jealousy or ignorance of his own motivation may prevent him having full control over his fate, so a more general inability to do what he sees as necessary may afflict him.

To have personal autonomy, then, is to behave, act and hold opinions in the light of one's own reasoning. It is to be master of one's fate in the sense that one's reasoning directs one's life and controls one's emotions and desires rather than the reverse, with the proviso that one's reasoning shall not involve self-deception and shall indeed represent one's sincerely held viewpoint.

Since the concept of personal autonomy is very much a philosopher's creation it will not be inappropriate at this stage to introduce the account that Dearden, who is one of those who have devoted particular attention to the concept, himself has to give of it. As he says,

'there is no clear guidance to be gained here from something called "ordinary usage". On the contrary, what one is doing is attempting to formulate a concept of something often still rather vague and inchoate, but nevertheless implicit in a variety of educational innovations and changes'. He then goes on to say that 'a person is autonomous to the degree that what he thinks and does in important areas of his life cannot be explained without reference to his own activity of mind. That is to say, the explanation of why he thinks and acts as he does in these areas must include a reference to his own choices, deliberations, decisions, reflections, judgements, plannings or reasons'.

The reference to the fact that in practice autonomy will be a matter of degree as well as Dearden's admission that there are other ideals that may conflict with autonomy are important qualifications. But these qualifications apart, the concept of personal autonomy, now that we have given a more precise account of what is meant by 'reference to his own activity of mind' which seems to be in accord with what Dearden means, is not difficult to grasp.

There remain, however, two extremely important questions. How does one recognize a person as being relatively autonomous in practice? And does the notion of autonomy involve by definition any reference to standards of reasoning? And these questions, it seems to me, have not been adequately dealt with by philosophers such as Dearden.

It is clear that the concept of autonomy, as thus outlined, does not necessarily involve being either correct or morally good; there is no suggestion that moral rectitude or an ability to produce the right answers is written into the concept of personal autonomy. As Dearden points out, a master criminal might be an example of a man who is extremely autonomous, and he or anybody else might make bad mistakes in calculation or judgement, without thereby indicating a loss of autonomy. The distinction between the relatively autonomous and the relatively unautonomous man is between the man who works things out for himself and acts accordingly and the man who does not. Dearden cites as an example of somebody behaving autonomously Antigone in Sophocles' play of that name, inasmuch as she acts in accordance 'with her sincerely held view of what was right'. In the play, Creon, who is the king of the state and uncle of Antigone and her sister Ismene, issues the order that one of Antigone's brothers shall be buried honourably, while the other, who has died fighting against the city, shall remain unburied. Since the king has given the order the natural assumption is that it is to be obeyed. But Antigone disobeys the order because her reasoning – not her emotion or her truculent disobedience – tells her to do so. She does not unreflectingly allow an order to be imposed on her by someone else and she does not obey it because it is an order. She does what she regards as right – the question of whether we think that she does what is morally right being irrelevant – and our immediate assent goes to the statement that she is acting autonomously.

But what of Ismene who, after discussion with Antigone, decides to obey Creon? Dearden does not say that she is unautonomous, but one suspects that he would argue that she is, and that it is in contrast to her decision to do what she is told to do that Antigone stands out as autonomous. But what, after all, is the difference between Antigone and Ismene? Both reason about the matter – they actually discuss it together. Both do what they sincerely think ought to be done in the circumstances. Antigone decides that faced with an awkward clash between two principles dear to the Greeks – that the law, represented by Creon, should be obeyed and that the dead should be buried – her allegiance is to the latter. Ismene decides that hers is to the former. Both obviously have misgivings about ignoring the principle that in either case they choose to ignore. That, after all, is what the play is about: a clash of principles. But that does not alter the fact that each one does what she decides is right in the circumstances.

The point is that because Ismene obeys an order it is very easy to assume that she does not think for herself. But such an assumption ignores the possibility that she thought for herself and decided that the law ought to be obeyed. In other words this example is a particular illustration of the ambiguity of the phrase 'acting in obedience to authorities' which Dearden cites as a mark of the *un*autonomous individual. An autonomous person, by definition, must not act in a certain way, against his own better judgement, simply because an authority figure tells him to do so. But acting in obedience to authorities does not necessarily mean that the agent is acting against his own better judgement: he may think that in a particular instance the authority is right or, more significantly, he may think that, as a general principle, it is advisable or right that people should obey the authority of the state.

I do not wish to make too much of this particular example. Dearden may have chosen a bad one, he might concede that Ismene was also autonomous, or he might argue that there is no real evidence in the play that she did any thinking at all. The problem as I see it is that, no matter what example one chooses, once one has ruled out such obvious limitations on a person's autonomy as alcoholic cravings or drug addiction, it is in practice virtually impossible to distinguish between the more and the less autonomous individual. And if we cannot assess the degree of a person's autonomy, it is going to be very difficult to aim to promote it.

A particular individual who acts in conformity with the standards of behaviour that he was brought up to adopt may not *seem* to be very autonomous to you and me, but if all he has to do to be autonomous is to think for himself, there is no obvious reason to suppose that he is not autonomous. He is thinking for himself; he thinks that he should conform to these standards or he simply thinks that he should conform. The distinction between a person who acts in obedience to authorities and the person who acts on his own reasoned judgement is not a true antithesis, because people who act in obedience to authorities do so in general because they think it right to do so. Their reasoned judgement says that authorities should be obeyed, perhaps because they believe that in general those in authority know more than they do, perhaps because they believe that society can survive only with a degree of obedience to those in authority, or perhaps because they believe that those in authority are in a particular instance right. They may be *wrong* in making any of these claims, but that, on Dearden's admission, is irrelevant to the question of whether they are more or less autonomous.

The danger of making autonomy, as so far defined, an ideal to be striven for is obvious: forgetting that an apparently rather unintelligent conformist may nonetheless be autonomous, we shall tend to judge people's autonomy by the extent to which they are different or pursue idiosyncratic behaviour patterns, as, I suspect, Dearden has done in singling out Antigone rather than Ismene as an example of the autonomous individual. But, of course, being different from most people or being nonconformist is not in itself a mark of autonomy.

Not only is the concept of autonomy thus defined very difficult, if not impossible, to make use of in practice; it is also questionable whether it is an ideal of any worth. To aim to promote autonomy in this sense is to do no more than to attempt to bring people to hold opinions and to behave as they see fit. They are, ideally, to think for themselves whether an opinion is worth holding and whether to behave in this way or that, and to act in accordance with the results of their thinking. It should be noted that if we were sincerely to commit ourselves to this ideal, it is difficult to see what education has to do with it and why it should be regarded as an educational ideal. Why should one need to educate people to do this? If an autonomous person merely has to opine and act as he sees fit, then presumably one could be autonomous without any education at all.

But surely this in any case is *not* our ideal. In the first place it is not enough that people should simply think for themselves; ideally they should also think well, which is to say consistently, logically, with due regard to the facts of the matter and so on. Secondly, if the argument of Part Two of this book is accepted, then we have already agreed that ideally people should not be free to do what they see fit to do, but rather that they should be free to behave in any way that does not militate against the greatest happiness of the greatest number.

It therefore seems that to make the concept of autonomy an acceptable ideal, we have to define further the vague phrase 'think for oneself' and add a fourth necessary condition to the concept of autonomy. An autonomous person, besides thinking authentically, must also think well. Merely to go through the formal motions of thinking, e.g. I am blowing up the Houses of Parliament because Guy Fawkes did and I've always rather admired him, is not sufficient; one's thinking must embody standards; it must be of a certain quality.

On this claim two observations must be made. First it may well be argued that in adding this fourth necessary condition of autonomy, I am stretching the meaning of the term unduly. That is to say it may be argued that it is unreasonable to claim that being autonomous *means* thinking for oneself *and* thinking well. The answer to this is that it makes no significant difference to my argument: we can say either that autonomy means this and is a desirable ideal, or that it does not involve the idea of thinking well and is not a desirable ideal. My only concern is to argue that it is desirable that people should think for themselves provided that they do it well, and not otherwise.

Secondly it may be pointed out that even if we agree formally that thinking should embody standards, in practice there is the enormous question of what the standards of good thinking are and who decides them. Now it is certainly true that in the final analysis people disagree about whether, say, Marxism represents a well-thought position or whether the argument for utilitarianism in this book is to any extent sound. But this should not blind us to the fact that even in the realm of value judgements – notoriously difficult as they are – we can distinguish between arguments that are totally inadequate and those that at least deserve to be taken seriously. There are some formal standards – of coherence, consistency, relevance and so on – that we can and do agree on. And then there is the whole sphere of thinking concerned with the choice of appropriate means to ends, when the ends themselves are not in doubt, where it is simply not true to say that we cannot in principle distinguish between good and bad thinking. Likewise we can in general distinguish between good and bad thinking in the realm of the empirical sciences.

I therefore conclude that in principle there is no real objection to the notion of an autonomous person as being one who is subject only to the restraints of good reason. But does even this conception of autonomy constitute a desirable ideal? Considered as a political ideal, autonomy raises an exceedingly interesting problem for the utilitarian: convinced, as he is, that happiness is the ultimate consideration, is he to say that those who think well must agree with him and that therefore there is no clash between the ideal of autonomous individuals and the ideal of a society run on utilitarian lines? Or is he to concede that, convinced though he is, it is going too far to suggest that those who do not accept utilitarianism must be reasoning badly somewhere along the line? In which case, if he wishes to remain a utilitarian, he will presumably have to argue that the ideal of people behaving autonomously must be subordinated to the claims of happiness. That is to say he will argue that although it is important for people to think for themselves if they do it well, and although he is not prepared to say that people who reject utilitarianism are not doing it well, nonetheless people should not be allowed to *act* autonomously if their actions would go against the demands of utilitarianism.

It is quite conceivable that the dilemma here posed to the utilitarian – for neither way out seems obviously acceptable – will cause even some readers who up to this point have accepted the arguments for utilitarianism to think again. And I would not deny that the dilemma is great. However, our concern here is primarily educational. And considered as an educational ideal, then this conception of autonomy surely is desirable.

Promoting autonomy in this sense involves bringing people to question things for themselves rather than passively accepting the pronouncements of others, but doing so in an informed, able and pertinent manner. On utilitarian terms this is a highly desirable aim on the grounds that such questioning leads to understanding and paves the way to an increase in knowledge. It seems reasonable to suppose that a greater understanding spread more widely through the population and an increase in knowledge is a potential contribution to the long term happiness of society.

Finally it should be noted that the aim of promoting autonomy, understood as I have now defined it by four necessary criteria, will logically involve us in three immediate objectives: (i) It will be necessary to promote in individuals a concern to search out reasons and to think for themselves. (ii) It will be necessary to impart to children information and/or knowledge of where to look for various kinds of information and how to acquire it. It often seems to be forgotten by educational theorists that to think well or to come to reasonable decisions very often necessitates knowing some simple brute facts, as well as other, more *recherché* things. (iii) It will be necessary to promote in individuals a concern for the idea of *good reasoning* and some training in or initiation into the business of good reasoning. In particular, since the way in which one reasons may differ in various spheres – reasoning about moral values in an attempt to discover what ought to be done is quite different from reasoning about where the most appropriate place to locate an airport may be – it is vitally important that people should recognize the different kinds of approach that are necessary for different kinds of inquiry. (On this important point, see further Chapter 11.)

Perhaps one of the greatest threats to education at this time is that many of those who are pioneering against a view of education that discourages the child from questioning and thinking for himself simply ignore this need for *informed* and *rational* questioning.

REFERENCES

1 Dearden, R. F., 'Autonomy and Education' in Dearden, R. F., Hirst, P. H., and Peters, R. S. (eds), *Education and the Development of Reason* (Routledge & Kegan Paul, 1972).
   All references to Dearden in this chapter are to this article.

FURTHER READING

Much pioneering work on the concept of personal autonomy has been done by Dearden. See in particular his article 'Autonomy and Education' in Dearden, R. F., Hirst, P. H., and Peters, R. S. (eds), *Education and the Development of Reason* (Routledge & Kegan Paul, 1972), and his *Philosophy of Primary Education* (Routledge & Kegan Paul, 1968). The concept of autonomy is central to many of the papers collected by Doyle, J. F. (ed.), *Educational Judgements* (Routledge & Kegan Paul, 1973). See particularly in that volume Gewirth, A., 'Morality and Autonomy in Education' and Peters, R. S., 'Freedom and the Development of the Free Man'. See also, Quinton, A., 'Authority and Autonomy in Knowledge' in *P.E.S.G.B. Proceedings,* vol. 5, no. 2 (1971).

Chapter 9

Rights

Talk of 'rights' has a long history, and there is no reason to suppose that people are going to talk any less about 'rights' in the near future. In the past particular attention was given to what were called 'natural rights'; these were rights that were supposedly derived from and guaranteed by 'natural law' or the Roman *ius naturale* which corresponds to that 'which is always good and equitable'.[1] In other words a distinction was drawn between man-made law (or convention) and 'the notion of an eternal and immutable justice'[2] or 'a universal pattern of action applicable to all men everywhere'.[3] Philosophers, as one might expect, disagreed to some extent about what precisely were the natural rights that man had in consequence of this natural law. Locke, for instance, asserted that man had a natural right to property, life and liberty. Not all agreed on the first of these, at least. And they did not always have the same account to give of the foundation of natural law. Aquinas saw natural law as essentially the expression of God's will. Others saw no need for a religious foundation. But for a long time there was widespread agreement that there was such a thing as natural law and rights derived from it.

The phrase 'natural rights' gradually went out of fashion to some extent, but essentially the same idea was expressed by such phrases as 'inalienable rights' (used in the American Declaration of Independence) and 'human rights'. What is common to all such talk is the idea that there are certain rights that all people simply have, whatever the laws of the land in which they live, regardless of the circumstances of their birth or life, and even if in point of fact somebody is effectively denying them enjoyment of these rights. The preservation of such rights is, of course, the avowed purpose of the International Court at the Hague.

The sphere of education is increasingly beset by reference to 'rights'. There is the magazine *Children's Rights*; there are demands for children to have the right to determine their own dress, to opt out of religious worship and to participate in the management of schools. A. S. Neill refers to the child's 'right to climb trees'. Philosophers debate the question of whether everybody has a right to education. In the near future, if a Labour government keeps its promise effectively to put an end to all independent schools, the question is likely to arise as to whether parents do not have certain rights such as the right to have their children educated where they choose. So what rights do people have? What is the status of the various rights referred to here? Are they natural or human rights? Is it possible that utilitarianism offends certain human rights? What I want to consider in this chapter is not so much the question of specific rights as the language of rights itself. And I want to suggest that the language of rights is misleading.

Consider first the logic of the term 'rights'. A right is a thing to which one is entitled. What it means to say that somebody has a particular right is that that person has an entitlement. In the song 'Have I the right to hold you?' the singer means 'Are there considerations – in this case, let us say, such as that the two concerned are ex-lovers – that entitle me, as opposed to other people, to hold you?' Again 'You have no right to enter my house' means that you are not entitled to do so: there is nothing (no law, no permission, no custom) that entitles you to do so. 'I have the right to say what I think' is a claim to the effect that I am entitled to speak freely. When we say 'Parents do have the right to remove their children from R.E. lessons', we are saying that they are entitled to, and in this case we can point easily enough to the source of that entitlement: the 1944 Education Act.

Any right, then, involves an entitlement of some sort. One can have a right *to do* something (to exclude unwelcome visitors; to cast one's vote), a right to be free from something (to be *free from* imprisonment without trial), or simply a right *to* a thing (to one's possessions). But whatever the precise nature of the right, it is clear that any right logically presupposes some kind of rule-structure. For a right is an entitlement, and an entitlement presupposes some rule-system that provides entitlement. For example, suppose that we are watching a football match and I suddenly say that United have a right to a free kick. You ask me why. I reply 'Because X was offside'. My reply constitutes an acceptable reason; it reveals the source of the entitlement, but it only does so on the assumption that you and I and the players know the rules of football and are trying to abide by them. For it is the rule-structure lying behind the game that decides what entitlement what players have to do what in various situations. If we had no rules for football, if we imagine simply a free-for-all with a football, which by definition has no rules, it is obvious that it would make no sense to talk of rights. If there are no rules, there are no rights.

So far, so good. But although any reference to rights involves an appeal to some rule-structure, clearly there are different kinds of rights which therefore presuppose different kinds of rule-structure. There are various games which have their own rules and hence their own distinctive rights. There are institutions which have their own rules and hence their particular rights, as a club may have a rule that nobody should speak in the library and thereby confers on its members the right to enjoy silence. More significantly there are legal rights. These are rights that are dependent upon the law of the land. In theory therefore there is no problem about what legal rights we have: we have those that the law provides. We may not always like them, we may think that we *ought* to have others, but what one obviously cannot meaningfully do is claim that one has a right, if one means a legal right, that is not as a matter of fact guaranteed by the legal rule-structure.

Clearly the interesting type of rights, from our point of view, are the so-called natural rights, human rights, or, more simply, moral rights. The rights that, it is claimed, are not dependent on any local or temporal rule-structure. The question we have to ask is, What are people doing when they claim such moral rights? What was Locke doing when he asserted that man has a right to life, liberty and property? What are people doing when they claim a right to self-government, a right to choose their children's school, a right to work, to happiness or whatever? Quite obviously what they are doing is appealing to a presupposed moral schema or system of moral rules. They are assuming, and implicitly demanding that others share their assumption, that there is a particular system of moral rules binding on men, such that it is true that man ought to be free, ought to be self-governing, ought to be allowed to choose his children's school, and so on.

This of course is parallel to what is happening when a man says that he has a legal right and is thereby saying that there is a system of rules, embodied in our law, such that he is entitled to do such and such. But there is one crucial difference. Other rule-structures (legal, institutional, games) are in principle verifiable. There is no real room for argument as to what is involved in them. But, as we now know very well, the moral rule-structure is a hotly disputed entity. To claim a moral right involves claiming that a specific moral rule-structure has validity. In other words to substantiate that man has *any* specific moral right would involve substantiating a complete ethical position. We can only agree on whether or not people have particular moral rights if we share a particular moral viewpoint. We cannot say, for instance, that although it is well known that people have different over-all moral viewpoints, nonetheless everybody must agree that man has a right to provide his children with the best education he can, because on some moral viewpoints this would simply not be true.

What is the upshot of these considerations? Well, first, that the language of rights is in practice misleading. There is an air of finality about the phrase 'It's a right', no doubt due to the fact that in the legal sphere it can serve as a full stop to an argument. 'Why have the police not arrested him for doing such and such?' 'Because he has a right to do it.' That is all that needs to be said in that instance. But of course there is no reason why the claim that something is a right in the moral sphere should serve as a full stop. It is no step in an argument about whether people ought to be free, to say 'Man has a right to freedom', for that is precisely what the argument is about: whether he does or not, and if so, in what sense he does. Likewise those who object to totalitarianism on the grounds that it involves a denial of man's right to self-government are begging the question. They are not showing that totalitarianism is objectionable. They are merely pointing out that it involves something that they happen to regard as objectionable. The advocate of totalitarianism – if he had any sense – would not deny that it took away man's opportunity for self-government; he would deny that man necessarily ought to be self-governing. He would deny that there was such a thing as a right to self-government. To merely assert, in response to this, that man *does* have this right is not to argue at all. Again, those who object that utilitarianism might lead in practice to the suppression of various human rights, such as the right to freedom, are not really introducing separate considerations that have to be weighed against utilitarianism. They are really attempting to strike at the heart of it by saying that it is not true that the claims of happiness ought to be supreme. That is a point of view, but to substantiate it as the correct point of view it would be necessary to take on the whole argument for utilitarianism and to show where and why it is inadequate or at fault. It is simply meaningless to assert that utilitarianism *must* be unacceptable because it does not give priority to man's right to freedom.

What will the utilitarian say about all the proposed rights referred to as examples in this chapter? He will say that fundamentally man has a right to happiness. (The argument for this claim is contained in Part Two. If it is true that all people ought equally to have their happiness considered, then it is true that all men have a right to happiness.) The individual forfeits that right, however, if he attempts to gain his happiness at the expense of others. Beyond that, the individual has a right to whatever is, as a matter of fact, necessary to his happiness and its maintenance, provided that it does not militate against the greatest happiness of the greatest number. Thus the question of whether parents have a right to choose the type of education that their children should have must be decided by attempting to work out whether on balance, and taking the long-term view, allowing them to do so will contribute more or less to the happiness of the whole community. This will be an exceedingly complex calculation and probably there will always be disagreements about the accuracy of such a calculation. Nonetheless, this, according to utilitarianism, is the right way to approach the problem. Likewise the claim that men have a right to self-government, if it is true, as I believe it is, is true only because on balance people's happiness is more likely to be promoted by some form of self-government than by any other form of government. The question of the extent to which children should be entrusted with a share in the running of schools must be answered in the same way.

In sum, when people begin to talk of 'rights' we need to be on our guard, not because there are no rights, but because any assertion that there is a specific right is in fact a disguised appeal to some particular scheme of moral values. The appropriate response to any statement of the form 'man has the right . . .' is to ask what reasons can be given for claiming that man should have this right. Such a response will plunge one immediately into a full-scale discussion about ethics. Hard work, but there are no short cuts.

REFERENCES

1   *Digest*, Book 1.
2   Barker, E., *Traditions of Civility* (Shoe String Press, Connecticut, 1967).
3   Wild, J., *Plato's Modern Enemies and the Theory of Natural Law* (University of Chicago Press, 1953).

FURTHER READING

Melden, A. I. (ed.), *Human Rights* (Wadsworth, California, 1970) is a useful collection of classic philosophical texts on 'rights'. Cranston, M., *What are Human Rights?* (Bodley Head, 1973) contains a short essay and the texts of the main historical charters of human rights.

O'Connor, D. J., *Aquinas and Natural Law* (Macmillan, 1967) and d'Entreves A. P., *Natural Law* (Hutchinson, 1951) are useful.

At present little philosophical work has appeared in print relating to educational rights, though we may expect two such books from Routledge & Kegan Paul in the near future.

In the meantime see Gregory, I.M.M., 'The Right to Education' and Wringe, C. A., 'Pupils' Rights' in *P.E.S.G.B. Proceedings,* vol. 7, no. 1 (1973).

Chapter 10

Creativity

A number of colleges of education, schools and teachers set great store by the notion of developing creativity, and most of us are familiar with the idea of creative maths, creative English or, more generally, creativity hours and creative activity lessons. When it is suggested that creativity is important, the philosopher's first reaction is to want to know what is meant by the term. An obvious enough reaction, one would have thought, since though the word is impressive – it would be pleasant to be described as a creative thinker, for example – it is nonetheless mysterious and vague. What do I actually have to do to show that I am a creative thinker? How can we set about promoting creativity, how can we even be sure that it *is* important, unless we have a precise idea of what we are talking about? It is worth briefly illustrating just how out of control discussion can become when this task of elucidating meaning (conceptual analysis, as it is some-times called) is ignored or hastily and imperfectly carried out.

There is a little book by Hugh Lytton that seeks to summarise the psychological research carried out to date on creativity.[1] Lytton, like most of us, treats creativity as a normative concept; that is to say he values creativity, assumes that to call someone creative is to compliment them, and describes the fostering of creativity as providing 'the jam of education'.

Obviously if creativity is generally regarded as desirable, if we are all agreed that it ought to be promoted, it becomes particularly important to make sure that we are all talking about and concerned to promote the same thing. Lytton is aware of this need and his first chapter therefore attempts to clarify the concept of creativity. Unfortunately his attempt at definition does not proceed in a philosophical manner at all. The philosopher would be concerned to examine all the various uses of the terms 'creative' and 'creativity' in an attempt to arrive at a clearer understanding of what is common to all uses and the ways in which various uses may differ; he would seek to arrive at necessary and sufficient conditions for describing somebody as creative – that is to say, he would want to know whether there were certain conditions that would have to be met for some-body reasonably to be described as creative (these would be necessary conditions) and whether there were other conditions that, if they were met, would be sufficient to entitle us to call somebody creative. He would be particularly interested in apparently border-line cases, for it is by close consideration of such cases that one can most easily sort out precisely what one would demand of a genuinely creative person and what one would not. It is most important to stress that the philosopher engaged in conceptual analysis does not imagine that he is revealing some eternal truth and he does not see himself as entitled to lay down the law about how words must be used. He is concerned only with clarification. He does not, so to speak, assert that Shakespeare was creative and you may correctly describe him as such, whereas a 3-year-old child splashing paint on paper is not and you may not call him creative. You may do what you like. All the philosopher is concerned to do is to point out the great difference between describing Shakespeare and the child as creative.

Lytton's procedure, in attempting a definition, is to quote from various other authors whose views on creativity are for the most part expressed in terms no less obscure than the concept itself. Thus he quotes extensively from Koestler, whose concern is to express by analogy what the significance of creativity is felt to be, rather than to define the concept. But there is obviously a great difference between saying 'What I mean by a creative person is one who exhibits features A and B, and does Y and Z', and saying, as Koestler does,

'Every creative act . . . involves a regression to a more primitive level, a new innocence of perception liberated from the cataract of accepted beliefs. It is a process of *reculer pour mieux sauter*, of disintegration preceding the new synthesis, comparable to the dark night of the soul through which the mystic must pass.' (*The Sleepwalkers.*)

Only the former approach can help the reader appreciate what it is that he is being invited to value and promote in children. Lytton also quotes, and subsequently lays considerable stress on, Bruner's remark that 'it is implied that the act of one creating is the act of the whole man . . . that it is this rather than the product that makes it good and worthy', and he goes on, again following Bruner, to state that 'effective surprise' is the hallmark of the creative act. We thus arrive at two kinds of creativity – objective creativity and subjective creativity. Objective creativity is exhibited in works that cause others to feel 'effective surprise' when they see (or read or hear) them; subjective creativity is involved when the person producing the work himself feels 'effective surprise', as the child, for instance, may do when he produces a painting of square cows. We cannot, writes Lytton, 'deny the epithet "creative" to the five-year-old who with all his might and enthusiasm has given us an image of the world as he sees it, littered with square cows and people with round-bellied, neckless mums and dads'.[2]

Now this is all very well, but not to put too fine a point on it, it is getting us absolutely nowhere. Consider the obvious difficulties. First, what does it mean? What is the 'whole man'? What is 'effective surprise'? Is it to be identified with a feeling of satisfaction, of mute astonishment, of bewildered ecstasy, of reflective admiration or what? These phrases are every bit as obscure as the concept of creativity itself, which they are supposed to elucidate. Secondly, is this valuable? It was agreed that by common consent creativity was valuable, but then in agreeing that we use the term creative as a term of commendation, some of us at least may have had in mind the idea that Beethoven and Shakespeare were the sort of people who deserve to be called creative. If, as now appears to be the case, a child's drawing of square cows may be described as a creative work, it is surely at least open to question whether creativity is necessarily valuable. In any case, why can't we deny the epithet 'creative' to the 5-year-old's picture? Thirdly, do we accept Bruner's contention that a creative person is to be judged by reference to the *process* whereby he produces something (the act of the whole man) rather than by reference to the work he produces. Fourthly, in the case of objective creativity, whose 'effective surprise' counts as evidence that a work is creative? Is any body creative who produces any work that causes someone somewhere to feel 'effective surprise'? Finally, and above all, even if we knew precisely what was meant by 'effective surprise', how in point of fact does one judge whether people are feeling 'effective surprise'? How do we know, in the case of subjective creativity, whether the child does or does not experience 'effective surprise' when he paints his square cows? How do we know, in the case of objective creativity, whether the visitors at an exhibition of paintings are experiencing 'effective surprise' or not?

Lytton surprisingly, in view of the fact that it is his sole criterion for assessing creativity, but honestly, admits that we cannot judge or measure 'effective surprise'. The consequence on Lytton's own terms is inescapable: we cannot judge or measure creativity. If creativity is assessed by reference to 'effective surprise' and 'effective surprise' cannot be assessed, we cannot assess creativity. How then are we to set about promoting it, if there is no way of estimating our success? And what of all the creativity tests conducted by psychologists that Lytton is going on to review? What are they testing, since it cannot be creativity. What they really measure, for the most part, according to Lytton, is divergent and convergent thinking, but, although of the two types of thinking divergent thinking is the one that might most readily be associated with creativity, as Lytton admits, 'the evidence, such as it exists, that divergent test-scores are related to real-life creative performance is not very strong'.[3]

Examples of tests for assessing ability in divergent thinking are themselves not without interest. For instance children are asked to think of 'problems that might arise in taking a bath', to make a list of 'ideas for using an old shoe box' or to 'invent as many appropriate titles as possible for a given story'. But it is surely legitimate to question whether such tests are telling us very much about the children in question. 'Divergent thinking' (like creativity) sounds impressive, but there does not appear to be any evidence that success in one test will necessarily lead to success in other tests or in real-life problem solving. The fact that a child can think of many uses for an old shoe box would, therefore, strictly speaking, appear only to tell us that he can do precisely that, and that, if that shows he is an able divergent thinker, then all divergent thinking means is thinking of a lot of uses for old shoe boxes. So how valuable is it? There are, besides, two dangers inherent in the use of such tests that obviously need to be guarded against. First there does not appear to be any overt reference in such tests to the question of the quality of the answers given. For all that is said to the contrary, anything that the child proposes as a use for a shoe box might count as a legitimate answer. Consequently a high score on this particular divergent-thinking test might simply indicate that the child is unabashed about writing down as rapidly as possible a lot of nonsense. (Lytton quotes an example of a pretty silly suggestion for the use of the shoe box without indicating that he regards it as unacceptable in any way: 'Put a hole in it and use it as a watering can'.) Secondly, and more importantly, I think, if we assume that there must be some attention paid to the quality of the answers, then the conclusions about particular children, drawn from their performance at such tests, are going to depend to a marked extent upon the subjective judgement of the person giving the test as to what is a good answer. For example in Guilford's test that asks for as many appropriate titles as possible for a story, somebody has to judge the appropriateness of a given title. And Guilford himself went farther than this and divided the answers he received into 'clever' and 'non-clever': only clever responses count as evidence of divergent thinking. If we sweep away all the jargon (divergent thinking, open system thinking, lateral thinking), what we are really facing is the claim that it is valuable to be able to do things like think of uses for old shoe boxes and invent plot-titles. It may be, but we should remember that such tests involve the subjective assessment of 'good' answers by the tester, that there does not seem to be any evidence about the relation between success in such tests and 'originality', 'inventiveness' or 'problem-solving ability' in general, and that we have come a long, long way from the notion of bringing up a generation of creative individuals.

In a chapter entitled 'What Are Creative People Like?' Lytton refers to research carried out on various creative groups (creative architects and creative writers, for instance). He also mentions 'various checks' that were made to ensure that the individuals selected 'were really more creative' than other people, but he does not specify what the checks were. A moment's reflection at this point will lead one to see that something rather odd is going on. How could one specify ways of checking that a person was really creative without first defining the term? How can one begin to answer the question 'What are creative people like?' when one has just come to the conclusion that so-called creativity tests do not in fact assess creativity? How did the researchers in question ensure that the architects they selected were creative architects? Is it not transparently clear that the criteria used by the researchers to assess the creativity of those whom they are going to select for the experiment are going to govern the answer to the question 'What are creative people like?' It surely comes as no surprise that creative architects and writers are found to be 'well above the norm . . . in terms of the ability to achieve through independence rather than through conformity', since researchers who are preoccupied with such things as divergent thinking and originality would not select somebody whom they judged to be conformist as an example of a creative person in the first place. In other words there is at least a degree of circularity about the whole experiment: architects who are thought to be good and nonconformist architects are selected (for a bad, conformist architect would hardly count as creative) and the researchers conclude, after study of the selected group, that they 'achieve through independence'.

So much for the cautionary tale: the starting point was the assumption that creativity was desirable and that we ought to promote it – not an unreasonable assumption given the ordinary language connotations of 'creative'. But because the concept has not been clearly defined, before we know where we are we find ourselves apparently committed to the view that it is desirable that the child should 'effectively surprise' the teacher and pursue nonconformity. Perhaps it is, but so far no argument is forthcoming to support the contention: it rests entirely on the ambiguous nature of the concept of creativity.

Let us therefore start again, for it is surely not too difficult to make some brief and basic observations about the concept of creativity. First, I suggest, it is obviously a necessary condition of being creative that one should produce some original work that is one's own. 'Work' may be taken in this context to cover a wide variety of things ranging from a painting to an idea; 'original' need not mean startlingly out of the way or bizarre – the work may gain its originality from some small twist or new treatment of the material already used in the work of another, as composers have often written variations on a theme originally conceived by some other composer. By 'one's own' is meant that the work is the product of the agent's own working out, design or calculation, rather than produced by him in accordance with somebody else's instructions or by way of imitation. All I am saying here, then, is that if a man simply copies the work of others, or painstakingly works things out for himself but always produces something that we already have, or, of course, fails to produce anything at all, then he may be a number of excellent things, but he is not creative.

Fairly obviously the crucial question that arises in relation to the concept of creativity is the one already touched upon in reference to divergent thinking tests: does a creative person, by definition, have to produce work that embodies some standard of excellence, or may one appropriately refer to someone as creative when the work he produces, though original and his own, is absurd, poor or incoherent? (Incidentally the question of how in practice one decides whether certain works, such as art works, are works of excellence or not must not be confused with the separate question of whether, formally, creative people by definition must produce excellent works. Only the latter question concerns us here.)

Clearly, if we say that a creative person must produce works of quality, it is at once clear both that creativity has some value and why it does so. But in this case it is by no means clear that the sort of activities deemed to promote creativity in schools or to test it are in fact doing so: there is no obvious reason, despite Lytton's contrary claim, why we should regard the 5-year-old child's picture of square cows as evidence of his creativity, nor yet his list of uses for a shoe box or his sincerely written story. Nor is there any reason to assume that practice at such activities will lead to real creativity in later life – it is certainly not *necessary* to the development of creativity as we can see from countless historical examples: Mozart, Shakespeare and Goethe did not have the benefit of lessons devoted to thinking of uses for bricks, for example. Certainly a creative person must think for himself and sincerely express himself, since his work must be his own, and therefore one could hardly claim to be fostering creativity in children if one deliberately tried to destroy their spontaneity. But the creative person, on this view of creativity, has to be considerably more than spontaneous. He must express himself sincerely, but he must do so in deference to standards: his autobiography (or autobiographical essay) is only creative work if it is well-written work as well as sincere, from which it follows that if we wish to promote creativity in any sphere one of the things that we shall have to do is initiate children into the standards of excellence appropriate to that sphere.

If, on the other hand, we say that to be creative is not necessarily to produce works of value, or, alternatively, that the only measure of value is spontaneity or sincerity, then, of course, the 5-year-old child may well be creative when he paints square cows or writes autobiographically. But in this case the question arises as to whether creativity is particularly, if at all, valuable. Let us not be dictated to by words and their associative ideas. Granted that 'creative' sounds flattering and that we unreflectively assume that creativity is valuable, if all that creative means is 'production of work that is original and one's own' without reference to quality, which is what some apparently do mean by it, then we are nonetheless perfectly entitled to ask why it should be regarded as valuable.

The situation is this: there are certain activities that some would have us commend in schools on the grounds that they are creative activities. As examples I have taken thinking of uses for an old shoe box, writing that is ideally subject to no correction in respect of objective standards, drawing or painting that is similarly divorced from the claims of objective standards of quality, and thinking up titles for a story. The simple claim that these activities must be desirable because they are creative is unacceptable because it is ambiguous. If we attempt to clarify the situation it seems that one or more of the following claims might be being made:

1.   The work produced by children, when given the opportunity to express themselves or think for themselves, is creative in the sense of original and of quality judged by objective standards.

2.   The work produced in such circumstances is of quality because the only measure of quality is spontaneity and sincerity.

3.   The work actually produced in schools in these circumstances may very often lack quality in itself, but as a result of the opportunity for such work – unencumbered by corrections and reference to standards – children will become creative, in the sense of producers of original work of quality, at a later stage.

4.   The argument for creative activities does not lie in an appeal to the quality of the work done at all, but in the fact that children take pleasure in them. To this may be added some such claim as that the opportunity to engage in such activities may have great therapeutic value or serve to boost confidence in children whose schooling would otherwise consist of repeated corrections and criticisms.

As far as the first claim goes no more needs to be said. It simply is not true, in general, that spontaneous and uninhibited activity in any of these spheres (let us take writing as the central example) results automatically in productions of quality. To be able to produce writing of quality one needs to be initiated into certain standards of excellence. Great writers may go beyond or break the existing standards, but they do so with understanding of what it is that they are going beyond and why they are doing so. To take a pretty basic example: writers such as Joyce dispense to a large extent with the conventional rules of punctuation. But there is obviously a considerable difference between doing this with understanding and for specific purposes, and doing it because one does not know anything about punctuation. If children are to be left to express themselves in words without any understanding of punctuation then they are denied the use of one tool that the writer uses precisely to bring quality to his work and the rest of us are left in a position where it is virtually impossible to assess the quality of the work. More generally (returning to the fundamental point) the writings of children (and indeed of most adults) that are the product of however sincere an attempt to express themselves just are not creative works in the sense of original works of quality judged by objective standards.

The second claim would get round this objection. For if the only criterion of excellence in writing is sincerity, then obviously the spontaneous and sincere product of the child would be excellent. But despite the fact that some educationalists do claim that sincerity is the only criterion of quality, I shall dismiss the suggestion as absurd. All one can say is that if one were to accept it, that would merely invite the further question of whether there was any value in creative work. If we grant that by definition any sincerely expressed piece of writing is excellent writing (so that a letter to the *Times* expressing the writer's conviction that the world is going to the dogs is by definition as good a piece of writing as a Pinter play), then we may quite reasonably go on to ask whether there is any particular value in 'excellent writing'.

The third claim lacks any real evidence to support it. By citing creative writers who became such without having experienced any opportunities for creative writing, simply in the sense of writing that was not subject to any criticism or correction, at school, one can show that these opportunities are not necessary for the development of creative writers. On the other hand, since *one* criterion of the creative individual is agreed to be originality, there may well be something to be said for the view that in general some encouragement for children to write freely as they wish to, without being concerned about and restricted by considerations of objective standards of excellence, may contribute to the development of creativity. This is obviously a matter of degree, and the essential point remains that they will not become creative individuals, unless, as well as developing the ability to express themselves sincerely, they also acquire the ability to express themselves well by objective standards. This point can be most effectively made by consideration of the notion of a creative mathematician (because the standards of excellence in mathematics are more obviously recognisable than the standards of excellence in literature). A creative mathematician will be one who produces original work in the sphere of mathematics, but whose work is also valid. He must be a good mathematician as well as an original one. We are not likely to produce creative mathematicians therefore if, besides encouraging people to think for themselves and be original, we do not also promote competence in the field of mathematics as it now stands.

The fourth argument for creativity introduces an entirely new dimension. Up to this point we have taken it for granted that ideally we would like to produce creative individuals in the sense of individuals who display originality and quality in their work. On almost any view, no doubt, there would be an argument for saying that this is something that society ought to be concerned to do. From the utilitarian point of view it is desirable on the grounds that the existence of creative individuals is likely to contribute in the long term to the promotion of happiness in the community. This is obviously so in respect of such things as the sciences. For instance, it seems that at the present time the world faces something approaching an energy crisis. We need original and valid ideas for new sources of energy, if the world is to avoid a breakdown in energy supply and the resultant confusion and misery. In respect of the arts the case is perhaps not so clear: nonetheless it does not seem unreasonable to argue that the pleasure given directly by creative art and the indirect consequences of art, such as the fostering of heightened perception and understanding of ourselves and others that can come about, both contribute positively to the sum of human happiness.

The fourth argument goes directly to this question of happiness. It is suggested that the value of creative activities in schools lies in the satisfaction that in one way or another the individual may find in them, rather than in any objective value in the work produced. Is the utilitarian, with his emphasis on happiness, committed to a stress on creative activities on these grounds? Is it good – to exaggerate the point – that children should scribble away and splash paint about because it enables them to relax and feel happy, and that they should not be subject to the attempt to restrict their spontaneity by introducing them to the notion of standards of excellence? The answer to this is yes and no. Yes, of course, the utilitarian must regard it as desirable that children, as much as anyone else, should be happy and that their education should not be a misery, and insofar as it is true that such activities are enjoyable (both immediately and in the long-term sense that they promote confidence which is liable to contribute to happiness) that is a good reason for encouraging them. But, and it is a large but, if the teacher is really committed to the value of happiness, then he is clearly going to have to do a lot more for the children in his care to prepare them for a life in which they will be happy, and will help to contribute to the sum total of happiness in society, than leave them to doodle away. In particular it would probably ultimately contribute considerably to their happiness if they do not grow up with an inflated idea of the value of spontaneous scribbling.

In short, for reasons that have already been given, it is desirable that we should attempt to promote creativity in children, in the sense of a tendency to produce original and good work in various spheres. In order to do this it is logically necessary to introduce children to an understanding of the standards of excellence that apply in various spheres as well as to promote a willingness to display originality. Clearly, despite all this emphasis on creativity, only a minority of children actually turn out to be creative writers, mathematicians and so on. That being the case, it may be suggested that the emphasis on quality is relatively more important than the emphasis on originality. Original (and sincerely produced) work in literature, mathematics or anything else that actually lacks any quality is a hollow achievement; whereas work that, though unoriginal, has quality and thereby indicates a grasp of the relevant standards of excellence has at least that to be said for it. On the other hand some degree of concern with encouraging children to work in various spheres without feeling hampered by the thought of the teacher's red pencil poised to expose its weaknesses may well be defended on the grounds that it has value in the immediate pleasure it gives and helps to promote in the child the willingness to think for and to be himself. But it is a matter of degree. What has to be rejected in my view, is any suggestion that the question of standards can be ignored. The long-term happiness of the human race is dependent on maintaining a formal commitment to the importance of standards.

REFERENCES

1 Lytton, H., *Creativity and Education* (Routledge & Kegan Paul, 1971).
2 Ibid., p. 3.
3 Ibid., p. 42.

FURTHER READING

'Creativity' is perhaps an overworked concept in the philosophy of education. A seminal article so far as clearing away some of the confusion and nonsense surrounding the concept goes is White, J. P., 'Creativity and Education: a philosophical analysis' in Dearden, R. F., Hirst, P. H., and Peters, R. S. (eds), *Education and the Development of Reason* (Routledge & Kegan Paul, 1972). Articles that pursue the concept farther than I have allowed myself to do in the text include Elliott, R. K., 'Versions of Creativity' in *P.E.S.G.B. Proceedings*, vol. 5, no. 2 (1971) and, by the same author, a reply to Olford, J. E., 'The Concept of Creativity' in *P.E.S.G.B. Proceedings*, vol. 5, no. 1 (1971).

Much of the educational literature relating to creativity is in fact psychological in kind and this aspect of the topic is well summarised by Lytton, H., *Creativity and Education* (Routledge & Kegan Paul, 1971).

Chapter 11

What is Worthwhile?

It has been convincingly argued that by definition 'education' involves 'initiation into worthwhile activities'. And, at any rate, I take it as axiomatic that anybody who feels a commitment to education, anybody who wants to teach or who regards the business of education as important, must be concerned in principle to ensure that children come to engage in worthwhile activities. What activities *are* worthwhile is of course another question, and one about which there may be widespread disagreement, but one cannot conceive of someone who believed that education was important and yet who believed at the same time that children should, or quite acceptably could, devote all their time at school to worthless pursuits. If what is happening is altogether worthless, then, by definition, it is not important.

In this chapter I am concerned with the question: how do we evaluate any proposed educational activity? I shall not try to be very precise about what specific activities are valuable, since that would involve detailed knowledge of what was actually entailed in all the activities in question and a considerable amount of empirical information, as well as evaluative considerations. For example, to answer the question 'Is studying chemistry valuable?' one would need to be able to say: (i) Studying chemistry involves such and such. (ii) Children of specific ages may study chemistry in this way, and the result will be such and such. (iii) This result is valuable. I am concerned only with the question that nobody can ultimately avoid: on what criteria does one assess something as more or less valuable?

My answer is simple (and not, I imagine, unexpected, in view of Part Two of this book), although, for the reasons indicated in the previous paragraph, it will not make the actual decisions as to what specific activities ought to be pursued in schools easy to make.

The criterion of worthwhileness is pleasure, but that is not to say simply that an activity is worthwhile if it gives the agent pleasure. Rather we have to say that an activity is worthwhile *insofar as* it promotes pleasure and/or diminishes pain in general. We have to take into account not only the degree of pleasure immediately experienced by the individual agent, but also the pleasure arising out of the activity for other people. And furthermore we have to take into account any aspects of the activity that may indirectly contribute to an increase in pleasure. For example, even if as a matter of fact no one took any pleasure in being a doctor, the pursuit of medicine would still clearly contribute indirectly to increasing pleasure. All these factors have to be taken into account in estimating the worthwhileness of an activity, because our concern is to produce as much pleasure as possible for all people.

It follows from this that no activity is *necessarily* worthwhile. No activity just is and must be worthwhile for all time, for it is always conceivable that an activity that does as a matter of fact provide great pleasure might cease to do so. It also follows that worthwhile is in fact a *relative* term. Things are not simply worthwhile or worthless – they are more or less worthwhile. We therefore do not need to concern ourselves with a question such as 'How widespread does the pleasure arising from an activity have to be before it becomes worthwhile?' An activity is relatively worthwhile insofar as it promotes relatively more pleasure than other activities. To describe an activity simply as 'worthwhile', as we undoubtedly sometimes do, is thus in effect to say that it is particularly worthwhile or that its propensity to promote pleasure is so marked as to make it indisputably worth pursuing.

Thus, to take an example, we can reasonably say that the study and practice of law is a worthwhile activity; for that is to say that it is particularly conducive to pleasure or that it is relatively worthwhile in that it is more conducive to pleasure than certain other activities such as making mud pies. And this it certainly is, although we are now heading for trouble which we have already met in Chapter 6 relating to the problem of calculation. The practice of law is relatively worthwhile and certainly more worthwhile than making mud pies, because even if the unlikely circumstances arose that everybody actually found more pleasure for themselves in making mud pies than practising law, it is entirely reasonable to claim that the community would ultimately lose more in terms of pleasure from having no legal system than it would gain from making mud pies. In realistic terms the practice of law is a relatively worthwhile activity because it is an activity that can both give pleasure to the individual practising it and contribute greatly to the overall pleasure of the community.

I have already argued in Chapter 6 that, although it is true that the quantity of pleasure arising from various activities or rules cannot be literally quantified, this does not mean that one cannot make reasonable estimates. Particularly where formulating moral rules is concerned, it is not only possible to make such estimates, but it is entirely unreasonable to suggest that there can be any doubt that a rule such as 'Thou shalt not kill' is justified on utilitarian grounds. However, when we turn to the question of grading activities in order of worthwhileness, it is true, I think, that we must be content to accept that there will be a range of activities in the middle that it is neither possible nor profitable to try to compare in terms of worthwhileness. That is to say that insofar as different people happen to take pleasure in playing cricket, playing chess, watching films, going to the theatre, mountaineering, cooking, or stamp-collecting, they are all to some extent worthwhile activities. It would be absurd to try to establish that playing cricket was more worthwhile than mountaineering.

But we now come to a crucial stage in the argument of this book. For it is clear that one of the central problems in estimating worthwhileness is that very often we are faced with a straight conflict between what it gives the individual pleasure to do and what will contribute to the pleasure of people in general if done. For example, there cannot be much doubt that if as a matter of fact people took as much pleasure in reading literature as in playing Bingo the former would be *more* worthwhile. Why is this so? It is because of the respective natures of the activities themselves. Bingo has virtually no instrumental value. That is to say, essentially the playing of Bingo carries with it no further consequences beyond the immediate pleasure it gives. Whereas literature by its nature has the potentiality to bring about significant changes in the individual; it may affect his outlook, his insight, his perception and his ideas, which may in turn have significant repercussions on the sum total of pleasure in the community. To put the same point another way, to play Bingo involves only limited capabilities and does not affect the pleasure of those not playing at all, either directly or indirectly. To read literature may indirectly affect the pleasure of others and requires rather more in the way of human capacities. People who are so constituted as only to be able to take pleasure in playing Bingo are by definition lacking in those capacities that are necessary to enable one to take pleasure in literature and which may contribute indirectly to the maintenance and promotion of happiness in a community. To keep the matter simple, we can say, for example, that to take pleasure in literature it is necessary to be to some extent interested in and aware of the complexities of human relationships, since these are the subject matter of a great deal of literature. Conversely to read literature is to gain some increase in one's understanding of the complexities of human relationships. Such understanding may indirectly contribute to an increase in one's own happiness or one's ability to contribute to that of others.

Two things must be stressed. First, insofar as the above example involving reference to understanding the complexities of human relationships is accepted, it must be understood that I am not trying to claim that such understanding is in itself valuable. Nothing is valuable in itself except pleasure. Nor am I suggesting that understanding is itself necessarily pleasurable. The claim is that such understanding may indirectly contribute to an increase in pleasure in a community. Secondly the claim is only that it *may* contribute, not that it necessarily will. It would obviously be absurd to claim that those who take pleasure in reading are *ipso facto* greater contributors to the happiness of the community than those who play Bingo.

But it is not necessary to make such an extravagant claim. All that is necessary to support the claim that the reading of literature would be more worthwhile than the playing of Bingo, assuming that people could take the same amount of pleasure in doing both, is the suggestion that the nature of literature is such that it is likely to call forth from people and develop in them characteristics that will contribute to the sum of happiness in the community or provide them with an awareness which may likewise contribute to the sum of happiness. This is to suggest that the community as a whole would suffer more if it lost the sort of people who take pleasure in literature than if it lost the sort of people who take pleasure in Bingo. This is not of course a provable contention, but it is none the worse for that. If it is a reasonable contention, it is worth acting on.

The significance of this line of argument is as follows. Insofar as there are some activities that contribute more than others, directly or indirectly to increasing pleasure generally, it would obviously be desirable, if possible, that people should come to find their immediate pleasure in such activities. And this is where education comes in. For through education we can be initiated into and come to take pleasure in activities that we would not otherwise have taken pleasure in.

The task of education is therefore, broadly speaking, to develop people in such a way that they will be enabled to take pleasure in life, while contributing to the maximization of pleasure in the community as a whole. What is educationally worthwhile is whatever will contribute to that end. Since people are not born with a pre-ordained capacity to take pleasure only in a certain restricted range of activities, it is the task of education to initiate children into those activities that seem most likely to contribute directly or indirectly to pleasure, discounting the immediate pleasure of the agent. For the object is to bring people up so that they will find their pleasure in such activities. Now since the crucial determiner of the extent of happiness in a community, over and above the opportunity for people to pursue those activities that they do take pleasure in, are the qualities or characteristics of the people in that community, it follows that ideally children should be introduced to those activities that may contribute to the development of desirable characteristics. These are the activities that they should be brought to take pleasure in; these are the activities that are particularly educationally worthwhile.

So the next question is, What characteristics are desirable? What characteristics are most likely to contribute to the happiness of a community? I feel some embarrassment in listing the characteristics I have in mind, since it will at once be clear that, before one could make effective use of them as guide-lines, they would require close philosophical analysis which they are not going to get in these pages. Nonetheless I think that my general point can be understood in advance of that analysis. The characteristics are:

1. A tendency to want to know the reason why.
2. A concern for coherent reasoning and ability in reasoning.
3. A concern to understand other people and an ability to do so ('understand' here in the sense of 'have empathy for').

The development of such characteristics in people, I suggest, insofar as these characteristics serve to prevent unjustified and dogmatic conviction, error and the failure to take account of others, must contribute to the sum of human happiness. Consequently those activities that promote such characteristics are educationally particularly worthwhile.

It would, of course, be an enormous undertaking to attempt to establish precisely what activities were indispensable or most worthwhile from the educational point of view, even in the light of the utilitarian criterion that has been clearly expounded and taking into account the further considerations that I have mentioned. This is that dreaded point at which the philosopher, much to the dissatisfaction of most, retires, mumbling that to go further than this is not a philosopher's job. And, of course, he is quite right that once objectives have been sorted out and terms clarified it is largely an empirical matter as to what are the most effective means to achieve ends. My intention here has been to indicate the sort of way in which I believe that one should set about considering what is educationally worthwhile. Nonetheless I shall add in the following paragraphs some broad suggestions of a slightly more practical nature for consideration.

'The tendency to want to know the reason why' can presumably only be cultivated in an atmosphere where one is allowed (possibly encouraged) to demand to know the reason why. Concern for this characteristic therefore commits one to rejecting any educational system that attempts to suppress questioning and teaches that all is known and must be accepted uncritically from those in authority. But at the same time 'wanting to know the reason why' is a hollow kind of quality if one is in no position to understand the reason why. Likewise concern for and ability in coherent reason presuppose understanding of what reasoning is coherent. Now although we cannot ensure that all people will be proficient in reasoning in all matters, what we can attempt to do is to provide all children with some understanding of the formal demands of coherent reasoning and the logically distinct ways in which different kinds of questions have to be approached. Thus we can attempt to promote respect for such formal principles as those of consistency and relevance, by drawing attention to examples of inconsistency and irrelevance, by studying examples of coherent reasoning and by encouraging children to reason coherently for themselves. Fairly obviously one cannot envisage something like 'coherent reasoning' lessons in the abstract. Coherent reasoning is context-bound: a coherent argument for Communist presupposes information, considerations and ways of proceeding that are not all to be found in a coherent argument to establish a hypothesis in physics. But, from the point of view of promoting respect for the formal notions of consistency and relevance, it is presumably not particularly important in what spheres practice is obtained. Consistency is consistency, whether it occurs in a scientific demonstration or an argument about a film.

On the other hand it is also important, if error is to be avoided, that it should be appreciated that different kinds of questions have to be approached in different ways. It is not simply that to resolve different kinds of problems different kinds of evidence may have to be adduced, but also that different kinds of question are logically distinct. Essentially there are two types of knowledge or ways of reasoning, each of which encompasses various spheres of human inquiry. These two types of knowledge I shall call, respectively, philosophical knowledge and scientific knowledge. (If the reader is acquainted with Hirst's work on the forms of knowledge, he will appreciate that I am both drawing on that work and disagreeing with it to a substantial extent. See Further Reading.)

Philosophical knowledge is that way of reasoning that is appropriate to all matters that cannot be decided by empirical inquiry; scientific knowledge is that way of reasoning that is appropriate to all empirical inquiry.

It may perhaps reasonably be argued that the sphere of mathematics represents a third type of knowledge that is neither philosophical nor scientific pure and simple, but sui generis. However all other spheres of human inquiry may be subsumed under the heading of either philosophical or scientific knowledge. Thus questions such as 'How ought people ideally to behave?', 'What makes a painting or a work of literature good art?', 'Does God exist?' are philosophical questions. Whereas 'What proportion of working-class children attain university places?', 'What happens if nitric acid and water are mixed in equal proportions?' or 'What sources of energy may there be, besides those with which we are familiar?' are scientific questions. It will be at once apparent that some subject matters may be approached either philosophically or scientifically. Thus one may explore morality from a philosophical point of view ('What is morality?', 'What principles ought we to adopt?'), or from a scientific point of view ('What moral values do people hold?'). Furthermore some areas of inquiry, such as history, may invite both ways of reasoning. 'Was Athenian democracy a shambles?' To answer the question it would be necessary to ask 'What were the features of Athenian democracy?' and 'Were these features, in sum, shambolic or not?' The latter, involving as it does the need for value judgements, requires philosophic reasoning; the former, scientific.

Hirst argues that there are eight distinct forms of knowledge (mathematics, physical sciences, human sciences, history, religion, literature and fine arts, philosophy, and morals) and that ideally children ought to be initiated into all these forms, not so that they become expert physicists, historians and so on, but so that they understand what is distinctive to being a historian, a physicist and so on, and so that they do not confuse historical questions with questions in physics.

I am suggesting, as against that view, that these are not all distinctive forms of knowledge. Morality, for instance, is not a form of knowledge at all; it is a specific area for human inquiry, which may invite philosophical or scientific questions. It is not necessarily important that all children should have some understanding of the ways in which all eight of these spheres of inquiry are or may be explored. It is not, for instance, necessarily important that all children should have some understanding of the physical sciences as such. What *is* important is to understand the distinction between philosophical and scientific knowledge and, ideally, to recognise in any given inquiry which type of knowledge or way of reasoning is appropriate. In other words, it is important to recognise that to ask 'What paintings are popular?' is logically distinct from asking 'What paintings are good?' and has to be approached in a different kind of way. It is not necessarily important that all children should actually have some experience in dealing with either of these specific questions relating to the sphere of fine arts. In order to promote understanding of the two types of knowledge all that is necessarily required is initiation into some sphere of inquiry that exemplifies either type.

How one may hope to promote empathy or understanding of and concern for others would seem to me to be the single most interesting and difficult question in education. I certainly do not know the answer to it. But it may be suggested that since empathy involves the ability to move beyond one's own limited way of looking at the world and responding to it, at the very least it will be necessary to impart to children the realisation that other people may be different and some awareness of the possible range of different ways of looking at and responding to the world. In other words it is necessary to widen the child's experience of human feelings, reactions and motivations, beyond the limits set by his personal experience. Although one must resist the tendency of some advocates of the study of literature (and to a lesser extent history) to talk as if it were self-evident or proven that such study does lead to greater empathy, it is surely plausible to regard these areas of study (particularly literature) as more likely than most other areas of study to do so. Literature is, after all, a body of work that is by and large about human feelings, reactions and motivations. To read the novels of D. H. Lawrence is to meet certain types of people; to read the novels of George Gissing is to meet, on the whole, very different types of people. To study and reflect upon these new acquaintances is to widen one's understanding of different people and their different ways of looking at the world. (It seems much more difficult to feel convinced that the study of literature tends to promote an actual feeling of concern for other people.)

Attempting to draw these general (and insufficiently worked out) points together, I would argue that what is educationally worthwhile for all children, insofar as they have the capacity to handle it, is initiation into the study of literature, moral philosophy, mathematics and history. Beyond that there are many worthwhile pursuits that might be encouraged according to the individual interests and talents of the child (e.g. music, science, fine arts), some of which it is important for the future welfare of the community that some should be initiated into – most notably the human and physical sciences. Literature I advocate on the hypothesis that it is liable to contribute to the promotion of empathy; mathematics in view of its sui generis status and its evident utility up to a certain point. Moral philosophy I advocate as the most suitable area in which to initiate the child into philosophical knowledge, partly on the transient grounds that it is an area that seems more widely appealing than most other areas of philosophical inquiry, partly on the grounds that it is a matter of importance, from the point of view of concern for the welfare of the community, that people should examine the question of human conduct, and partly for reasons relating to the concepts of indoctrination that will be explained in the final chapter on moral education. The inclusion of history as an ingredient in a common-core curriculum, is perhaps the least well argued. I select it as the vehicle for initiating the child into scientific knowledge not because it is the purest example of that type of knowledge (it isn't, as I have already indicated), but because it may be hoped (a) that the study of history gives more scope for individual questioning and for thinking for oneself, even at the school level than, say, chemistry does, and (b) that through a study of the past our understanding of the present may be informed. One important aspect of any question relating to the general problem of 'What should society be like?' is to have some idea of what is likely to happen if such and such occurs. History cannot, any more than anything else, predict the future: but history can inform us of the sort of things that tend to happen if . . . For example, the study of Athenian democracy cannot be allowed to dictate our views on democracy; but in considering the question of a form of democracy involving direct rather than representative government, besides considering the evaluative questions and the practical problems of the mechanics of the matter, it surely might be no bad thing to have a thorough understanding of the only truly direct democracy there has ever been, notwithstanding the differences in circumstance between then and now. (*Was* it a shambles?)

. . . . . .

If what I have said about the *way* in which the question of what is educationally worthwhile is accepted – as it may be, of course, without any commitment to my attempts to outline what *specifically* might be regarded as worthwhile being involved – then it follows that certain other approaches to the question have to be rejected. In order to redress the balance slightly, I shall now briefly consider some of these approaches and explain why they seem to me to be inadequate.

1. I share the view of those radicals who scorn an approach to the question of what is worthwhile that proceeds by assuming that there are certain subjects that just are self-evidently inherently worthwhile, without giving reason for that judgement.

> 'There are thousands of teachers', according to Postman and Wein-gartner, 'who believe that there are certain subjects that are "inherently good", that are "good in themselves", that are "good for their own sake". When you ask "Good for whom?" or "Good for what purpose?" you will be dismissed as being "merely practical" and told that what they are talking about is literature qua literature, grammar qua grammar, and mathematics per se.'[1]

No doubt there are some such teachers. But I have *not* argued that literature, for instance, is inherently good qua literature. And what I do not see any reason to accept is the apparent conviction of these same radicals that this argument shows that none of the traditional subjects in schools are worth studying. It may very well be worthwhile for children to study literature, classics or chemistry for the sort of reasons that have been given. (Although, of course, there may also be good reason for arguing that the subjects should be taught in different ways or that they should not be treated in the self-contained compartmentalized ways that they often have been.) The fact that some subjects are taught and defended by people who refuse to justify the teaching of those subjects, though it may point to a poverty of good sense in the defenders, obviously does not show that justification could not be given or that the subjects in question are not worthwhile.

Furthermore the criterion for producing a worthwhile curriculum put forward by Postman and Weingartner is quite unacceptable as a sufficient or sole criterion. They argue, with magnetic verve and dash, that the entire curriculum might 'consist of questions'. For example: 'How can "good" be distinguished from "evil"?', 'How can you tell what something "is" or whether it is?', 'Of the important changes going on in our society, which should be encouraged and which restricted? Why? How?' 'What are the conditions for sustaining life in plants?'[2] It is suggested that the teacher should not attempt to structure or control any discussion that might follow from these questions: he 'is interested in the students' developing their own criteria or standards for judging the quality, precision and relevance of ideas'. No idea from a student should be 'excluded . . . because it is not germane. (Not germane to what? Obviously, it is germane to the student's thinking about the problem.)'³ As a specific example of the sort of way not to proceed they cite the study of Ancient Greece and dismiss as 'pretentious trivia' questions such as 'Why was Athens the leading city in Greece?'

If persuasive oratory, rather than sound reasoning, deserves to win arguments, then Postman and Weingartner deserve to be regarded as the great educationalists of our time. Enormous skill is devoted to the sophistic game of making 'the worse cause appear the better'. But surely the incoherence of this is manifest, if we care to *think* about it. The questions are (to me) fascinating and well worth pursuing. But they happen to be extremely sophisticated and complex questions, the first two philosophical, the last scientific and the third both. To want students to pursue such questions is one thing; to define 'pursuing' them as saying *anything* that seems to be a good idea to oneself is just absurd. If, in response to the first question, I say that 'good' can be distinguished from 'evil' by counting the number of times that an action is performed, I am simply wasting everybody's time including my own; I evidently do not even understand the question. The truth is that these questions could not be seriously pursued without (a) some degree of understanding of the nature of the question, (b) some skill in handling the question in the appropriate manner, (c) some concern for the formal standards of good reasoning, and (d) some information. What changes, for instance, *are* going on in our society? Which are 'important'? Consequently the 'entire "curriculum"' could not consist of questions. Furthermore the implication of the scorn attached to a question such as 'Why was Athens the leading city in Greece?' is that Postman and Weingartner are determined to exclude from the student's mind whole areas of inquiry that might be germane. 'Germane to what?' Germane to the question immediately to hand. If students are not allowed to study 'any century but this, or any country but [their] own' – which Postman and Weingartner do not say, but which seems to be the logical implication of their dismissal of history and the exclusively contemporary nature of their questions – their answer to questions about 'important changes in our society' will presumably take on a horrifically insular, not to say unimaginative or just plain ignorant tone.

What the 'questions curriculum' may perhaps give us is a desirable suggestion of a *way* in which to conduct education in respect of older students. In other words, if we presuppose that education has already provided skills in reasoning technique, awareness of two types of knowledge, practice and information, then it may be very much better to encourage the pursuit of these complex questions than to 'feed' allegedly indisputable answers. What this notion does not give us is any criterion for assessing what in general is educationally worthwhile.

2. Secondly I do not accept that the criterion of worthwhileness can be the child's own evaluation or his own view of what is important, relevant or worth doing. The term 'relevance', incidentally, is rapidly achieving the status of a slogan that we could well do without. We are repeatedly being told that this, that and the other are irrelevant, as if there were no doubt about what or whom it ought to be relevant to. But that is precisely what there is doubt about. It is all very well to assert that the speeches of Cicero are irrelevant to a working-class child in this century; in one sense of course they are: they do not directly relate to his present experiences, they do not seem relevant to him because they are new to him and he does not see what there is about them that might relate to him and his experience. In this sense, *nothing* is relevant to him that is not already a part of his experience and something which he regards as important to him. If we attempt to make education relevant, in this sense of relevant, we therefore condemn children to grow up within the confines of the environment into which they were born, or, at best, to move out of those confines only so far as the children themselves immediately desire to move. If, on the other hand, we do not arbitrarily define relevance in this limited way, it is not at all clear that even the speeches of Cicero are necessarily irrelevant. They may well be very relevant to certain objectives such as increasing the child's awareness of the way in which words may be skilfully manipulated in such a way as to win a legal case against all odds; and increasing that awareness might be very relevant to improving the child's chances of seeing through attempts to con him. By the end of this chain of reasoning even he might agree that it was of immediate relevance to him that he should be able to see through persuasive but fallacious arguments that might be put before him.

It may well be that a lot of what goes on in schools at the moment is nonetheless irrelevant in the straightforward sense that it does not have any bearing, even indirectly and taking the long-term view, on the life that the child is ultimately going to lead. It may also be that the child's view of what is relevant to him and his evaluation of what is worth doing are significant factors to be taken into account in trying to decide what should be done in schools. To lay down a programme while totally ignoring these factors might result in a situation in which children could scarcely be motivated to proceed and in which they were thoroughly miserable, for instance. But the child's own evaluation of what is worthwhile cannot be accepted as the sole criterion of what is worthwhile.

To say that it is leads to the conclusion that there is in fact no distinction between any activities in respect of worthwhileness, since it is conceivable that some child somewhere might be found to value any activity one can think of. But if all activities are equally worthwhile, it is logically absurd to refer to anything as the criterion of worthwhileness. Consequently one ends up in the contradictory position of asserting on the one hand that there are no criteria for worthwhileness and on the other hand that the criterion of worthwhileness is the child's view of what is important. Besides which, if we do accept the child's evaluation as the sole criterion of worthwhileness, there is no escaping the conclusion that things like stamping on goldfish, eating chocolate cake until one is sick, teasing people, and any other imaginable activity may in principle be worthwhile. I appeal to the reader to concede without argument that such activities are not and cannot be worthwhile. If he insists on argument I can only refer him back to my positive argument that nothing is worthwhile that does not contribute to the long-term sum of human happiness, and these activities do not. Time devoted to stamping on goldfish is time that might have been better spent. If such activities cannot be worthwhile, then, since a child (or an adult for that matter) might think that they were, the child's evaluation cannot be the sole criterion of worthwhileness.

3. It is often suggested that the essential criterion in deciding what is a worthwhile educational activity is children's needs. The objection to this approach is that it is insufficiently precise. What do children need? Need for what? One cannot have needs in a vacuum. One needs something in relation to some objective, as one needs money to buy things with. If one does not want to buy things one does not need money.

Some take children's needs to be synonymous with children's expressed needs or what they think they need. The suggestion that what is educationally worthwhile should be decided by reference to this criterion is, however, obviously open to exactly the same objections that were raised to the suggestion that the criterion should be the child's own evaluation. But if we assume that children's needs are not to be identified with what they think they need, we have to establish what they do need before we can proceed. One will find no shortage of arbitrary lists of alleged children's needs: security, love, happiness, routine, knowledge, independence, good food, exercise, opportunities to express themselves, freedom and so on. My point here is not that they do not need some or all of these things, nor that it is not true that if children need security they ought to be provided with it. My point is the logical one that to say that children need to have independence or anything else must imply some end or objective: they need independence on the assumption that such and such that cannot come about except through independence is desirable.

Now there are no doubt certain basic needs that we would all agree that children have and that should be fulfilled; for example, who would dispute that children need affection, food, security and exercise in some degree? But the reason that we agree on such needs is that we agree, broadly

speaking, on the objective of bringing people up to be healthy and psychologically at ease, to which end these needs are fairly obviously necessary
means. But these basic needs, though important, are scarcely adequate to
serve as the foundation of a complete programme of educationally worthwhile activities: besides which it is not these needs themselves that serve
as the criterion but the objective that they are intended to meet.

In short, one must accept the formal point that what it is worthwhile
for children to do must be decided by reference to their needs. But this
solves no problems, since we still have to decide what they do need and
that cannot be decided except by reference both to the nature of children
and one's objectives. The utilitarian will argue that what children need is
whatever relates to their happiness as flourishing members of the community and contributors to the general happiness.

4. The suggestion that children's interests provide the criterion of worthwhileness is ambiguous. Children's interests may be taken to mean either
what is in their interests or what does as a matter of fact interest them.
Clearly the two are distinct: what interests an individual is not necessarily
in his interests, and vice versa. Thus it is in my interests to keep a check on
the state of repair of my car, but it does not happen to interest me at all.

The objection to the claim that what is worthwhile must be decided
solely by reference to what interests children is the same as that raised
against the claim that the criterion should be the child's evaluation or his
expressed need. It simply is not true that whatever interests the child must
for that reason be worthwhile. It might of course be true that in general
it is worthwhile for teachers to take *some* account of what does interest
children, but that is a quite different claim, and one that incidentally
indicates that the criterion of worthwhileness cannot be what interests the
child.

On the other hand, it is true that whatever is educationally worthwhile
must be in some way in the interests of the child. But this is not a very
helpful point since it is true by definition. It is only true because both
'educationally worthwhile' and 'in the interests of the child' *mean* 'what
it is desirable that children should do'. The question remains, What is it
desirable that they should do? What is educationally worthwhile? What
is in their interests? We obviously cannot make 'what is in the child's
interest' the criterion for deciding what *is* in his interest. We have to find
some other criterion for deciding that, and hence for deciding what is
worthwhile.

Once again the utilitarian will say that it is in the child's interest to
equip him to find happiness in life in such ways as contribute to the happiness of others and cause no misery.

5. Peters argues that education should be concerned to initiate children
into activities that are intrinsically worthwhile. He puts forward what has

become known as the 'transcendental argument' to show that some activities are intrinsically worthwhile. According to this argument, anyone who seriously asks himself the question 'Why do this rather than that?' *thereby* commits himself to valuing certain theoretical activities. He writes:

'How can a serious practical question be asked unless a man also wants to acquaint himself as well as he can with the situation out of which the question arises and of the facts of various kinds which provide the framework for possible answers? The various theoretical inquiries are explorations of these different facets of his experience. To ask the question "Why do this rather than that?" seriously is therefore, however embryonically, to be committed to those inquiries which are defined by their serious concern with those aspects of reality which give context to the question which he is asking.'[4]

Thus, in essence, the claim is that in asking 'Why do this rather than that?' one commits oneself to the value of rational appraisal, which presupposes the knowledge and understanding acquired through such theoretical pursuits as science, history and philosophy. Hirst similarly attempts to justify his claim that education should involve initiation into the eight forms of knowledge that he delineates, on the grounds that initiation into whatever forms of knowledge there are is one and the same thing as the development of the rational mind. He then argues that it would be peculiar to ask for justification of the attempt to develop the rational mind. 'To ask for the justification of any form of activity is significant only if one is in fact committed already to seeking rational knowledge. To ask for a justification of the pursuit of rational knowledge itself therefore presupposes some form of commitment to what one is seeking to justify.'[5]

Now it is surely clear that the transcendental argument will not in fact do the job required of it. That is to say, it will not establish that philosophy or any other theoretical pursuit concerned with the development of knowledge, understanding and rationality, just is intrinsically worthwhile. What it does indicate, which may be important, is that certain people do as a matter of fact implicitly value rationality, even though they may not admit as much to themselves. Most people *do* value the giving of good reasons, as is witnessed by their concern to be given them. From this it follows that it would be odd for such people to deny *any* value in those theoretical pursuits which are concerned with the search for good reasons in some sphere. Thus, insofar as the research chemist seeks to explain chemical phenomena and thereby provide us with data that will enable us to proceed rationally in respect of the use we make of chemicals, we can see that this pursuit has some value. And insofar as the good scientist proceeds with respect for the formal rules of scientific procedure, we must approve the rationality of his procedure.

But to admit this is not to admit that the study of science is intrinsically worthwhile. All that the transcendental argument establishes is that most people do value rational rather than irrational behaviour. It does *not* establish that *all* people *necessarily* do, for some people might conceivably just live out their lives in a random way without concerning themselves with question of the form 'Why do this rather than that?' It does *not* establish that those people who as a matter of fact are committed to rational behaviour are right to be so committed. For, from the fact that most or even all of us are committed to rational behaviour, we cannot conclude without further argument that we ought to be. Above all, it does *not* establish that theoretical pursuits such as the study of science, history or philosophy are intrinsically worthwhile. For to say that one values rational rather than irrational conduct is to say something about *how* people should proceed, and it is to say nothing about the direction or sphere in which they should proceed. To commit oneself to the value of having good reasons for action is quite different from committing oneself to the value of proceeding rationally in some particular sphere. The sort of person who asks a question like 'Why study science?' does thereby commit himself to rationality and therefore to the ideal that if people are going to pursue scientific questions they should do so with proper respect for the procedural rules of science. But he does not thereby commit himself to any particular view about the value of pursuing scientific questions. Surely there is nothing logically odd about saying 'I value rational conduct and I see that science produces a certain amount of data that is germane to the attempt to settle certain issues rationally, but I do not see any intrinsic value in studying science'.

Similarly, though Hirst is right to suggest that it would be logically odd for us to question the value of the rational as opposed to the irrational mind, he is wrong to suggest that it would be logically odd to question whether we ought to enable people to proceed rationally in all of his eight forms of knowledge. There would be nothing logically odd at all about concluding that, though it is desirable that people should proceed rationally rather than irrationally in any sphere in which they wish to engage, there are some spheres in which it does not matter if some people do not engage at all. It matters that one who wishes to discourse on the fine arts should do so rationally, perhaps, but it is a separate question whether or not it matters that people should discourse on the fine arts at all.

In short, although most of us probably do value the ideal of the rational rather than the irrational mind, it is still not clear that we have any good reason for so doing. There is nothing paradoxical about querying whether we have good reason to be concerned about good reasons. Secondly, the transcendental argument has not established the intrinsic worthwhileness of the various theoretical pursuits, since valuing rationality is not the same thing as valuing the pursuit of various studies that happen to involve rational procedures. Some argument is therefore still needed to show why it is worthwhile to initiate children into such pursuits as the study of history or philosophy.

The utilitarian offers the suggestion that some of the so-called forms of knowledge, as outlined by Hirst, are more important than others in that their subject matter is more crucial to the sort of decisions that necessarily affect our daily life: it is of more concern to us all that people should proceed rationally in the sphere of moral values than in the sphere of fine art. The development of the rational mind, in the sense of a mind that proceeds rationally in whatever sphere it does operate, is to be valued as a means to happiness. Utilitarianism does not claim that a society of rational beings must necessarily be happier than a society of irrational beings. It claims that insofar as we have reason to believe that, in present circumstances, the development of rationality is likely to contribute more to the happiness of the community than a lack of concern for rationality, the development of rationality is to be valued for that reason. Conversely, if we had reason to believe that concern for the development of rationality would be likely to lead to more misery than the cultivation of irrationality would do, then the cultivation of irrationality would be preferable. But, of course, we have no reason to adopt the latter belief.

In summarising this chapter it is important to stress its limited objective: to answer the question 'What is the criterion for estimating worthwhileness?' I have written the chapter from a utilitarian point of view, taking the opportunity to explain why certain other approaches to the question are not acceptable, but not so much concerned to defend the utilitarian approach as to expound it more fully. Because of the nature of my reply to the question, specific suggestions as to the sort of thing that is educationally worthwhile have inevitably been tentative and insufficiently justified. 'Inevitably', because the question of whether, for instance, studying history is likely to be worthwhile becomes to a large extent an empirical question on the utilitarian criterion. My concern has been to indicate the sort of way in which utilitarianism demands that we proceed.

The argument has been as follows: the question of what constitutes worthwhileness is central to the task of curriculum-planning. Suggestions such as that what children need, what they value, what interests them or what is in their interests can serve as the criterion of what is educationally worthwhile are unacceptable, either because, being formal, they offer no practical guidance, or because they plainly are not the sole criteria of worthwhileness. On the other hand the claim that the sorts of things traditionally valued by schools just are worthwhile is also plainly unsatisfactory; in the face of sincere dissent from the view that the traditional subjects just are worthwhile some attempt to explain why they are, or to give reasons for valuing them, is clearly required of their supporters. The transcendental argument, which seeks to establish the worthwhileness of a range of activities connected with the pursuit of truth in various spheres, fails to establish the intrinsic worthwhileness of the various theoretical disciplines. But that is not to say that, for instance, the study of history might not be a relatively worthwhile pursuit.

The utilitarian argument is that pursuits or activities are the more worthwhile insofar as they tend to promote pleasure. It is not disputed that, as things are, different people may take pleasure in a variety of different kinds of activities. But if worthwhileness is linked to considerations of pleasure, then it follows that it would be more worthwhile for people to take pleasure in those activities that contribute to the promotion of pleasure in general rather than in activities that only provide immediate pleasure for the agent.

From this nothing *necessarily* follows. It is not a *necessary* truth that, say, the study of science will contribute more to the sum of pleasure in a society than lying about in the sun all day. Furthermore, insofar as people happen to prefer doing the latter, that is *one* factor that will contribute to its relative worthwhileness. There is no necessary reason why at some point in history a society should not evolve which was capable of maintaining itself on very simple conditions and happy to lie in the sun for most of the day. If such a society were to come into being, the utilitarian would argue that it was an admirable society.

But, having conceded this logical point, the utilitarian may reasonably go on to make the empirical claim that, as things are, if everybody were to reach the point at which their only pleasure in life came from lying in the sun all day, then either people would in fact be extremely miserable, since they would have to do a lot of things they didn't want to do, or else the community would just collapse. Furthermore it is highly improbable that all people would come to find their sole pleasure in lying in the sun, in the natural course of events. Different people come to find pleasure in different activities at least partially as a result of being introduced to various activities. The utilitarian therefore argues that, given that we want to maximise pleasure, the rational thing to do is to bring people up to take pleasure in pursuits that contribute to pleasure generally and in behaviour that likewise contributes to pleasure generally.

Specifically he may argue that the promotion of rationality and awareness of and concern for others would be likely to contribute to the sum of human happiness, and that therefore to seek to enable children to take pleasure in those pursuits which may be thought to be likely to contribute to the promotion of these qualities would be particularly educationally worthwhile. The fact that it is not a proven contention that rationality will contribute to the sum of human happiness more than irrationality and that it could not in the nature of things be literally demonstrated is not important. The important questions are two: (1) Is there reason to accept the utilitarian contention that it is pleasure alone that matters? (2) Assuming that there is, is it reasonable to suppose that rationality will contribute more to the sum of pleasure than irrationality? It is quite possible for something to be a reasonable supposition without its being a provable contention.

One point that was conceded was the futility of trying to make even reasonable estimates about the relative worthwhileness of a range of activities in the middle ground between the manifestly more or less worthless and the plainly pretty worthwhile. Therefore if the utilitarian argument is basically sound, the conclusion would be that there would be some particularly worthwhile pursuits which ideally all children should be initiated into (I suggested moral philosophy, history, English literature and mathematics), but that beyond that the important thing would be to provide opportunities for children to see which of a range of activities they took most pleasure in. The teacher's task would be to attempt to reveal to the child what was involved in any given activity in such a way as to enable him to make an informed judgement as to whether there was any potential pleasure for him in that particular activity.

REFERENCES

1 Postman, N. and Weingartner, C., *Teaching as a Subversive Activity* (Penguin, 1971), p. 50.
2 Ibid., p. 68 ff.
3 Ibid., pp. 44–5.
4 Peters, R. S., *Ethics and Education* (Allen & Unwin, 1966), p. 164.
5 Hirst, P. H., 'Liberal Education and the Nature of Knowledge' in Dearden, R. F., Hirst, P. H., and Peters, R. S. (eds), *Education and the Development of Reason* (Routledge & Kegan Paul, 1972), p. 403.

FURTHER READING

Peters, R. S., devotes considerable space in *Ethics and Education* (Allen & Unwin, 1966) to the question of what is worthwhile. Essentially he takes the view that the pursuit of knowledge is intrinsically worthwhile and offers in support of this view what has become known as the transcendental argument. White, J. P., *Towards a Compulsory Curriculum* (Routledge & Kegan Paul, 1973) criticises the transcendental argument and suggests that neither it nor any other argument that he knows of will establish that anything just is intrinsically worthwhile. Wilson, P. S. and Peters, R. S. engaged in debate over the educational value of Bingo in *British Journal of Educational Studies* (June, 1967).

Hirst, P. H., 'Liberal Education and the Nature of Knowledge', in which the forms of knowledge are introduced, has been reprinted most recently in Peters, R. S. (ed.), *The Philosophy of Education* (O.U.P., 1973). Criticisms of Hirst include White, J. P., *Towards a Compulsory Curriculum* and Hindess, E., 'Forms of Knowledge' *P.E.S.G.B. Proceedings*, vol. 6, no. 2 (1972).

Wilson, P. S., has argued for the central place of what interests the child or what he values in education. See his *Interest and Discipline in Education* (Routledge & Kegan Paul, 1972) and his 'Child Centred Education' in *P.E.S.G.B. Proceedings*, vol. 3 (1969).

Needs and interests are both considered by Dearden, R. F., in his *Philosophy of Primary Education* (Routledge & Kegan Paul, 1968).

Chapter 12

The Free School

What is a 'free school'? What is meant by the demand for free schools or
for more freedom in schools? Clearly there is not some single ideal pattern
of a free school, to which all schools that claim to value freedom conform.
In order to proceed, therefore, I shall take as an example of a school that
appears to value freedom highly, and which most would regard as a free
school, A. S. Neill's Summerhill. What exactly is the nature of the freedom
provided at Summerhill?

The distinguishing feature of Summerhill is that children there are to a
large degree free from rules and restrictions that have been imposed upon
them by adults. This means in particular: (i) The day-to-day government
of the school is provided by a council that consists of all the children who
wish to partake in it and the staff. Each child and each member of staff
has one vote and numerically the children are therefore in a position to
over-ride the staff. (ii) There is very little that the children are forbidden
to do except by a vote made by themselves in council. (iii) Specifically,
attendance at lessons is voluntary for all children at all times.

These are aspects of Summerhill freedom. But to describe these aspects
is not to give the kind of answer that we want to the question, What is the
nature of Summerhill freedom? This tells us in what respects the children
are as a matter of fact free. But we want to know why they are free in
these respects. In other words, on what principle or principles does
Summerhill function? What good reasons are there for giving children
these freedoms? Only when it is clear what the reasoning is that lies behind
these aspects of Summerhill life can we be in a position to assess for
ourselves or meaningfully argue the merits of such a free school.

The first thing that we need to know is precisely what kind of a claim is
being made by those who want free schools along Summerhill lines. For
one might argue in favour of the type and amount of freedom to be seen
at Summerhill in two logically quite distinct ways, either by making an
empirical claim or by making a simple evaluative claim. (Or, of course,
one might attempt to combine the two kinds of claim.) Thus champions
of Summerhill might argue from the assumption that we all hold certain
broad values in common, and make the empirical claim that as a matter
of fact if schools provide children with the sort of freedom they enjoy at
Summerhill then certain desirable consequences are likely to follow. For
instance, it might be said, we value happiness and self-reliance, and

children brought up in this kind of a school become happy and self-reliant as a consequence of the freedom they are given. Alternatively, the direct evaluative claim might be made that children ought to be given these freedoms, regardless of the consequences, because it is wrong to deny children such freedoms. On this view, although one might still value happiness, self-reliance or anything else, and hope to promote them as well, nonetheless the point would be that children should have this freedom, even if it could be shown that they were not in fact very happy, self-reliant, etc., as a result.

In other words, Summerhill freedom might be commended either as an end in itself or as a means to some other end or ends, rather as the manager of a small firm might accept workers' representation on the management board either because he believed that it was right that they should be represented or because he believed that it would have desirable consequences such as promoting harmony in the firm or, more cynically, causing him less trouble in the long run.

Although nobody, I imagine, would accuse a man such as Neill of granting various freedoms to children in order to avoid trouble for himself and his staff in the long run, there is nonetheless a real question as to which of the two types of claim he was making. Did he assume certain educational aims, certain objectives that ideally should be met, and believe that the free situation he provided was an effective means of promoting those ends and achieving those desirable consequences? Or did he say to himself 'To hell with all this desirable consequences stuff; this is the morally right way to treat children?' Was his argument of the form: 'It is desirable that people should acquire a love of learning and that they should learn certain things. A school that provides the sort of freedom that Summerhill does promotes such learning and love of learning better than a more restricted traditional school does'? Or was it of the form: 'Giving children the freedom to decide whether they want to learn anything is more important than seeking to ensure that they do learn anything. We therefore ought to give children that freedom even if as a matter of fact the result is that relatively little learning takes place?'

In my experience most students and disciples of Neill take the view that he stood for the latter, immediately evaluative, position. And it is certainly true that he was not apparently much impressed by the specific aim that I have taken as an example – that of promoting learning in the traditional sense of becoming competent or knowledgeable in some sphere, subject or discipline. He was not saying that the freedom at Summerhill is desirable on the grounds that it is an effective means of producing good scholars and academics. But although promoting learning was not one of his aims, it was by no means clear that his argument for freedom was not of the empirical type, and that he did not advocate freedom for the sake of some further end. For Neill not only talked and wrote a lot about freedom. He also talked a lot about happiness.

More than once he wrote of his desire to promote happiness and we therefore come to the specific question: is the freedom provided at Summerhill desirable because it leads to an increase in happiness, or would Neill have claimed that, though he valued happiness, it would nonetheless be right to provide the sort of freedom that Summerhill provides even if as a matter of fact it could be shown that such freedom militated against happiness? Neill, who at the best of times had a certain contempt for fine argument, would probably have replied that it was a bit of both: his school treats children as they ought to be treated and happens thereby to promote happiness. End of argument. Exit hair-splitting philosophers in confusion. So, at any rate, many of Neill's supporters would hope.

But why should we give up so easily? There are matters of real importance here. The answer that I suggest Neill might have given simply avoids the interesting question of what we are to do in specific instances where granting freedom to children can be seen to militate against concern for promoting happiness. And we still have to consider whether it is *true* either that children ought to be treated in this way or that such freedom does promote happiness.

The latter question, precisely because it involves an empirical claim, is not strictly speaking a philosophical question. It can only finally be answered by carrying out some empirical research, some kind of survey, in an attempt to discover whether it is or is not the case that schools run on Summerhill lines do more to promote happiness than schools that are markedly less concerned with freedom.

Sad to relate, no such research has ever been undertaken, so that all we can say for certain at this juncture is that if this was Neill's claim (or part of it) it stands only as a hunch. However, certain observations may be made on this hunch. In order to attempt to verify it – and surely ideally one would like to make the attempt – one would need to do some preliminary conceptual analysis on the concept of happiness, so that one knew what one was looking for. I have not set a very good example here by the way in which I have confined myself to making a few general points about happiness sufficient for the argument I was trying to outline in Part Two. But we can see, from the confusion caused by attempts to test 'creativity' without first analysing the term clearly, the sort of mess that we would get into if we attempted to assess the amount of happiness around without a clear idea of the concept. A survey that contented itself with remarks such as 'It was my impression during my two-hour visit to Summerhill that the children were happy' would be pretty unsatisfactory to anybody concerned with precision and truth. Secondly, and more importantly, one would have to do more than establish whether or not the children at Summerhill were happy. For if happiness is of importance, then, presumably, ideally our concern ought to be to ensure a community in which people are happy and contribute to the happiness of others; it would not be enough that children should be happy at school. (I have made this point before in reference to utilitarianism; but it applies no less to those who are not utilitarians, but who nonetheless feel that happiness is *one* important value.) Just as free-schoolers (and deschoolers) have rightly criticized some traditionalists for forgetting that childhood is itself a part of life to be enjoyed rather than something to be seen only as a preparation for adulthood, so we may legitimately criticize free-schoolers if they ignore the fact that childhood *is only a part* of life and *does* lead on to adulthood.

Ideally, of course, anybody who values happiness at all would want to see happy children and happy adults. But it is an unfortunate fact of social life that if we want all adults to be happy there are certain ways in which we cannot allow individual adults to pursue their happiness. And if we wish to promote the happiness of all as much as possible, then we are bound to attempt to lead individuals to find happiness in certain necessary features of social life, or at least not to find such features irksome. It is surely not patently absurd to suggest that if all children were educated along Summerhill lines, enjoying that degree of freedom (I am thinking here particularly of the freedom to opt out of all lessons, or, to use a less old-fashioned term, deliberate teaching activities), the community would be a less happy body. I do not say that this *is* so. I say that it is a contention that deserves to be taken seriously. I am merely drawing attention to the fact that, if the justification of Summerhill-type freedom is supposed to lie in considerations of happiness, then the argument is about nine times as complex as some people would have us believe. It is not clear that the traditional, relatively unfree school has to be miserable as an experience; it is not clear that children necessarily gain in terms of happiness from self-government and the freedom to opt out of lessons; it is not clear that the community does not benefit, in terms of happiness, from an attempt deliberately to cultivate a high level of competence in various spheres; it is not clear that children cannot be more happy as a result of being initially directed into the pursuit of knowledge and understanding than if they are given the freedom never to begin the pursuit. It is not clear that deliberate (call it enforced, provided that one remembers that enforcement does not have to be harsh or brutal) initiation into various complex fields such as history, English literature or science cannot lead to a positive gain in happiness both for the individual and the community, taking the long-term view.

Bantock has written that utility, by which he means essentially an emphasis on happiness rather than specific commitment to the ethical doctrine of utilitarianism, is the curse of our age. 'A supine acquiescence in the notion that happiness is the ultimate value has led us to under-estimate the importance of achievement, even at a temporary loss of personal content. Child-centred education has been much imbued with the desire for happiness.'[1]

My reply would be that it is not the aim but the practice of much pro-gressive education that is questionable. If the claim is that the sort of freedom that Summerhill provides and any other so-called progressive aspects of education are desirable because they promote happiness, in the sense of contribute to the sum of human happiness, then the utilitarian must in principle approve of the progressive ideals. He must side with Neill, as against Bantock, to the extent of saying that if excellence does not in any way contribute to happiness, it is of no worth; it is not its own reward. But this, I stress, is a conditional claim. *If* free or progressive education does this, utilitarianism is its justification. But *does* it do this? As I have already indicated, that is a question of stunning proportions. In keeping with my general desire not to sit on the philosopher's fence, I will merely add that I suspect that by and large it does not, and that the objection to many of the moves to increase freedom in schools is that they will finally result in a less happy society. (I 'suspect.' I do not 'know'.)

At any rate, the claim that the sort of freedom provided at Summerhill is desirable on these grounds is at least coherent. What of the other kind of argument, the direct evaluative claim that it is wrong to control, direct and manipulate children and that therefore it is right for children to be free?

As we have seen, the suggestion that we have no 'right' to impose any-thing on children or to coerce them into doing anything, or that children have a 'right' to freedom, although it looks like an appeal to some kind of fact, is in reality no such thing. It is only a way of making the claim that, in the speaker's opinion, we ought not to impose anything. We should not therefore be misled into thinking that we may not quite reasonably ask on what grounds the claim is made. Why have we no right to impose? Why ought children to be free?

We have also seen that it is meaningless simply to assert that people ought to be free; some specification is needed as to what they ought to be free from or to do before we can begin to make sense of the claim. Now there are some educationalists who would argue that children should be free to determine all aspects of their life for themselves and hence their own development. Self-regulation, which seems to be synonymous with self-determination, is in fact an ideal advocated by Neill. What is there to be said about this claim? Three things:

1. In respect of young children at least, it is surely meaningless to talk of the child 'determining' his life or development. To 'determine' anything involves asserting one's control over it, rather than merely automatically

responding to it, and it therefore involves at least a degree of cognitive ability. The 6-year-old child who walks out of a lesson because he feels bored is not 'determining' anything. (At least there is no necessary reason to suppose that he is.) He walks out in response to his feeling of boredom. He is not in a position meaningfully to determine his life and his development because he lacks (relatively, but to a marked extent) the information and the reasoning capacity to structure that information that are necessary to determining the course of events. If one does not know what options are open to one, if one does not know how to evaluate them, if one does not know what means are most appropriate to selected ends, if one does not know what demands are going to be made on one in the future, if one does not know what the consequences of various courses of action are likely to be, how can one 'determine' the future course of one's life? To describe young children as determining their lives or development, therefore, is simply a misuse of language.

2. Whatever anybody *says*, we none of us in fact literally leave children to determine their own development. We all do impose on children's freedom to some extent and cannot help so doing. That we all do so does not constitute a good argument for concluding that we ought to (no 'ought' direct from an 'is'), but that we cannot help so doing obviously makes the claim that we ought not to a trifle absurd. (Another little philosophical aphorism runs: 'ought' implies 'can.') The mere fact of sending a child to school is a limitation on his freedom to determine his own development, and this is so regardless of the nature of the school.

Rousseau has often been thought of as one who championed the complete freedom of the child, because he insists, in *Emile*, that the tutor should leave everything to natural consequences and do nothing. But to make the positive effort to create a 'natural environment', as Rousseau would have Emile's tutor do, even going to the lengths of keeping Emile away from other children, not to mention adults, who for some reason do not count as part of the natural world, is fairly obviously to interfere: one cannot really claim to be giving complete freedom to an individual to determine his own development and pattern of life if one first of all structures his environment to one's own ideal. In the same way schools in which adults refrain from overtly interfering with the freedom of children cannot sensibly claim that each child thereby acquires complete freedom to determine his life. All that happens in such a situation is that the limitation on the freedom of the individual now comes for the most part directly from his peer group rather than from adults, and that this should be so was decided by and imposed by adults. This may be a desirable state of affairs, but it does not amount to refraining from imposing on children's freedom, and therefore it cannot be desirable simply on the grounds that children's freedom ought not to be imposed on. And it is simply untrue to pretend, as some have done, that such a school does not impose values: it imposes (or attempts to impose) the values enshrined in that kind of school. To set up a school, however 'free', or to join the staff of one, is to have already made a deliberate move to structure a particular kind of environment, presumably with the avowed purpose of having some kind of effect on the development of the children within it.

3.   Older children are, of course, capable of determining the course and pattern of their lives. Are we to conclude that they should be given the freedom to do so? Are we to accept that, notwithstanding the fact that the nature of the school will inevitably have constituted a source of various pressures on the child in his formative years, which may or may not materially have influenced the course of his development, once he is technically in a position to determine the course of his own life, he should be free to do so? (So that we have something firm to hold on to, let us say that children are technically capable of determining their own lives at least by the time they enter secondary education.)

There is really nothing for me to add to the argument of Part Two. There I tried to show that one cannot accept that anyone, whether child or adult, should simply be free to determine his life in all respects as he sees fit. The consequences of taking such an absolute position are just unacceptable. All of us must concede, or so I argued, that there are some things that people should not be free to do. Once that is admitted we are obliged, unless we do not mind proceeding in a totally arbitrary fashion, to attempt to formulate some criterion or criteria whereby to assess the limits of freedom. My criterion was the utilitarian one, and I am sticking to it, unless such time as somebody gives me good reason to drop it. Therefore I say that the sort of freedoms that children should be given has to be decided by reference to the tendency of specific freedoms to contribute to the happiness of the community. If we have reason to believe that the involvement of children in running the school contributes to the general happiness, that is a good reason for encouraging the practice. But, in this case, let us remember that *this is* the reason for advocating the practice. Consequently we are off the point if we drone on about a right to freedom, and we may quite consistently add that there should be certain limitations to the power of a management body or council thus constituted. There are certain things that we will not let children decide to do, whether individually or by vote in a council, because we cling to our belief that they will be to the detriment of the happiness of society. For example, they certainly may not vote to encourage bullying. Well, perhaps they never would, but the point is that *we* need to do some thinking about precisely what are the limits of the power of such a council to be, before we set it up. Can the children, for instance, be free to decide that all lessons should be voluntary (assuming that that is not a freedom that they have already been specifically given)? I can think of nothing more likely to spread resentment and disillusion, and hence unhappiness, than inviting children to participate in school management, without specifying the limits of their competence, and then using one's authority to over-ride half of their decisions. And yet, in my experience that is precisely what most schools that countenance some form of council do.

I am aware that the sort of view I am here putting forward is one that is abhorred by many radicals. They point out, correctly, that the sting is in the tail: all this talk of freedom, giving the children the freedom to decide about the running of the school – and then, wham, bam, the limits come down: they are free to decide, provided that they decide as I do. Yes; that is what I am saying and I have given my reasons for saying it. Nothing that I have heard yet has persuaded me that I should subscribe to the view that children should be free to do precisely what they want nor, specific-ally, that they or anyone else should be free to behave in ways that militate against the long-term happiness of the community. I have indicated my feeling – and admitted that it is by no means a proven contention – that in terms of happiness the community will lose if all attendance at lessons, or whatever you want to call them, is voluntary. Suppose the children in a particular school sincerely feel that I am empirically mistaken? I can only say that there seems to me good reason to claim that as a general rule adults, in view of their greater experience and knowledge and reasoning ability, are better equipped to make such judgements than children. And it is important to note that we are not concerned with *value* judgements at this point, but empirical judgements. Therefore we should adopt the rule, in the interests of the long-term welfare of the community, that teachers remain the *final* arbiters of the limits of freedom. To a certain frame of mind such a pronouncement is intolerable; I only hope that it will be discussed and considered with the seriousness due to what is after all the most complex aspect of the debate about freedom in schools: who decides?

Finally, having acknowledged the difficulties in my view, let us turn once again to a rival view. What did Neill actually have to say about the limits of freedom? – for he certainly imposed limits on the freedom of children at Summerhill. Despite his talk of self-determination or self-regulation, there are clear examples of things that children may not deter-mine to do. He argued, with scathing scorn for people who do not appreci-ate that his solution is the correct one, that the answer lies in a distinction between liberty and licence. But we must weather the scorn, for we have already seen that such a distinction solves no problems at all. It merely restates the problem: how do we decide what freedoms are licence and hence unacceptable? After careful consideration of the examples that he incidentally gave of various freedoms that are and are not allowed at Summerhill, I can only conclude that he committed himself, whether he knew it or not, to the utilitarian criterion. For he said that children should not be free to jump out of windows, jump on sofas, smash pianos or kick doors; they should be prevented where possible (bars on windows), and corrected where prevention is impossible. Now on what grounds could he cite these examples, except that they constitute behaviour that either harms the child himself or annoys other people? But this notion of harm, whether physical or psychological (i.e. causing annoyance), whether to the individual or others, is merely another way of expressing the utilitarian criterion. But if this is so, if Neill, or anyone else, would argue that children ought not to smash pianos because to do so involves causing harm to others, then we may surely reopen the question of whether all the freedoms that he would have granted to children are in fact desirable on his criterion. As ever, all we are after is consistency: if 'harm' is the criterion, then the only remaining question of interest is whether more or less harm is caused, taking individual and community into account, by self-government for children to the extent that Neill advocates and complete freedom for children to decide whether or not to attend any lessons.

I have not been concerned either to dismiss or accept Neill's view of education. I am concerned with the way in which we should approach the sort of issues that a school like Summerhill raises. Presented with the example of such a school, we ask 'Why do you do this and that?' My own view is that Neill was not actually very clear why. He seemed to proceed to a considerable extent by intuition and he was not in fact entirely consistent. But that is not the point at issue, which is rather that we do not want talk of 'rights', 'self-regulation' and unqualified 'freedom', so much as some coherent account of the criteria necessary for determining rights and the limits of freedom for children. The most interesting issue seems to me to be the question of voluntary attendance at lessons. I conclude with a question: surely on the assumption that we have something to offer, on the assumption that our schools are attempting to initiate children into worthwhile activities, it must by definition be worthwhile to take steps to ensure that children are initiated into them?

REFERENCES

1 Bantock, G. H., *Education, Culture and the Emotions* (Faber & Faber, 1967), p. 139.

FURTHER READING

Neill, A. S., *Summerhill* (Penguin, 1968) is the most convenient source for his over-all educational views. For an account of the way in which they developed, see Hemmings, R., *Fifty Years of Freedom* (Allen & Unwin, 1972).

Chapter 13

Educational Distribution

Independent sector

Argument about the independent sector of education is often confused by forgetting that there are many different types of independent schools and by failing to distinguish between three different types of argument. Within the independent sector there are schools as disparate as Summerhill and Eton; there are religious and secular foundations; boarding and day schools; schools where the emphasis is on a traditional academic curriculum, schools which could only fairly be described as progressive and experimental; besides the well-known public schools, there are schools for the handicapped, for the blind and so on. It is conceivable that there might be good reason for adopting a different attitude to different kinds of school within the private sector. The three different questions (and hence types of argument) that must not be confused are: (1) Are independent schools good schools? (2) Are independent schools in principle acceptable? (3) Are independent schools in practice acceptable or desirable in our society? The first of these questions is about the schools themselves, the second about the system of private education, and the third involves consideration of both the previous questions in relation to other features of our society.

Of the many points that have been made at one time or another on one side or the other of this argument I shall single out five that are commonly put forward in justification of an independent sector and three that are put forward by way of objection. It is argued that an independent sector is desirable because: (1) It provides a good education, not otherwise available. (2) It caters for certain specific needs that some children at least may have, such as the need for a boarding school. (3) It serves various minority interests. (4) It provides the opportunity for experiment that is lacking in the state system. (5) A principle of freedom justifies an independent sector. In the words of Walter Hamilton,

> 'To take away from such parents as at present have the means to exercise the right to educate their children at their own expense would be an invasion of liberty unheard of West of the Iron Curtain, an act of tyranny which would not lose its tyrannical character because it was exercised by a constitutional majority.'[1]

As against these points it may be argued (1) that the independent sector provides a bad education, (2) that it leads to social division, and/or (3) that it is in principle unacceptable that the education in question should be the privilege of the few.

Clearly whether the education provided in the independent sector is good or bad is an exceedingly complex question that depends for its answer on such factors as what one's view of a good education is, which of the great variety of schools in the sector we are talking about, and, in some cases, what children we are talking about (for example, there may be certain children for whom distinctive schools such as Abbotsholme or Gordonstoun would provide a good education and others for whom they would not). In any case, since the question of the quality of education provided is a question about the schools, whereas we are primarily interested in the principles that may or may not justify an independent sector, and since any blanket assessment of private education will obviously be a ludicrous oversimplification, it seems best to concentrate primarily on that part of the independent sector that people generally seemed concerned about – namely, the traditional public schools. Now although there is certainly a wide difference of quality in the education provided, on any criteria, by the various public schools, and although there may be some whose objection to the public schools is that they deny their pupils a good education, it seems best that we should proceed by assuming that a public school education is in some sense a good education. That, at any rate, would seem to be the view of those who pay large sums of money to obtain it for their children and the view of those who resent the fact that it is confined to the few. The people concerned may have very different reasons for regarding it as a desirable education (some may see it simply as a passport to a better job, some as a good training ground for character, some as academically stronger), but that it is generally regarded as desirable can hardly be doubted.

On the assumption, however, that the public schools provide a good education, what we are being presented with here is merely the beginnings of an argument for certain features of the public school education being brought into the state system. If, for example, boarding be singled out as a desirable feature of education, for whatever reason, for at least some children, that is an argument for boarding facilities being provided by a good educational system, whether it be private or state controlled. Neither of the first two points put forward above as possible arguments for the independent sector, therefore, are in fact any such thing. They do not justify the system in principle; they merely offer possible reasons for admiring specific schools.

The next two points (that an independent sector caters for minorities and allows of experiment) *are* about the system, as opposed to being merely about specific features of specific schools. Furthermore it is as a matter of fact true that within the independent sector there has been considerable experimentation and that minorities have been catered for. But these truths are only contingent truths. That is to say that, although it is as a matter of fact true, there is no necessary reason why it should have been true or should be true in the future; nor is there any necessary reason why there should not be experiment and a catering for minorities within the state system. There obviously has been, and is, experiment within the state system, though perhaps it has a less distinguished record for catering for minority interests. So even if we accept the need for continued experiment and for some concern for minority interests, and even if we acknowledge the contribution of the independent sector in these respects, we cannot conclude that therefore the independent sector is justified.

We thus arrive at the only argument that could hope to establish that an independent sector of education is in principle justifiable – an appeal to freedom.

The question before us is whether it is right that a desirable education should be available and reserved for those who can afford it. One does not have to be a philosophical genius to see that opponents of the independent sector are obviously correct in their assertion that the wealth of parents is not a relevant criterion for differential educational treatment. It has nothing to do with education. It is as bizarre as the claim that having red hair is a relevant reason for being provided with a distinctive kind of education. Furthermore they are probably right that the existence of a private sector is one factor that may contribute to social division. However, it seems to me that we should not make too much of this, since it is at worst only one factor, and it is difficult to believe that the abolition of a private sector of education is going to make very much practical difference. The whole question of the independent sector is therefore finally seen to rest upon the question of freedom. Do we accept that justification is to be found in the principle of freedom?

Obviously we do not. Hamilton's argument simply will not do. Passing over his emotive hysteria about iron curtains and his question-begging reference to a 'right' as rapidly as possible, let us nonetheless note that one point he makes is true: to take away this freedom from those who can afford it would indeed, by definition, be an 'invasion of personal liberty', and those who are in the habit of ranting on in other contexts about the importance of freedom without qualification or substantiation are of course hoist on their own petard in the face of Hamilton's impassioned cry. But we, I trust, do not have this habit. As we have seen, talking about freedom without qualification is meaningless. The question must be whether there are reasons that can be given to defend this specific freedom of the few who can afford it. Is there any reason why those who are rich enough to afford it should be given the freedom to acquire preferential education for their children? Any such reason, to be acceptable, would, I have argued, have to appeal to the ultimate consideration of equal concern for the welfare of all. Beyond question, I suggest, in principle there can be no such reason. A private sector of education is thus, in ideal terms, indefensible.

However, before leaving this topic, we should not allow a concern with principle and abstract theory, such as philosophy predominantly displays, to blind us to practicalities. It would not be at all unreasonable to suggest – although the suggestion will irritate those who expect a revolution to build Rome in a day – that in practice we have to take into account a number of other factors, and that as things are it would be worse in terms of the welfare of society as a whole to sweep away the independent sector than to retain it. Two reasons in particular might be given to support this suggestion: (1) Given that the distribution of wealth in our society is as a matter of fact unequal, a private sector of education is a useful means of taxing the rich and effectively increasing educational resources for the rest of us. (2) Given that the private sector provides a good education in some sense, the community as a whole may be thought to gain from the existence of such well-educated people.

I am not personally convinced by the second point, and in any case I should have thought that the idea of calculating whether in fact the community gains from the existence of ex-public school individuals constitutes an impossible task. As for the first point, one can think of a variety of other ways of taxing the rich and increasing educational resources if that is what one wants to do. (Since we are dealing with practical considerations it is worth adding that if all parents had their children at state schools this might serve to bring a certain amount of influential pressure to bear on the demand for increased educational resources.) However, this is a point of view which it would have been churlish not to mention.

What we surely have to conclude from this discussion is that ideally the state system of education should incorporate whatever of those features of the private sector (be they features of individual schools or of the system) can be shown by reasoned argument to be desirable and offer them to all or to all whom they would benefit, rather than simply to those who can afford them. The independent sector is not to be justified in principle, but, if at all, as a practical expedient prior to the self-sufficiency of a universal state system.

The state system

The suggestion that ideally a state system should offer the good things to be found in the independent sector to all conveniently raises the question of whether this means offering the same kind of school to all children. Does it, for instance, commit one to comprehensive schools as opposed to the tripartite system? It has been suggested to me that to raise this question at this point in time is to be out of date before one begins: the tripartite system is on the way out, whether one likes it or not. I find this suggestion peculiar. Assume that it is true that a comprehensive system is here to stay – is that any reason to stop considering the merits of alternatives? If advocates of comprehensive education had taken the view that since we had a tripartite system there was no point in considering the rationale behind it or of examining alternatives, we would probably never have had a move towards comprehensivisation. I take the view that whatever system we have or will have in the near future has got nothing to do with the question of what system we ought to have, and that there is still a lot to be said on both sides of the question; the one thing we must resist is any tendency in the next generation of teachers unthinkingly to assume that a comprehensive system of education is obviously an improvement on what it has replaced.

There are, of course, many variants on the comprehensive plan, and many alternatives that might be considered, besides the simple tripartite model of grammar, modern and technical schools. Such variants cannot be examined minutely here, where my purpose is to focus on the simple question of whether it is desirable or acceptable to offer quite distinct types of education to different children on some criterion or criteria other than the wealth of parents, which was, of course, the assumption behind the 1944 Education Act. Conversely, it may be thought, the assumption that it is not desirable on any criteria lies behind the move towards comprehensive education. But does it?

The initial problem is that no two people necessarily seem to mean the same thing by a comprehensive school. To some it means simply a single community in which the interests of children of all types and abilities are catered for; on this view the essence of a comprehensive school is not that the distinctions of the tripartite system are avoided, but that they do not involve social segregation as well. A related view is that a comprehensive school should take in pupils from every social stratum and background. But some would go further and see a comprehensive school as, by definition, also involving a less rigid distinction between practical and academic curricula; at the very least the individual pupil who, let us say, is essentially non-academic would not thereby forfeit the chance of pursuing whatever slight academic interests he might have. Some, it would seem, want to go farther even than this and argue that a comprehensive school should, again by definition, break down the division between academic and practical completely and offer essentially a common curriculum for all. Finally it is not unheard of for the question of streaming to crop up, with some arguing that comprehensive schools are only truly comprehensive if there is no streaming at all.

It is not to the purpose to attempt a philosophical analysis of the notion of a comprehensive school. The term means 'all-embracing', and we simply have to recognise the fact that essential to its use is the idea of a contrast with any system that involves distinctive kinds of institutions for different children, but that beyond that advocates of comprehensives may be committed to any combination of the above demands. What we have to do is to consider each of these demands in isolation and attempt to discover what can be said for or against them.

But let us begin by considering the arguments for and against the tripartite system.

The 1944 Act demanded that such educational facilities should be provided as were desirable for children in view of 'their different ages, abilities and aptitudes'. In practice this was deemed to involve a distinction between three types of pupil: the academically gifted, those gifted in respect of practical skills or in respect of aptitude for specific occupations such as engineering, and those (the vast majority) who, given the implications of the Act, can best, if bluntly, be categorised as simply relatively less gifted in either respect. Corresponding to each group there arose the grammar school, the secondary technical school and the secondary modern school.

Now we surely cannot dispute that in principle differences of ability and aptitude are eminently reasonable criteria for providing different kinds of education. Conversely we cannot accept the simplistic argument that equality demands that people should all experience the same kind of education. Equality, as we have seen, demands impartial treatment, which means similar treatment except where there are relevant reasons for differentiation. The relevance of reasons is judged by reference to the nature of what is being distributed in the light of the ultimate consideration of concern equally for the welfare of all. On these terms it seems absurd to deny that, if one child has an obvious flair for the academic pursuit of mathematics and another does not, that constitutes a relevant reason for treating them differently.

What then are the objections to the tripartite system? There seem to me to be essentially four that are worth taking seriously:
1. The claim that although in principle such distinctions may be reasonable, in practice they are made extremely inaccurately.
2. The claim that whatever the theoretical justification of the distinctions, in practice they lead to social divisions that are unacceptable.
3. The claim that the specific education provided by one or more of the three types of school is inadequate or unacceptable as an education.
4. The claim that the system presupposes some kind of assessment, which is unacceptable.

Before proceeding to examine these criticisms in greater detail, I should like to put forward, simply for consideration, the suggestion that all of them are to a considerable extent attempts to rationalise a feeling of objection to the undoubted fact that, as a generalisation, secondary modern pupils in particular become second-class citizens in terms of our materialistic culture. In other words the real objection to secondary modern schools is, in the uncompromising words of Rubinstein and Stoneman, that, by being classified as secondary modern pupils, many of our children 'have their future determined as manual workers at the age of eleven'.[2] Secondary modern pupils tend, as adults, to lose in the race for secure and well-paid employment, which may have the incidental corollary that some children (or their parents), in their anxiety to avoid the secondary modern, struggle and gain grammar school places to which they are not entirely suited. If there is any truth in this suggestion, then I wish to make one simple but extraordinarily important observation on it: objectionable as this may be (is), there is no purely educational solution to it. I am not arguing, as some have done, that education *should* not concern itself with what are essentially social or political points, but that educational changes or reforms *cannot* affect them. If, for whatever reason, society differentiates between various roles in respect of status and pay and thereby renders some less desirable, then no educational system can get round this and any educational system will *be* a selective system, whether it wants to be or not. Whatever is meant by a comprehensive system, it cannot prevent an ultimate distinction between those who are better suited for some roles and those who are better suited for others. If some roles are judged to be superior in a society, that cannot be attributed to the system of education. Second-class citizens are the product of a socio-economic structure and not an educational system. One cannot therefore legitimately object to the tripartite system simply on the grounds that some can be shown to gain more in material terms than others at the end of the day.

What one can do, of course, is argue that the wrong people are gaining. This takes us back to the first objection: that the categorisation of children at the age of eleven has been inaccurate. There really seems very little doubt that this is true, and true in two senses. First, it is clear that examinations such as the 11-plus have been far from satisfactory in terms of accurately predicting potentially successful and unsuccessful grammar school material. Secondly, there is the more subtle argument that, in any case, children respond to the expectations made of them, and that therefore there may be many secondary modern pupils who seem to have been well placed but who, had they had the opportunity to go to a grammar school, would have seemed well placed there as well. Taking these points on their merits, it follows that (a) ideally there is a need for a better system of selection – and perhaps there are more suitable ages at which to select than eleven, (b) there is a need for increased facilities for transference at later stages between the various kinds of education, and (c) there is a need to remove the pervading ethos of a particular kind of school with its inbuilt expectations. Now it may follow from these considerations, although it obviously does not necessarily do so, that a comprehensive school in the limited sense of a single physical community is therefore to be desired. This would be an empirical point, but it seems reasonable to suppose that if all three types of education were provided in a single community, it would be easier to rectify misclassification, and the atmosphere of the school and the expectation that it put over to the children would be considerably less stereotyped. What we do not have here is an argument for anything more than a comprehensive school in this limited sense. However true it is that children's performance can be affected by what is expected of them, it is palpable nonsense to pretend that all children could do well in any kind of school. What one cannot accept is the argument that simply because some children under a tripartite system may turn out to be what they need not have been, therefore nobody ought to be allowed to experience a distinctive kind of education. Though some non-academic children in secondary moderns might have been academically successful in grammar schools, we cannot conclude that therefore it must be wrong to distinguish between the relatively academic and the relatively unacademic child.

That the tripartite system leads to social divisions is an argument that is frequently to be encountered. How pertinent a criticism is it? The first question is what precisely is meant by social division? Mere differences between groups of people are surely not in themselves objectionable; indeed it is difficult to conceive of a society in which a competent sociologist could not rapidly arrive at various criteria for classification such that he could refer to distinct social divisions or classes. If the classless society means a society in which no criteria could be found for classifying distinct groups of people, then the classless society is not going to come. Clearly if social division is taken to be undesirable then what must be meant is either divisions between groups in respect of advantages desired by all or else divisions in the sense of dissension between groups. It seems indisputable that the tripartite system has tended to contribute towards social division in both these latter senses (and indeed that it has actually served as a way of transferring people from one social group to another): the grammar school tends to be a path to advantage, and no doubt dissension can arise between grammar school and secondary modern school pupils. Here then we have another plausible argument for a single physical community and for the comprehensive conceived of as a neighbourhood school. Though it is unlikely that the mere housing of different kinds of education and pupils from different backgrounds in the same community will solve the problem of social division, and though it must again be stressed that the nature of society and its outlook in respect of the relative esteem to be accorded to various social roles is the key factor in determining social division, it surely is reasonable to suppose that the less children from different backgrounds and of different aptitudes are treated as different species in their own private world, the more chance there is of creating a spirit of homogeneity, which anybody committed to the overriding importance of equal concern for the welfare and happiness of all must welcome.

In a way the suggestion that the objection to the tripartite system is really that one or more of its constituent parts provide a bad education is the most interesting. It is also the most complex of the objections, requiring for its satisfactory resolution considerably more than a book the length of this one to itself. I have already argued that ideally education should be concerned to develop in the individual those embryonic talents that he has which are not anti-social, a sociable attitude, and those abilities which may be of value to him, either directly or indirectly, and of value to the community as a whole – value being assessed ultimately by reference to happiness and welfare. I have also suggested that on these grounds a modified form of Hirst's forms of knowledge should provide the basis of the education of all and that beyond that specialisation in whatever area the child has interest and aptitude is to be desired. On these terms one could certainly criticise all three of the forms of education provided under the tripartite system on points of detail. But it is not clear that any of them deserves to be dismissed as inherently bad education. However, one may well feel that the central criticism to be made is that there has been too exclusive a preoccupation with the academic at the expense of the practical: that grammar schools have ignored the practical completely and that technical and modern schools have in fact, surprisingly, followed suit with an unnecessary emphasis on a watered-down academic curriculum. To solve such problems there is obviously no *need* for a new system of education, but the comprehensive school, still conceived of as essentially merely a single community catering for all types of child, might well in practice facilitate the provision of a more flexible curriculum.

Finally there is the objection to the notion of assessment to be considered. Now let us face this allegedly burning issue coolly. Unless all children are to do exactly the same things or else be left free to do just what they want, then some form of assessment is inevitable. So long as we retain the notion that some people are better at certain things than others, and that some things cannot be done without certain prior conditions being met (as one cannot discuss the merits of Aeschylus' style if one cannot read Greek, or cannot play football if one does not know the rules), then we are stuck with the notion of assessment – although, of course, it may take a variety of forms. Finding the best way of assessing people, if by 'best' we mean that way which is most accurate and causes least anguish, may be difficult, but we cannot avoid it so long as we continue to make reference to people's 'readiness' to do things, or their 'suitability' or 'competence'. In short, unless we are prepared to drop altogether the idea that things may be well or badly done, that one can distinguish between the quality of various performances, and that there are standards of excellence in various spheres – whatever those standards may be, which is an entirely separate point – we are committed to assessment. For assessment is logically tied up with the concepts of quality, standard and excellence.

Now of course we are aware – who could not be with the recent spate of Penguin Educational Specials to remind him? – that there are some who apparently either do not understand this logical point or are not interested in the question of whether things are well or badly done provided that they are done. (An interesting philosophical question here: at what point is a thing being so badly done that it does not count as being done at all?) They advocate a total absence of streaming and a common curriculum for all in the sense of a curriculum consisting of various options from which the child takes his pick. With such a scheme assessment would, of course, be reduced to a minimum – perhaps age would be the only criterion of qualification.

What is wrong with this view? With the basic idea that a wide variety of options should be available, perhaps nothing. But to adopt this policy in its entirety is effectively to claim either that children have sufficient knowledge of what is involved in the various options, before they undertake them, to make a sound judgement as to which they will most enjoy, which they will undertake with success, and which will in the long run benefit them most, or that it does not matter whether they do enjoy, succeed or benefit. It also involves the presumption that anybody can 'do' anything, if he is so minded, and that it is unimportant how well equipped he is to do it. There may be some things of which this is true: for instance, to take up an example from a previous chapter, it may be unnecessary to discriminate between people in respect of their ability to think of uses for a brick, or in respect of their ability to talk about 'democracy', if 'talk about' simply means utter points of view. But this merely raises the question once again of whether such activities are particularly worthwhile. I suggest that there is a very limited value in discussing democracy unless one has some inkling of the historical evolution of democracies, the historical facts about various democracies (how they worked, how they arose and fell, what they achieved, what they failed to achieve), the actual workings of contemporary democracies, and some philosophical competence at handling abstract concepts and, in relation to such a topic as this, ethical concepts; it follows that to make the exercise valuable something more than the random decision to undertake it is required. Why should we accept the naïve oversimplification of such men as Postman and Weingartner that to question is all that matters? Anybody can question – what is surely needed is some competent and informed answering. Similarly if we accept, as I have argued we should, that there is a value in people coming to understand the various forms of knowledge and a value in expertise in the various branches of science, in history, in literature, in art and in philosophy, then clearly it is not true that anybody can 'do' any of the things that we are concerned with in education.

With the empirical claim that within limits the relatively less able may achieve more in the company of the relatively able, I am not here concerned. The evidence, such as it is, seems far from conclusive either way. But it should be noted that to use this argument in favour of non-streaming involves acknowledging that there *are* standards of ability and competence (otherwise it would be meaningless to distinguish between the less and more able). And if it is admitted that there are standards of competence, which can be judged, there seems no obvious reason why reference should not be made to them. What must be resisted, according to my argument, is the view that because A can gain something from the study of Z, therefore B must be allowed to study Z regardless of the question of his competence to do so.

Attempting to pull the various strands of the section together, I would suggest that there is a fairly obvious middle road to be adopted between the die-hard proponents of the tripartite system and the more extreme of the many different people who have to be lumped together as pro-comprehensive. Proponents of the tripartite system are surely right in their claim that such things as the study of English literature, modern languages, science, etc., at a relatively academic level (though not necessarily in the manner and the extremely departmentalised form often associated with the grammar schools), is worthwhile (evaluative claim); that some people are better suited to these activities than others and some not suited at all (empirical claim); and (probably/possibly) that the task is better done with a degree of streaming. They are therefore right to conclude that we ought to distinguish between children in respect of their ability and aptitude for such an education, and to resist a common curriculum and an absence of streaming across the board. But there is good reason to suppose that they are wrong to insist on the isolated existence of different types of school. For the sake of promoting social homogeneity and of ensuring more efficient consideration of what children's aptitudes and abilities really are, and possibly to allow of a greater flexibility in curriculum, we see the need for comprehensive schooling in the sense of the provision of institutions that embrace all kinds of children and, hence, curricula.

Universities

It has been argued that educational provision should be made for all, although the principle of impartiality might demand or allow different kinds of education to be provided for different people. Does it follow that all should go to school for the same length of time and that, turning to higher education, universities should be open to all?

No. It does not follow. The essence of the argument for universal education is that education is by definition something advantageous. What we actually provide in the name of education may not be advantageous, but what we *mean* to provide is something advantageous. In broad terms, education consists of a concerted effort to help the child enter on paths that are advantageous to him and not disadvantageous to society, and this is so whatever one's view of what is advantageous and hence of what education ought to involve. No relevant grounds can be discovered for refusing this advantageous process to any individual.

But, of course, what is as a matter of fact 'advantageous' may differ from child to child. Some things may be commonly advantageous to all such as, perhaps, acquiring the skills of reading, writing and coherent argument; but, thereafter, one child may be drawn to music, another to carpentry – one to studying classics, another to engineering – and so on. Therefore, although education in the sense of advantageous help is due to all, different individuals may benefit to different degrees from different educational programmes. Only if all individuals were identical in respect of their interests and abilities, and if society wished to maintain this identity, would the case be otherwise.

The concept of education, however, has no time element built into it. It is not a condition of being educated that one should have gone through a process or have 'experienced education' for any specific length of time. One can refer to education as something that never ceases, as something that is contiguous with life itself, as something that only ends with death, and so on. But when we are talking about education in respect of the deliberate activities of various institutions it has no specific time limit. However one judges the 'educated man', it is not by reference to time.

To decide how long a child ought to be at school (or, on deschooling terms, free to take advantage of educational provision) one has to decide, in theory, at what point the 'advantage' he is supposed to be gaining ceases to be provided effectively, or at what point it would be more to the advantage of him and society that he should cease to belong to a specific institution. This will clearly differ from individual to individual and will, to some extent, be affected by the specific nature of the education or schooling being undergone. The unacademic child, for instance, who has no interest in or talent for a continuation of study in much of the school curriculum, but who has a talent for mechanics, may well benefit from leaving the confines of the institution relatively early and becoming instead an apprentice mechanic. Conversely the student of modern languages may benefit from, and may wish to benefit from, continued institutional help.

The principle of equality, therefore, certainly does not demand that universities should be available to all. In fact, as things are, it demands the reverse. For, although the concept of a university may be difficult to define, although historically the concept has come to be modified to some extent, and although at present it may be thought to be undergoing change, the fact remains that a university is not just a collection of buildings put there for any old purpose. A university, by definition, could only meaningfully be thought to have a certain *kind* of purpose and there are a variety of purposes that it simply does not have. It may be taken to mean some things, and there are other things which it cannot be taken to mean. It is not, for instance, a place in which people are trained to become soldiers or practice nudity.

Whatever precise definition might be given, it is clear that one part of the meaning of a university is that it is an institution for academic pursuits available to people with certain qualifications. That is to say that by definition there are relevant reasons why some should be excluded. Now of course one may criticise the actual qualifications in question from a number of points of view: one may argue that A level passes do not in fact accurately measure or predict the relevant competence; one may argue that those who do badly at A level might nonetheless have done well at university; one may argue that the importance of A levels as qualifications puts a strain on children and impairs their performance or that it leads to the wrong kind of teaching; one may argue that luck plays too great a part in the selection of candidates for university places or that too much attention (or not enough attention) is given to other factors, besides academic qualifications, such as subjective impressions of the character and personality of candidates, and so on. But all such criticisms are criticisms of the actual process of selection: they involve the claim that injustices may be done in selection and that there are unsatisfactory features of the system of selection as it exists. They do not amount to an argument to the effect that the business of selecting is in itself unjust. For whatever the faults of the actual procedure for selection, the fact remains that built into our conception of a university, part of what we mean by a university, is the notion that there are in principle certain standards or degrees of competence in specifiable respects that are necessary to the business of undertaking a university course, and which some people do not as a matter of fact come up to or have.

It may, of course, be pointed out that these qualifications are only necessary because of the way we regard universities, and suggested that they ought to be abandoned. But if the notion of qualifications is abandoned, then, by definition, the concept of a university is altered. Carried to extremes (let us say to the extent that no qualifications are looked for at all, so that anybody can go to university), the concept becomes modified to such an extent as to be altered beyond recognition. If anybody can go and, when there, do more or less anything (as they would have to be allowed to do, since not all would be *able* to do the sorts of thing traditionally associated with universities), then a university becomes indistinguishable from a social club. By opening universities to all, one finally destroys universities. This would only cease to be true if as a matter of fact every individual was capable of undertaking and profiting from a university education essentially similar to the traditional idea of what a university education is, which is palpably not the case.

My argument is this: historically speaking a university is to be understood as an institution of research and teaching at a relatively high level in fundamentally academic areas. On this definition there are relevant reasons for refusing to offer such an education to all, and there is nothing inegalitarian about such a refusal. The principle of impartiality may well lead us to say that all people should be able to continue with some form of higher education and that they should not be effectively disbarred from such by factors such as poverty. But that is a different point. There are in fact a number of other higher educational facilities (polytechnics, colleges of education, medical schools, art colleges, etc.) whose function is precisely to provide alternatives suitable for different people. To insist on a university education for all is, in reality, merely to play the verbal game of calling every such institution a university. For one could not meaningfully insist on a university education, as at present understood, for all, so long as all are not capable of undertaking what is involved in it.

Once again we come up against the argument based on considerations of worldly success and status; it is pointed out that a university education provides a passport to better jobs; other higher education facilities are seen as poor relations. Insofar as this is true, and it is obviously true to some extent, I can only repeat the point made above in regard to secondary education: the fault, if it be one, is a socio-economic one. Employers, by and large, are presumably not so foolish as to prefer candidates simply on the grounds that the word 'university graduate' can be technically and correctly applied to them. When a university graduate is selected for a post, it is presumably at worst because he has undergone an education that the employer sees reason to regard as desirable. Employers will not cease to look for employees with particular types of qualification and educational background, just because we make their job harder by referring to everything as a university education.

198 | *Moral Philosophy for Education*

1 Hamilton, W., speaking at the Headmasters' Conference, 1965, quoted
   by Winn, C., and Jacks, M., *Aristotle* (Methuen, 1967), p. 29.
2 Rubinstein, D., and Stoneman, C. (eds), *Education for Democracy*
   (Penguin, 1970), p. 23.

Since it is out of fashion to discuss the sort of issues raised in this chapter
from a philosophical point of view there is no noteworthy literature to refer to.

Chapter 14

Indoctrination and Moral Values

In this final chapter I am concerned with the limited question of what, if anything, parents and teachers may legitimately do in respect of cultivating adherence to moral values in their children. The central issue, as will become apparent, is the spectre of indoctrination which floats ominously around any talk of guiding, shaping or forming moral values. I shall not be going into certain other equally important questions about moral education in any detail: questions such as, What is the most *effective* way to morally educate children? What is the distinction between moral *education* and moral *training*? What is logically involved in having a moral concept? This is therefore in no way a complete account of moral education. It concentrates on one major issue that has to be resolved before anything else can profitably be said: given the uncertain nature of moral propositions, are we morally entitled to contribute deliberately to the formation of specific moral values in children, and, if so, in what way?

'I know a man,' writes Hare, 'who has a child of one year old, and he keeps on saying that he is absolutely determined not to influence his child's moral growth in any way; the child must find its own morality.' This view Hare goes on to dismiss as 'obviously absurd', for 'we cannot help influencing our children; the only question is, how, and in what direction'.[1] Is it absurd? Well, the initial claim that we ought not to influence the child's moral growth in any way surely is absurd. For Hare is right to point out that we cannot help influencing its moral growth, and it is absurd to insist that we should not do what we cannot help doing. There is no need to go into the complex question of precisely *what* effect various kinds of influence that we may have on the child will have. All that is necessary is to point out that children inevitably do, to some extent, acquire moral attitudes from their environment, and that that environment includes parents and teachers. The example that a parent or teacher sets by his own behaviour, indications that he approves or disapproves of some aspect of the child's behaviour, even seemingly irrelevant factors such as that the father is divorced from the child's mother, will all have some effect on the growth of particular attitudes or behavioural patterns in the child, even if it is not always possible to predict precisely what effect a particular influence will have. And the growth of such attitudes and behavioural patterns is itself a part of moral growth. Even if adults were willing and able to refrain from giving any overt indication of their own actual values, they would still be influencing children; the situation would simply be that instead of *deliberately* influencing children towards the view that bullying is wrong, say, they would be influencing children towards the equally evaluative view that bullying didn't matter. Children just do initially pick up values from the environment in which they find themselves. Since we are part of that environment we cannot avoid influencing them to some extent.

It follows that in one sense children cannot 'find their own morality'. That is to say, they cannot be in a position to set out to find a morality completely untouched by and unaware of the existence of any moral values. They cannot start the search from scratch, with no evaluative pre-conceptions at all, because, before they are in a position to make a meaning-ful search, they will inevitably have acquired some rudimentary notions of examples of good and bad behaviour. But is Hare perhaps moving too fast in concluding that it is absurd to talk of children finding their own morality in any sense? What one might claim is that children should find their own morality in the sense that adults should make no *deliberate* attempt to structure and control the influences that come to bear on them. Thus, although children would still be susceptible to outside influences, as they must inevitably be, what these influences were would be a matter of chance, depending simply on such factors as what their parents and friends were like, what films they watched, what books they read, and so on. Thus, it might be argued, children should find their own morality in the sense that no adult should deliberately attempt to influence by commenting on or overtly indicating his attitude to all the other random influences at work. Of course, now that the idea that children should find their own morality is revealed as only making sense if it is understood as meaning that the influences that come to bear on them should be random rather than controlled, it is less obviously appealing. But still some might wish to defend this claim. On what grounds might they try to do so?

According to Neill there is no need to worry about the rights and wrongs of attempting to promote adherence to certain values in children, because there is no need to make the attempt.

> 'There is no need whatsoever to teach children how to behave. A child will learn what is right and what is wrong in good time – provided he is not pressurised. Learning is a process of acquiring values from the environment. If parents are themselves honest and moral, their children will, in good time, follow the same course.'[2]

Now despite this apparently clear statement, it is not entirely clear what Neill's thesis is: is it that if children are susceptible only to honest and moral influences, then they will be moral (as seems to be implied here), or is it that if children are left to their own devices (i.e. ideally removed from adult influence) they will become honest and moral (as Neill often seems to imply elsewhere in his writing)? If the former claim is made then we must face the fact that children are *not* only susceptible to honest and moral influences, besides which it is simply not true that children from honest and moral backgrounds are necessarily honest and moral. But what of the latter claim, that provided at least that no adult is deliberately trying to cultivate dishonesty and immorality, children just will learn what is right and what is wrong in good time?

There are a number of objections to this thesis. First one might argue that even if this were true, it is objectionable that children should behave dishonestly and immorally in that period of time before they come to see what is right. What about the unfortunate children who are bullied before the bullies come to see that bullying is wrong? Secondly it will be seen that this is essentially an empirical claim – it purports to tell us what as a matter of fact will happen under certain conditions – and yet there is not in fact any real evidence to support the claim. Nor could there be at present, for as it is *not* the case that children are left to their own devices, there is no way of testing the claim one way or the other. There are, of course, a few schools, such as Summerhill itself, where children are left relatively to themselves, but these schools hardly provide satisfactory or conclusive proof of the claim, for the following reasons:

1. Even in free schools the children are generally subject to some adult control, and they still come from homes where in the all-important early years (and in the holidays) they are almost certainly subject to some kind of influence. We have no way of knowing how crucial a factor this may be in their moral development.

2. Such schools are as a matter of fact the exception in our society. Consciousness of this *may* contribute to the children's willingness to make the system work. Again we have no way of knowing whether this is so or not. In any case, it would surely be rash to generalise from such a small sample.

3. It is not even clear whether there is any evidence to show that those children who did attend such schools do exhibit morally acceptable behaviour as adults. There have been no empirical studies that I know about of the adult behaviour of children educated at free schools.

This last point raises a third and considerably more important point about the broad claim that children left to their own devices will adopt morally acceptable values and attitudes. What is meant here by 'morally acceptable'? If somebody were to attempt a survey of the extent to which a specific group of adults exhibit morally acceptable behaviour, what would he be looking for? For Neill to even put forward this claim it is necessary that he should have some clear idea of what counts as moral behaviour.

What does count? Is what *he* counts as moral behaviour necessarily what you and I count as moral behaviour? If it is, if that is to say there is some general agreement on what constitutes honest and moral behaviour, it is difficult to see why we should not inform children of what it is and attempt to steer them towards this ideal, rather than leave them to discover it for themselves.

This is not to say that the claim is evidently false, although one might be forgiven for remaining sceptical of the absolute claim that any child left to his own devices and the influence of other children will necessarily become a virtuous adult. It is only to say that there does not appear to be any obvious reason to accept the claim. And the fact remains that, even if we believe in this ideal, we have to cope with reality for the time being. And the reality is that, whether we like it or not, most of us as teachers have to deal with children who have already begun the process of acquiring behaviour patterns and embryonic values which may as a matter of fact strike us as objectionable and which may as a matter of fact be there to stay if something is not done about them. It really is absurdly improbable to suggest that everyone would be a saint if only teachers would shut up.

There is only one other way, so far as I can see, in which one could hope to defend the thesis that children ought not to be subject to any deliberate attempt on the part of adults to steer them towards the acceptance of certain values. This would be to argue for an extreme subjectivist view of ethics such that nothing is good or bad but thinking makes it so. Clearly if to behave morally is one and the same thing as behaving in a way that one regards as moral or that one approves of, without any other conditions being written in at all, then the child who is free to behave as he sees fit must necessarily come to behave morally. My objection to this view is contained within the body of this book, where I have tried to argue that only certain kinds of behaviour can be moral. There is no need to re-introduce those arguments, but two points are worth stressing. The reader might well reject my arguments for a form of utilitarianism, but still feel that there are *some* necessary conditions of morality such that not just anything that an agent might happen to approve of can be moral. Secondly, the extreme subjectivist view considered here is, of course, as contentious as any other ethical view.

It therefore seems that Hare was correct. It is absurd to suggest that the child should be left to find its own morality from the start since this claim is either meaningless or, when interpreted to mean that adults should make no deliberate moves to influence children, it lacks any convincing argument to substantiate it. And again it is difficult to find fault with Hare when he continues: 'If we are going to influence them anyway, what can we do but try to influence them in the best direction we can think of?' Now this, of course, means in practice that different people will want to influence their children in different directions, and it also probably means in a society such as ours that there will be a certain amount of pressure on teachers to influence children towards what may loosely be termed 'our democratic values'. But it is extremely important to distinguish three different questions at this point: (1) What values ought a society to adopt? (2) What ought the individual to do when his conscience is at odds with his society? (3) What may teachers or parents legitimately do about forming values in children, assuming that they have an answer to (1) and are not faced with the problem of (2). Our concern at this point is only with (3).

And so we come to the main issue of this chapter. Assuming, for the sake of argument, that we are agreed that the utilitarian view that I have outlined is more reasonable than other moral views, can we legitimately influence children towards the behaviour and beliefs implicit in that view? Or must such influence constitute indoctrination? What is indoctrination?

To observe that philosophers are not agreed on what constitutes 'indoctrination' would be an understatement. All are agreed that it has something to do with promoting beliefs in other people, but beyond that there is very little agreement. Thus for Green, the hallmark of the indoctrinated man is that he holds a belief without having evidence for it; according to Sargant what is crucial to indoctrination is the use of non-rational techniques of persuasion to cause somebody to believe something; Wilson argues, on the contrary, that use of non-rational techniques does not necessarily imply that indoctrination is going on, but that what picks out indoctrination is the nature of the beliefs being imparted. To indoctrinate, on this view, is to make people regard as certain beliefs that are in fact uncertain. Hare claims that it is the aim of a teacher to 'stop the growth in our children of the capacity to think for themselves' that turns him into an indoctrinator. White similarly argues that it is the intention to implant a belief in such a way that nothing will shake it that marks out the indoctrinator, but adds that one may indoctrinate even simple falsehoods. Woods and Gregory disagree with White on the grounds that only beliefs that form part of a doctrine can be indoctrinated. An additional complexity arises from the fact that most (though not all) of the above philosophers regard indoctrination as necessarily objectionable, whereas Pincoffs, for instance, argues that there is such a thing as good or justifiable indoctrination.

It is clear that we can neither do justice to all these points of view here, nor very convincingly claim to offer the definitive analysis of the concept of indoctrination. In fact it is surely rather absurd to proceed as if there were one definitive analysis. The important thing is to consider various plausible conceptions of indoctrination, and to seek to form some conclusion as to which of them are necessarily objectionable and why they are so.

Naturally we are only concerned with conceptions of indoctrination that are objectionable, for our fear is that we may induce moral belief in such a way that we might be accused of indoctrination. But we only need fear the accusation if the term 'indoctrination' picks out something that is necessarily objectionable.

Bearing this in mind we can safely ignore certain conceptions of indoctrination, such as that of Green, not on the grounds that they are false or misuses of the word – for who are we to say that some people ought not to use a word as vague as indoctrination in ways that as a matter of fact they do – but on the grounds that they make indoctrination an acceptable practice, at least in some circumstances, by definition; and if indoctrination is taken to be an acceptable practice it represents no problem for us. By suggesting that anyone who comes to hold a belief without having evidence for that belief is *ipso facto* indoctrinated, Green is forced to the conclusion that all early moral education must be indoctrination, and that in practice all of us must be indoctrinated to a greater or lesser extent.[3] For children inevitably acquire values of one sort or another before they can meaningfully be said to have evidence for those value-beliefs, and most of us, even as adults, have certain beliefs the evidence for which for one reason or another we do not in fact have. But if everybody must be indoctrinated at least initially, there is no point in arguing that they ought not to be; there is no point in suggesting that indoctrination should be avoided.

There is another claim about indoctrination made by many philosophers, which we might also reasonably ignore in the context of this chapter, although in itself it is an extremely important issue in relation to the concept of indoctrination, and that is the suggestion that only certain kinds of belief can be indoctrinated. Thus Flew[4] argues that only doctrines can be indoctrinated and Wilson[5] that only uncertain propositions can be, while White[6] argues, on the contrary, that simple falsehoods such as 'Melbourne is the capital of Australia' or even straightforward truths might be indoctrinated. The reason that this issue is not crucial to the argument here is that nobody disputes that doctrines and uncertain beliefs can be indoctrinated (the argument is about simple falsehoods and truths), and the moral beliefs that we are concerned with must count as doctrines or uncertain beliefs. So whether one could indoctrinate a simple falsehood or not will not affect the point that one can indoctrinate moral beliefs. Nonetheless we should look briefly at this issue.

By 'uncertain beliefs' Wilson does not mean simply beliefs that people are not certain about in a psychological sense, as one might be uncertain whether the Labour Party won the 1945 General Election. He refers to beliefs that, whatever individual people think about them, are in fact logically uncertain. Beliefs, that is to say, which, though they may conceivably in fact be true or false, are not known to be either, because it is not certain what would count as evidence for or against them. They are beliefs of which it is not true to say 'that any sane and sensible person, when presented with the relevant facts and arguments, would necessarily hold the beliefs. We might put this by saying that there was no *publicly-accepted* evidence for them, evidence which any rational person would regard as sufficient.'[7] The distinction therefore is between on the one hand beliefs that are known to be true or false, such as the belief that a car engine works in a certain way, which according to Wilson cannot be indoctrinated in any circumstances, and, on the other hand, beliefs that are not known to be true or false, such as the belief that God exists. It *may* be true that God exists, but we do not know this: we do not have public agreement on what counts as evidence one way or the other. In the same way, moral beliefs are uncertain in the sense that even though one may argue for a particular moral viewpoint, as I have tried to do in this book, it would be absurd to claim that any such moral viewpoint was *known* to be true. It is simply not true that 'any sense and sensible person' must agree with the view that I have put forward. Thus 'Religious, political and moral beliefs are *uncertain*, in a sense in which mathematics and Latin Grammar are not uncertain'. To indoctrinate, according to Wilson, is essentially to teach as certain uncertain beliefs and it is, he suggests, necessarily objectionable.

Other philosophers, such as Flew, Woods and Gregory,[8] want to refine this yet further and argue that not even all beliefs that are not known to be true or false can be indoctrinated – they must also be doctrinal or ideological. That is to say that only beliefs that are part of a system of other interrelated beliefs, which taken together have repercussions for the way in which a man lives his life and that are not known to be true or false, can be indoctrinated. On this view, therefore, a simple proposition such as 'There is an abominable snowman', even though it is not known to be true or false, could not properly be said to be indoctrinated. It is only the substance of ideologies, such as Marxism, Catholicism, liberal-democratism or atheism, that can be indoctrinated.

It is very difficult to see how one can resolve the disagreement between such views and White's claim that a simple falsehood might be indoctrinated. The argument for the doctrinal view appears to rest on the claim that we regard the formation of belief in doctrinal systems such as Marxism and Catholicism as paradigm cases of indoctrination, and on the suggestion that the word *indoctrination* is plainly linked to *doctrines*. But, as White correctly observes, nothing much turns on a verbal point such as this, and it may well be that we only regard the inducement of belief in Marxism and Catholicism as paradigm examples of indoctrination for the contingent reason that as a matter of fact people are more concerned to indoctrinate ideologies than they are to indoctrinate simple falsehoods. My own view is that on certain conditions (shortly to be outlined) one might perfectly reasonably claim that even a straightforward falsehood or truth was being indoctrinated. But the important thing for us to note here, since our concern is with moral beliefs which are uncertain anyway, is that even if we do not accept White's claim that any kind of belief might be indoctrinated, we must accept one of the implications of that view, and that is that indoctrination cannot be defined *solely* in terms of a particular kind of content. In other words we accept that moral beliefs *can* be indoctrinated – regardless of what other kinds of belief can be – but only on certain conditions.

Wilson arrived at his conclusion that it was a certain kind of content that turned some teaching into indoctrination as a result of dismissing the view that it could be defined in terms of method. Some have argued that what marks out indoctrination is the use of non-rational techniques of persuasion such as the use of a charismatic personality, authority, praise or blame to induce belief. But Wilson claims that if we wish to retain the term 'indoctrination' as a meaningful pejorative term or, as he puts it, as a term to indicate 'a forbidden area', we cannot define it in terms of method. First he suggests, perhaps not very persuasively, that we would not object to 'hypnotising [a boy] to master A level physics' as we would object to hypnotising him to believe in communism. But secondly he makes the point, which we have already made, that, though we never *have* to use hypnotism, with young children we inevitably have to use non-rational methods of persuasion to some extent, since they cannot always understand rational explanations. Besides which, as we have also noted above, we cannot avoid using non-rational techniques of persuasion, since we cannot avoid setting some kind of example.

Wilson is therefore surely correct to say that the mere use of non-rational techniques is not in itself indoctrination. For a parent or teacher to set an example of kindness or to praise kind behaviour in children is not indoctrination in any objectionable sense. But then, I suggest, Wilson has made two mistakes. In the first place, having established that a certain kind of method is not sufficient to characterise indoctrination he seems to assume that it is not necessary either. And in the second place he assumes that content alone is sufficient. But this latter point leads him into an absurd position.

It will be remembered that for Wilson the 'criterion of indoctrination depends on the rationality of the content'. To teach certain beliefs cannot be to indoctrinate; to teach uncertain beliefs must be to indoctrinate. And moral beliefs are uncertain. It would therefore seem that any move on the part of the adult that contributes to the formation of moral belief in children is indoctrination. But this is precisely the conclusion that Wilson wanted to avoid, since he, like us, recognises the inevitability of teaching moral beliefs to some extent, and he too wants to keep 'indoctrination' as a clearly pejorative term. How does he attempt to avoid this dilemma? By arguing that avoiding indoctrination in the moral sphere 'consists in only educating children to adopt behaviour patterns and to have feelings which are seen by every sane and sensible person to be agreeable and necessary'.[9] But this is plainly unsatisfactory, for 'who are to count as sane and sensible people?' Wilson is ignoring one of the very premisses from which he started: that moral beliefs are uncertain, and that in the moral sphere it is just not true that every 'sane and sensible person' would necessarily hold certain particular beliefs. In this situation only one of two things can happen: either we identify sane and sensible people with those who think as we do, or else we identify them with those who take the view held by the majority in a society. But if we are to do justice to the complexities of the moral sphere, these are precisely the conclusions that we must avoid: an action is not necessarily good just because most people think that it is, or because we and those who think like us say that it is. A Catholic's view of a sane and sensible person in the moral sphere will not be the same as a Marxist's view. There is no way out of this problem for Wilson. Either indoctrination is to be defined solely in terms of teaching uncertain beliefs, in which case all early moral education is indoctrination, or else we must conclude that the content criterion (uncertain beliefs) is at best only one necessary condition of indoctrination. Clearly we must take the latter view if we wish to maintain that indoctrination is something that can and should be avoided.

This brings us to a third suggested condition of indoctrination. Hare and White take a roughly similar position in arguing that what is essential to indoctrination is a certain aim or intention on the part of the indoctrinator. White claims that to indoctrinate someone is to try 'to get him to believe that a proposition . . . is true, in such a way that nothing will shake that belief'[10] and Hare that it begins 'when we are trying to stop the growth in our children of the capacity to think for themselves'[11] about various beliefs. Here, I suggest, we get very near to the nub of the matter, but the stress on aim or intention itself will not quite do.

What is surely true is that the essence of being indoctrinated lies not in the fact that one has certain beliefs (whatever they are) nor in the fact that one came by them without basing them on rational evidence, but in the fact that one holds them in a certain way, namely, in an unquestioning way or with a closed mind. We surely cannot say that *all* Catholics, Marxists, liberal-democrats and atheists are indoctrinated, and yet we should have to say this on any analysis that defined indoctrination solely in terms of content or method or both. For atheism no less than Catholicism, liberal-democratism no less than Marxism, is an ideology, and since they are ideologies (i.e. being systems of belief that involve propositions that are not known to be true or false), one could not in the final analysis claim to have rational grounds for one's commitment to any of these sets of beliefs. That is to say that although one may put one's faith in Marxism, for instance, and even give reasons which explain why one does so, the ideology is based on certain fundamental axioms, such as that economic forces are the fundamental forces in social change, which though they may be true are not unquestionably known to be true. Such an axiom is rather a basic tenet of the faith. It can neither be proved nor disproved.

Faced with any historical example of social change, the Marxist will interpret it in terms of economic forces, whereas the non-Marxist will not. In just the same way the religious believer will interpret what he calls revelation as evidence for God's existence, whereas the atheist will deny that it is evidence (and probably call it something else, such as hallucination). If everybody who commits himself to any kind of ideology is thereby indoctrinated, then we are virtually all of us indoctrinated and the word once again becomes vacuous.

But in any case we do not as a matter of fact feel that all Catholics or whatever are *necessarily* indoctrinated. We surely want to distinguish between the man who recognises the logical uncertainty of a proposition such as 'God exists', but who feels the need to commit himself to the belief that God does exist, and the man who believes that God exists and treats this as an unquestionable truth such that those who fail to see it are just wrong, and must themselves either be stupid or else indoctrinated. To be indoctrinated is to regard as unquestionably true that which is not known to be true or false. (Or, if we allow White's claim that simple falsehoods or truths could be indoctrinated, it is to hold a particular belief without any regard for the actual logical status of that belief and the question of what kind of evidence, if any, is actually appropriate to deciding its truth or falsehood.)

If this is accepted, then to indoctrinate is to cause somebody to believe that a proposition is true in such a way that nothing will shake that belief. To indoctrinate somebody with moral beliefs is to cause them to hold moral beliefs in such a way that they are unable to recognise the uncertain nature of such beliefs, but rather regard them as unquestionable truths. And it follows from this that the use of non-rational techniques of persuasion is a necessary, but not a sufficient condition of indoctrination. That it is not sufficient we have already seen, but it must be necessary, for nobody could come to regard a moral belief as unquestionably true if he had been brought up to examine rationally the status of moral propositions. This is simply because the nature of moral propositions is such that reasoning cannot establish them as incontrovertibly true. Thus a man who comes to hold that killing people is wrong as a result of reasoned reflection must see that, though he can explain why he thinks that is a more reasonable view than its opposite, that reasoning has not established its unquestionable truth.

What, then, of the specific suggestion that the teacher must *aim* to close the mind of, or *intend* to plant unshakeable conviction in, the child, if he is to be classified as an indoctrinator? It seems to me that this contention is to be rejected, despite White's distinction between a real intention and an avowed intention. White does not dispute that an indoctrinator might claim that he did not intend to implant unshakeable belief (avowed intention), but, he argues, he must nonetheless *really* intend to, in the sense that he must assume that the belief that he is inculcating is unquestionably true, otherwise he could not hope to impart commitment to that belief if in fact it is not unquestionably true. This argument is rather complex, but what White seems to be saying is that when we are not dealing with simple falsehoods (in which case clearly one would need to intend to close the mind if one hoped to succeed) it is logically inconceivable that one should succeed in closing the mind without intending to do so, except on the assumption that one sincerely believed that the issue was not open to question. Thus I cannot cause a child to believe unquestionably in God's existence, if I myself recognise it as a genuinely open question, unless I intend to do so. Conversely, if I regard it as an unquestionable truth, then implicit in my teaching will be the assumption that it is true and hence the intention to get this point across.

What is worrying about this argument (apart from the fact that 'real intention' seems to be being made a necessary part of indoctrination by definition and leads to confusion between this special sense of intention and the more general sense such as Hare seems to have in mind when he talks of the teacher's aim) is that it leads to the conclusion that children cannot be being indoctrinated provided that their teachers do not intend to indoctrinate them. But this surely is not true. Children may generally only be indoctrinated if people attempt to indoctrinate them; but it is surely conceivable that an educational system as a whole might succeed in indoctrinating people quite accidentally as a result of what it does *not* do, rather than what it does do. For example, by avoiding altogether the question of moral beliefs and their logical status as an area of inquiry, schools might materially contribute to a situation in which children just do grow up regarding certain moral beliefs as unquestionable certainties. The question of who, then, indoctrinated them is not particularly interesting. But surely what is necessarily objectionable, because it involves error and falsehood, is the holding of a moral belief – any moral belief, and regardless of what incidental influences from parents, peer group or teachers caused it – *as if it were unquestionably true*, since no moral belief is unquestionably true. People whose moral beliefs are thus unquestioned and unyielding are indoctrinated, and it is important that teachers should not only avoid intentional indoctrination, but that they should intentionally combat the possibility of indoctrination by examining the status of moral beliefs.

To summarise: if indoctrination need cause us any worries in the moral sphere it must be defined in such a way that it picks out a clearly objectionable form of teaching that may apply in the sphere of moral beliefs. Definitions in terms of method or content alone will not achieve this, nor is it satisfactory to confine indoctrination to cases where teachers intend or aim to implant unshakeable belief alone, although, of course, any teacher who does have such an aim could be accused of trying to indoctrinate. To indoctrinate children is to cause them to hold beliefs in such a way that they do not recognise the true logical status of those beliefs but regard them as unquestionably true. I do not see why we should not regard someone who tries to make somebody believe even a simple truth such as that the world is round as an indoctrinator, if he were to cause the belief to be held in such a way that, should the evidence that we take to establish this truth change, or be found to be faulty in some way, the belief would nonetheless be stubbornly held to. But such examples are not in fact likely to occur. It is in such spheres as the moral sphere that the danger lies.

Indoctrination is not, therefore, a simple process that can be carried through in one lesson, one day or even one year. One is not indoctrinating just because one does not at a given point in time examine the logical status of a belief or because one influences the child by example or praise towards a particular belief. Such practice might in certain conditions *contribute towards* the process of indoctrination, but that is a quite different point and it does not necessarily do so. Since to indoctrinate is to cause a certain end result, the way to avoid indoctrination is to ensure that that end result is avoided.

The upshot of all this is quite simple. We must influence children's moral development, because we cannot help so doing. We cannot do better than influence them towards acceptance of those values that we regard as most reasonable. But if we are to avoid indoctrination we must seek ultimately to cultivate an open mind on the question. The most obvious symptom of a tendency towards indoctrination in an institution is *not*, as many popularly suppose, the fact that an institution does enshrine and can be seen to enshrine values, *nor* the fact that it openly stands by certain values, but the very reverse – the fact that it does not *openly* stand by them. For any institution such as a school *will* enshrine various values, and if we wish to make a positive attempt to combat the danger of indoctrination we must have them out in the open and be prepared to talk about them.

What does this mean in practice? First it does not necessarily have anything to do with encouraging each individual simply to opt for his own values. There is nothing necessarily open-minded about being idiosyncratic. An individual might have a set of moral beliefs that were peculiar to himself and yet have a closed mind, so that he could not conceive that he might be mistaken. Open-mindedness is characterised by having a true understanding of what kind of evidence is relevant to a particular belief, and hence according to different beliefs only that degree of certainty that is appropriate to them. This is not to say that an individual who firmly commits himself to a belief such as that God exists is necessarily not open-minded, but that an individual who also commits himself firmly to the further belief that such a belief is unquestionably true is not open-minded.

Secondly it means that where reasons can be given they should be given. Thus, even with young children, besides setting an example and influencing belief by non-rational means such as praise and blame, we should explain our values so far as we can. Thus instead of replying to the question 'Why shouldn't I kick him?' with a non-reason such as 'Because I say so' or 'Because I'll kick you, if you do', we should surely attempt to provide the reasons that do seem to us to be relevant such as 'Because it hurts him' or even 'Because you wouldn't like it if he kicked you'.

But this in itself is not enough, first because this kind of response invites the further question 'Why shouldn't I hurt him?' and secondly because to treat a reason such as 'Because you wouldn't like to be kicked' as a *relevant* reason is already to be involved in a particular ethical viewpoint (in this case the relatively uncontroversial claim that sincere commitment to a moral judgement involves recognising it as applicable to oneself as well as other people, other things being equal). And yet clearly we cannot meaningfully discuss fundamental questions such as the universalisability of moral judgements, or the question of whether considerations of harm are necessarily relevant to moral debate, with children, at least until the stage of secondary education. It is essential therefore that at the primary stage reasons should be given where they can be, so that children acquire the notion that the beliefs and behavioural patterns that they are gradually coming to adopt are supposed to be based on reason rather than on the dictates of authority, and that at the secondary stage those reasons themselves should be subjected to critical examination. For the whole point about morality, as we have seen, is that it differs from spheres such as science, because there is not even agreement on what reasons count as moral reasons or as evidence for a moral claim. An open mind in the moral sphere involves recognising this problem. And to undertake an inquiry into this problem is to do moral philosophy. Therefore a necessary antidote to moral indoctrination is an introduction to moral philosophy –

provided that nobody is so foolish as to assume that what a moral
philosopher says is the case must be the case. Look to his reasoning – not
to his judgements.

REFERENCES

1 Hare, R. M., 'Adolescents into Adults' in Hollins, T. H. B. (ed.), *Aims in
Education* (Manchester University Press, 1964), p. 51.
2 Neill, A. S., *Summerhill* (Penguin, 1968), p. 224.
3 Green, T. F., 'The Topology of the Teaching Concept' in *Studies in
Philosophy and Education*, vol. III, no. 4.
4 Flew, A., 'What is Indoctrination?' in *Studies in Philosophy and Education*,
vol. IV, no. 3.
5 Wilson, J., 'Education and Indoctrination' in Hollins, T. H. B. (ed.),
op. cit.
6 White, J. P., 'Indoctrination' in Peters, R. S. (ed.), *The Concept of
Education* (Routledge & Kegan Paul, 1967).
7 Wilson, J., *op. cit.*, p. 28.
8 Gregory, I. M., and Woods, R. G., 'Indoctrination' in *P.E.S.G.B. Proceedings*, vol. 4 (1970).
9 Wilson, J., *op. cit.*, p. 34.
10 White, J. P., *op. cit.*, p. 181.
11 Hare, R. M., *op. cit.*, p. 52.

FURTHER READING

All the articles referred to in this chapter have been conveniently collected
into one volume edited by Snook, I., *Concepts of Indoctrination* (Routledge &
Kegan Paul, 1972) with the exception of: Sargant, W., *Battle for the Mind*
(Pan Books, 1959) and Pincoffs, E., 'On Avoiding Moral Indoctrination' in
Doyle, J. F. (ed.), *Educational Judgements* (Routledge & Kegan Paul, 1973).

Index

Absolutism, moral 44 ff.
Aesthetics 60 ff.
Assessment 192 ff.
Authentic reasoning 133, 134
Autonomy Ch. 8

Categorical Imperative 121, 125
Children's values 166
Comprehensive Schools 188 ff.
Creativity Ch. 10
Curriculum 20, 25, 35

Deschooling 76
Divergent thinking 148 ff.
Duty 119, 124

Educational distribution Ch. 13
Educational theory 19, 27
Educationally worthwhile 159 ff.
Emotivism 49 ff., 67
Empathy 162
Equality 59, 79, Ch. 5, 91, 189 ff., 195 ff.

Forms of knowledge 161 ff.
Freedom 59, Ch. 4, 91, 113 ff., 186, Ch. 12
Free School Ch. 12

Happiness 91, 94–5

Impartiality 85 ff., 122
Independent schools 184 ff.
Indoctrination 203 ff.
Intentions 100, 124
Interest 168
Intrinsic value 169–71
Intuitionism 48 ff., 64

Knowledge, nature of 35, 46, 53

moral 9, 18, Ch. 2 (esp. 47 ff.) 143, 202 ff.
forms of 161 ff.

Moral philosophy, nature of 17, 18, Ch. 2
and philosophy of education 34–39
relevance to teachers 17, 211, 212
Moral Education 18, Ch. 14
Moral reasons 65–67, 91 ff., 111 ff.
Moral relativism 43 ff.

Naturalistic fallacy 68–69, 73
Needs 167, 8
Normative terms 29, 30, 38

Person 126
Pleasure 92 ff., 99, 156 ff.
measurement of 100
Philosophy, nature of 15 ff., 41, 146
Philosophy of Education, nature of 16, 17, 27–34
and moral philosophy 34–39
Prescriptivism 51 ff.
Progressive Education 179

Reason 132–3, 135 ff., 138 ff., 160 ff.
types of 139–40
Reasonable 54, Ch. 3
Relevance 166
Respect (for persons) 125 ff.
Rights Ch. 9, 179

Self-government 144
Self-regulation 179, 80
Sexual morality 113 ff.
Spontaneity 151 ff.
Standards of excellence 151 ff.
State system of education 187 ff.

Theory and practice 20 ff.
Transcendental argument 169–71
Truth, as a value 107

Universalisability 52, 120, 122 ff.
Universities 195 ff.

Utilitarianism 9, 45, 59, Ch. 6
 Act and Rule 95 ff.
Utility, principle of 93
 proof of 108 ff.

Worthwhile Ch. 11